PATRICIA BRIGGS'

# MERCY THOMPSON

## moon called

### VOLUME TWO

DYNAMITE®
ENTERTAINMENT

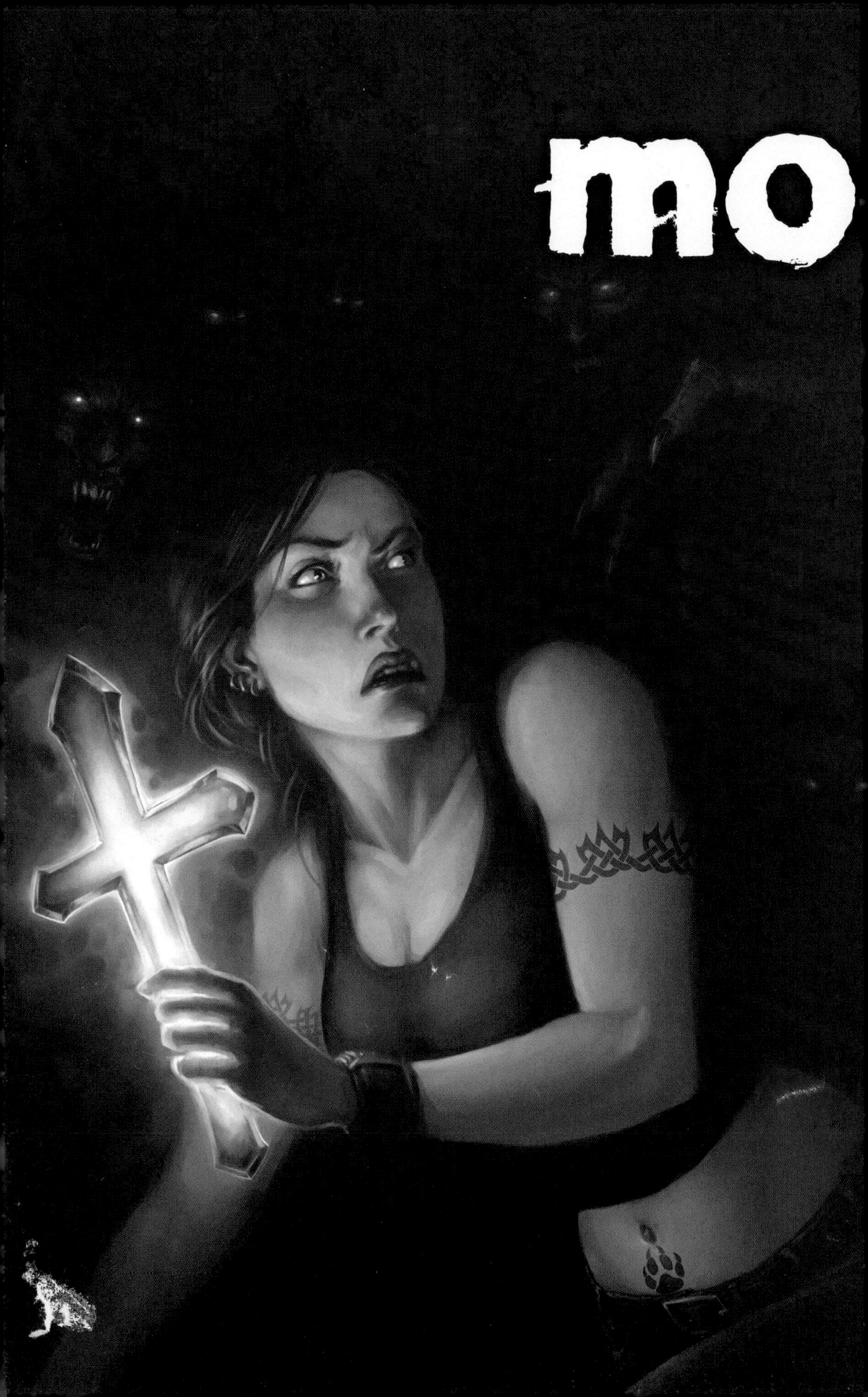
mo

# on called
## VOLUME TWO

WRITTEN BY:
# PATRICIA BRIGGS
## & DAVID LAWRENCE

ARTWORK & COLLECTION COVER BY:
## AMELIA WOO

LETTERS BY:
## ZACH MATHENY

THEMATIC CONSULTANTS:
## LINDA CAMPBELL, JENIFER LINTHWAITE & DEBRA LENTZ

CONSULTATION: **LES DABEL & ERNST DABEL**

COLLECTION DESIGN BY: **BILL TORTOLINI**

ISBN10: 1-60690-214-8
ISBN13: 978-1-60690-214-1

8 7 6 5 4 3 2 1

**DYNAMITE**
ENTERTAINMENT®

Dynamite Entertainment:

NICK BARRUCCI · PRESIDENT
JUAN COLLADO · CHIEF OPERATING OFFICER
JOSEPH RYBANDT · EDITOR
JOSH JOHNSON · CREATIVE DIRECTOR
RICH YOUNG · BUSINESS DEVELOPMENT
JASON ULLMEYER · SENIOR DESIGNER
JOSH GREEN · TRAFFIC COORDINATOR
CHRIS CANIANO · PRODUCTION ASSISTANT

www.dynamite.net

For media rights, foreign rights, promotions, licensing, and advertising: **marketing@dynamite.net**

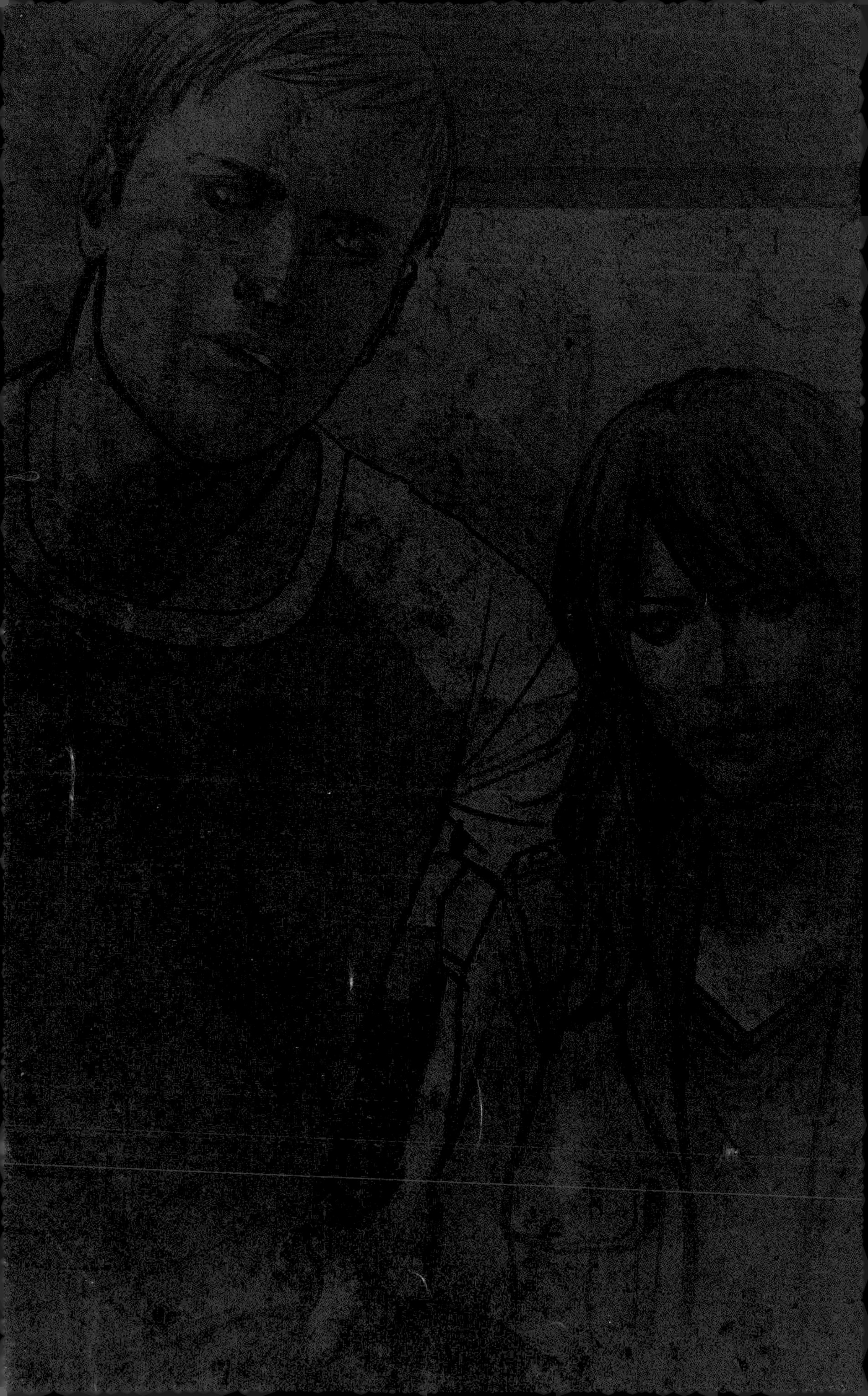

Mercy Thompson inhabits two worlds
without truly belonging to either.

To the human inhabitants of
Washington's Tri-Cities she's a bit of an
oddity, a fiercely independent woman
who repairs cars for a living.

To the town's darker residents,
werewolves, vampires, and fae, she's a walker,
a last-of-her-kind magical being with the
power to become a coyote.

Always an outsider, Mercy warily straddles
the twilight line dividing our everyday world
from that darker, inhuhman dimension.

But now her two worlds are about to collide.
Outnumbered and outmuscled,
can Mercy possibly survive?

ISSUE FIVE COVER BY:
**TYLER WALPOLE**

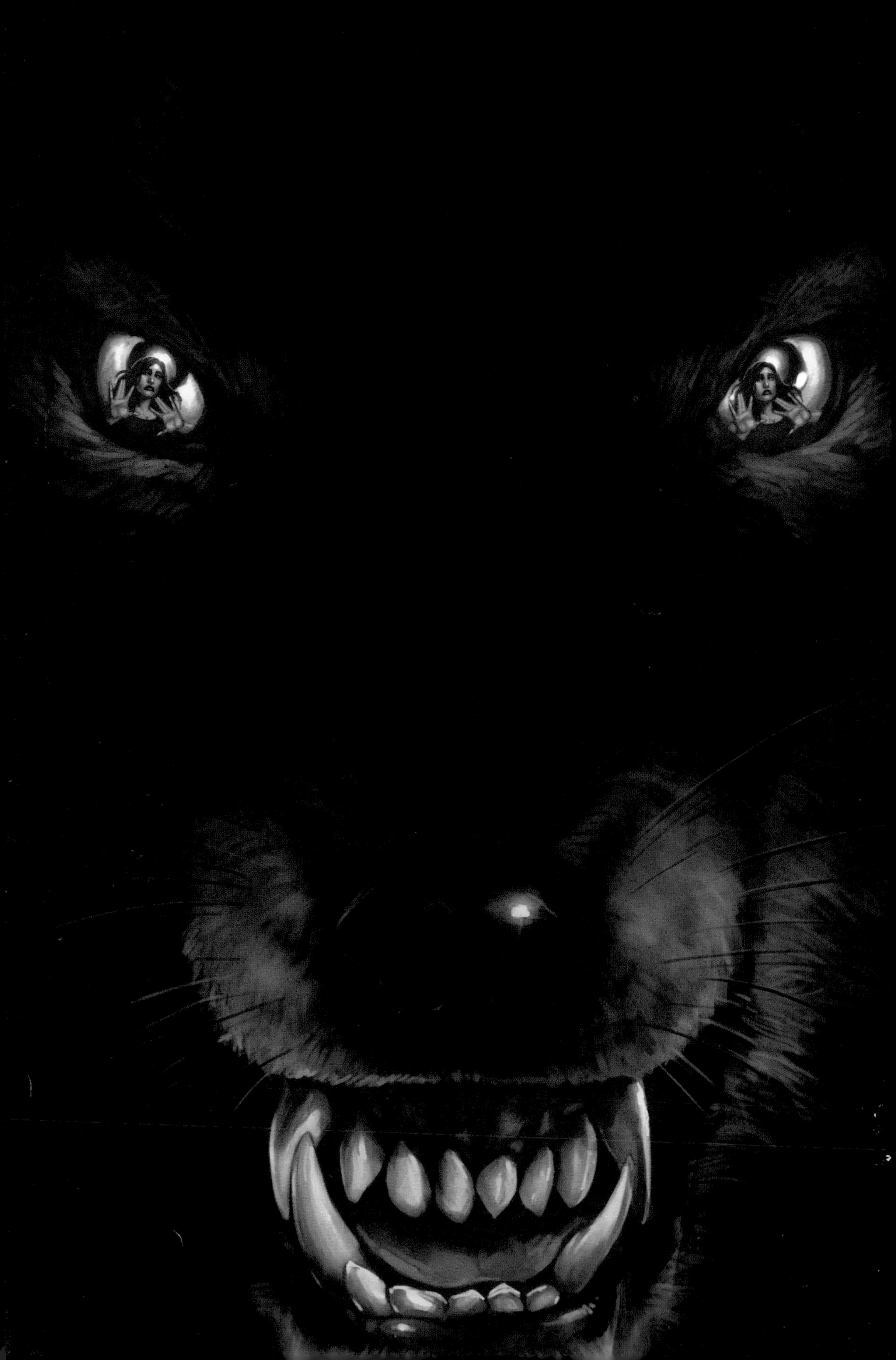

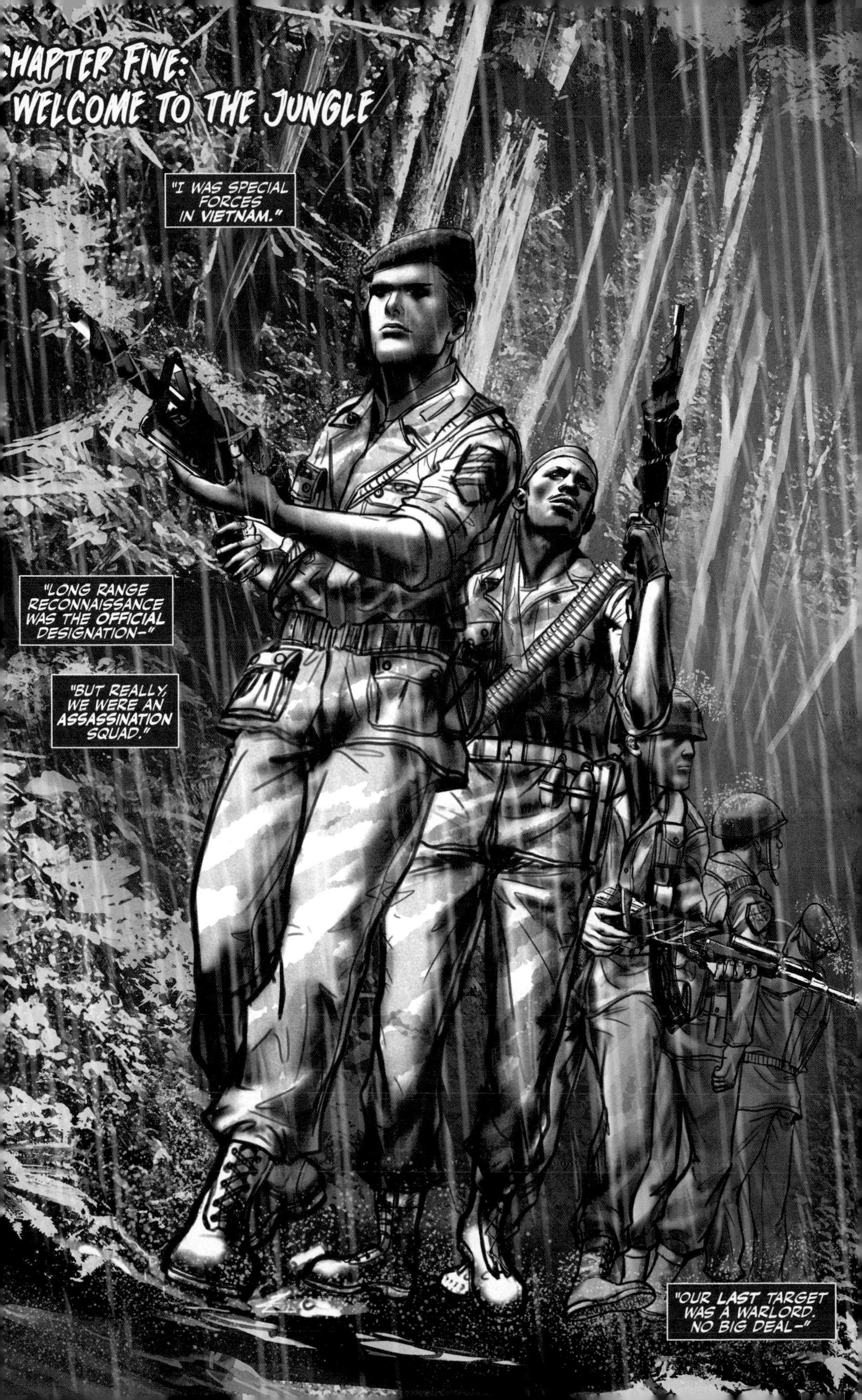
CHAPTER FIVE:
WELCOME TO THE JUNGLE
"I WAS SPECIAL FORCES IN VIETNAM."
"LONG RANGE RECONNAISSANCE WAS THE OFFICIAL DESIGNATION–"
"BUT REALLY, WE WERE AN ASSASSINATION SQUAD."
"OUR LAST TARGET WAS A WARLORD. NO BIG DEAL–"

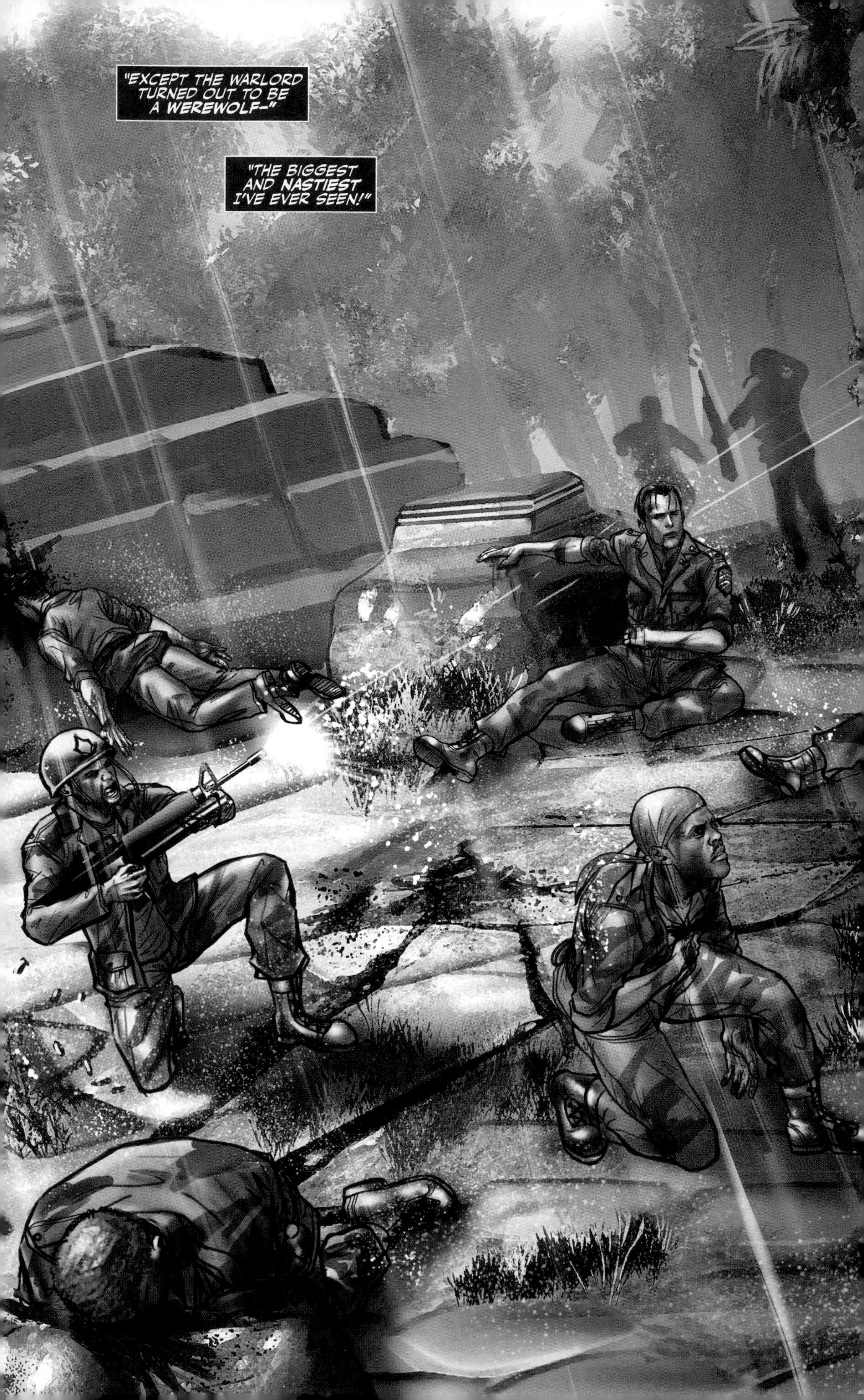
"EXCEPT THE WARLORD TURNED OUT TO BE A WEREWOLF--"
"THE BIGGEST AND NASTIEST I'VE EVER SEEN!"

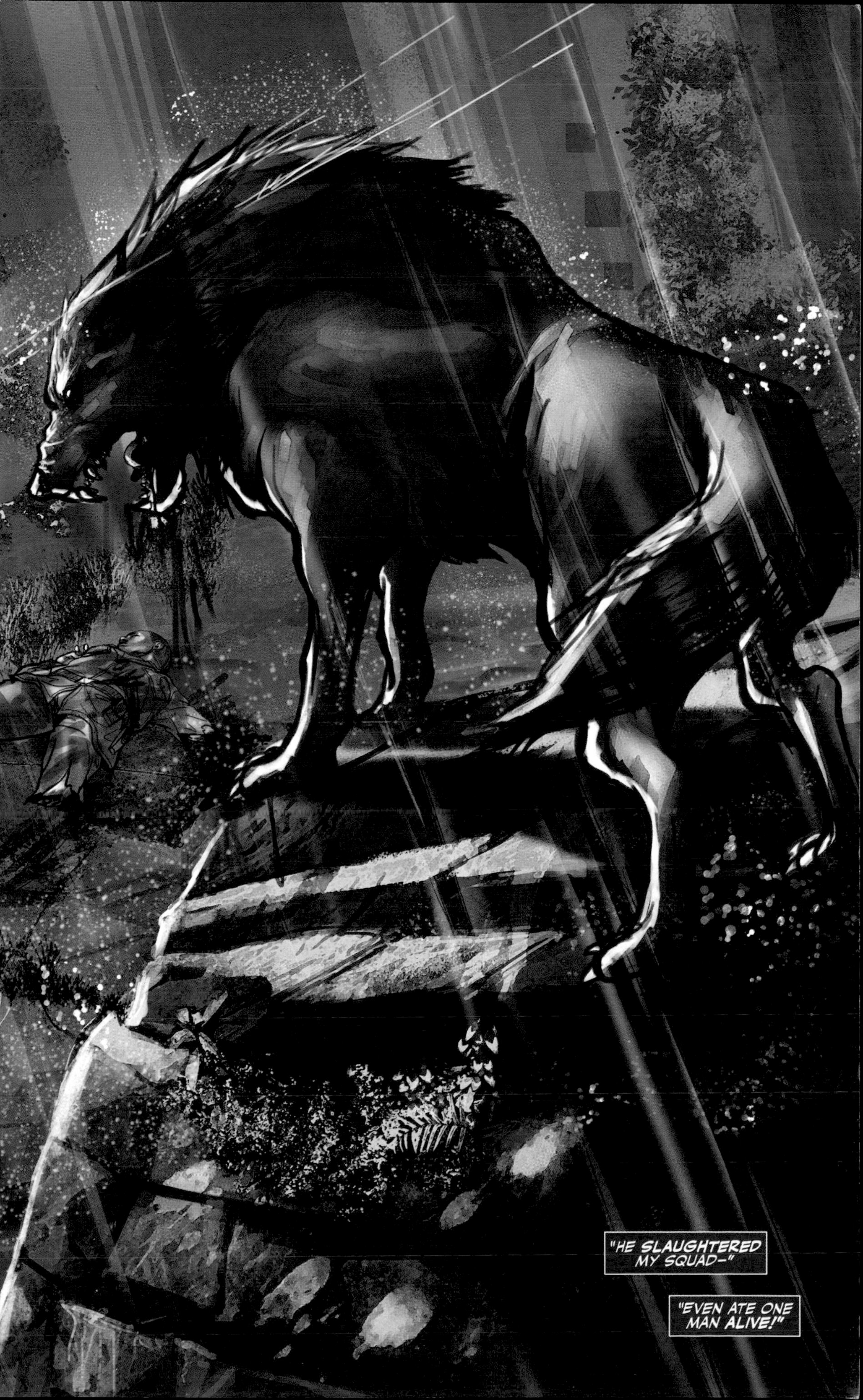
"HE SLAUGHTERED MY SQUAD-"
"EVEN ATE ONE MAN ALIVE!"

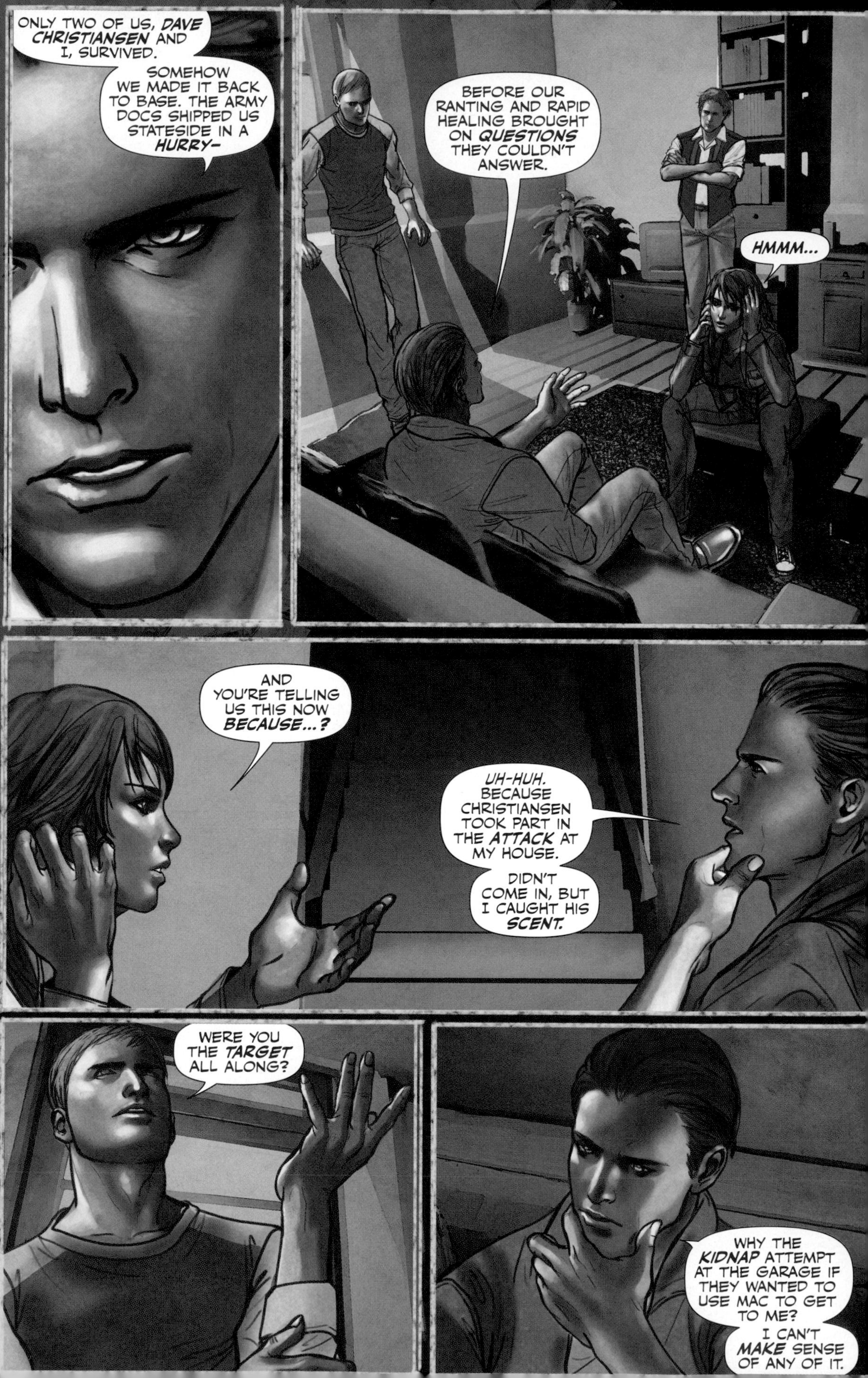
ONLY TWO OF US, DAVE CHRISTIANSEN AND I, SURVIVED.
SOMEHOW WE MADE IT BACK TO BASE. THE ARMY DOCS SHIPPED US STATESIDE IN A HURRY-
BEFORE OUR RANTING AND RAPID HEALING BROUGHT ON QUESTIONS THEY COULDN'T ANSWER.
HMMM...
AND YOU'RE TELLING US THIS NOW BECAUSE...?
UH-HUH. BECAUSE CHRISTIANSEN TOOK PART IN THE ATTACK AT MY HOUSE.
DIDN'T COME IN, BUT I CAUGHT HIS SCENT.
WERE YOU THE TARGET ALL ALONG?
WHY THE KIDNAP ATTEMPT AT THE GARAGE IF THEY WANTED TO USE MAC TO GET TO ME?
I CAN'T MAKE SENSE OF ANY OF IT.

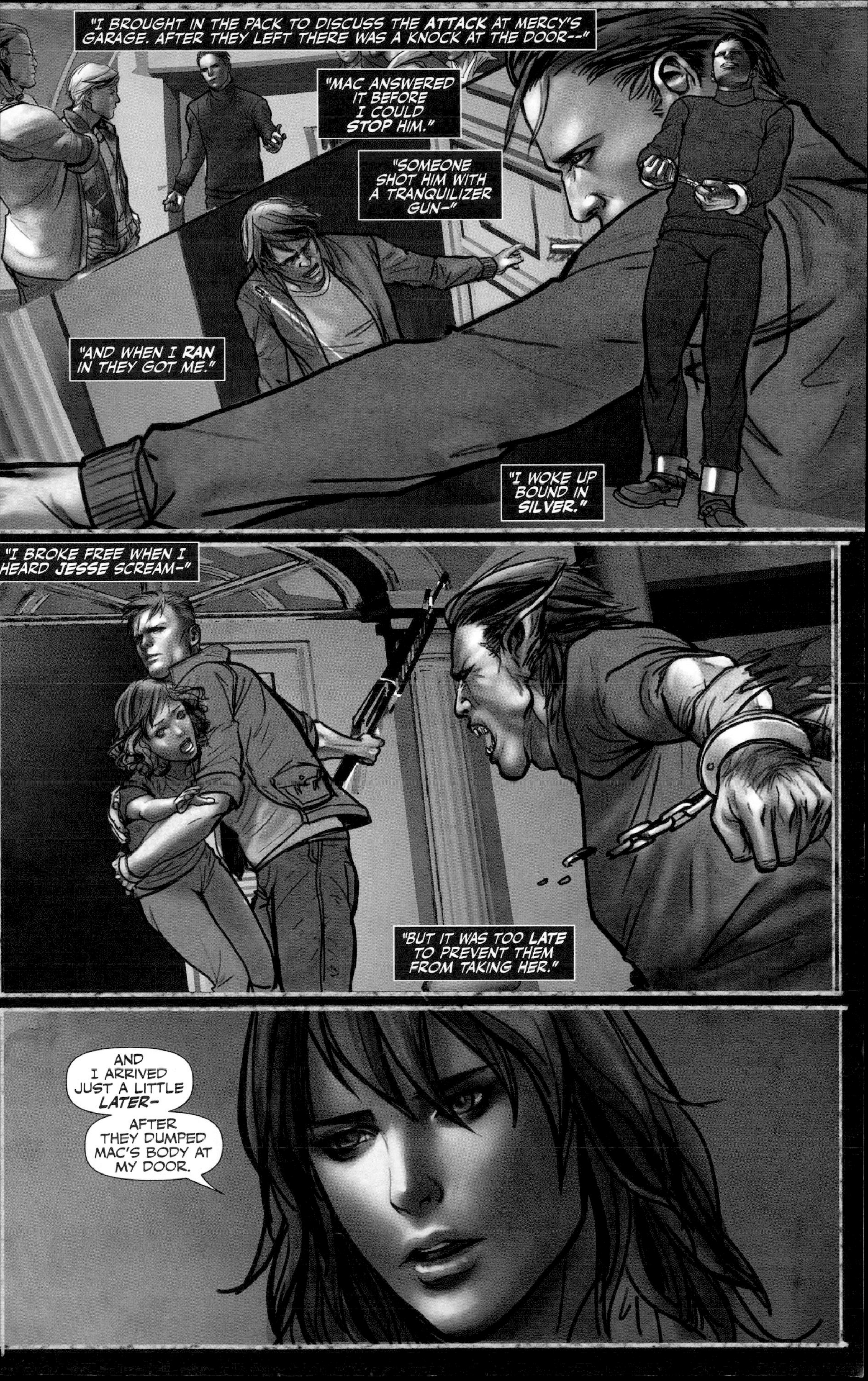
"I BROUGHT IN THE PACK TO DISCUSS THE ATTACK AT MERCY'S GARAGE. AFTER THEY LEFT THERE WAS A KNOCK AT THE DOOR--"
"MAC ANSWERED IT BEFORE I COULD STOP HIM."
"SOMEONE SHOT HIM WITH A TRANQUILIZER GUN--"
"AND WHEN I RAN IN THEY GOT ME."
"I WOKE UP BOUND IN SILVER."
"I BROKE FREE WHEN I HEARD JESSE SCREAM--"
"BUT IT WAS TOO LATE TO PREVENT THEM FROM TAKING HER."
AND I ARRIVED JUST A LITTLE LATER--
AFTER THEY DUMPED MAC'S BODY AT MY DOOR.

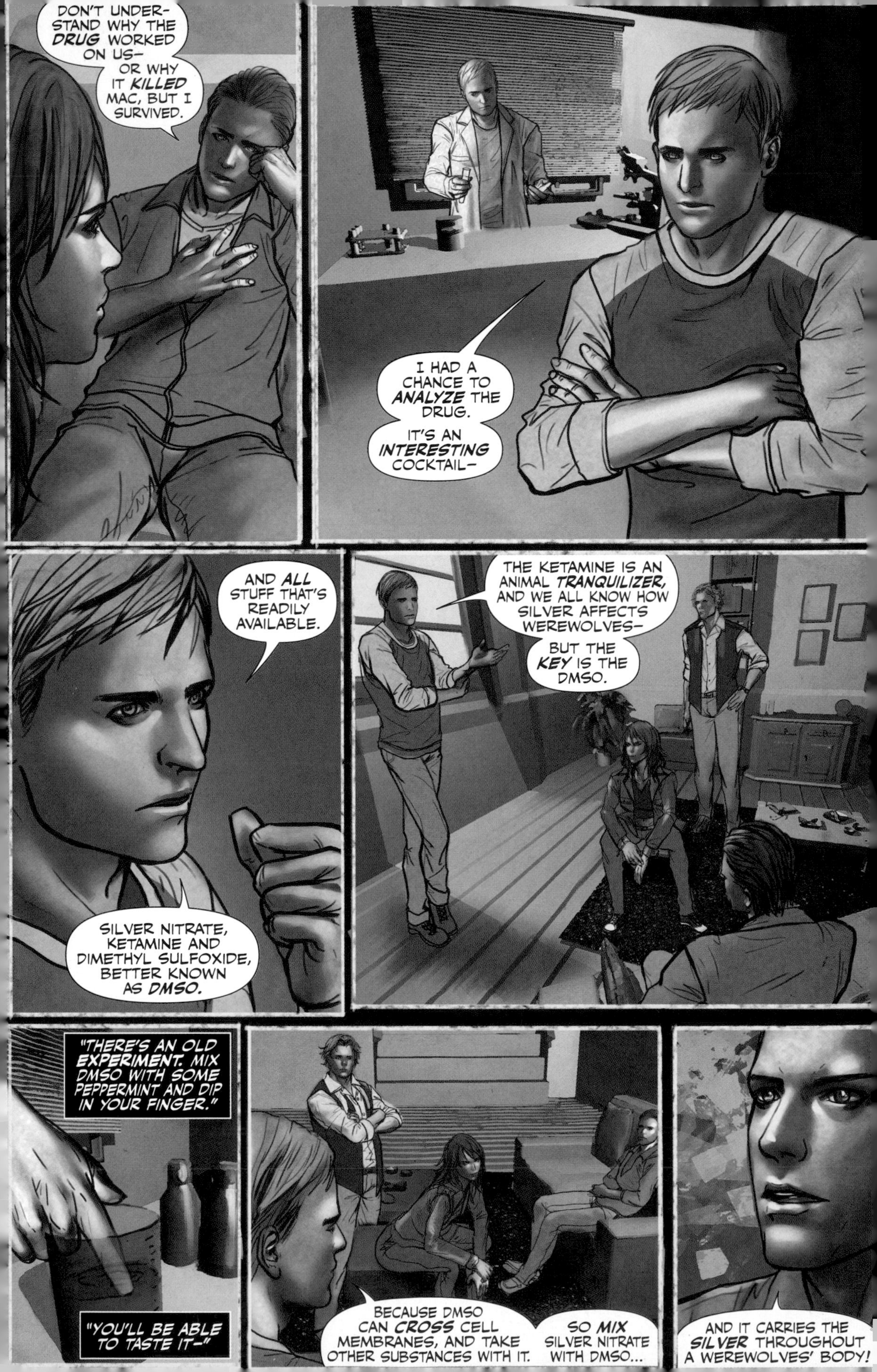
DON'T UNDERSTAND WHY THE DRUG WORKED ON US–
OR WHY IT KILLED MAC, BUT I SURVIVED.
I HAD A CHANCE TO ANALYZE THE DRUG.
IT'S AN INTERESTING COCKTAIL–
SILVER NITRATE, KETAMINE AND DIMETHYL SULFOXIDE, BETTER KNOWN AS DMSO.
AND ALL STUFF THAT'S READILY AVAILABLE.
THE KETAMINE IS AN ANIMAL TRANQUILIZER, AND WE ALL KNOW HOW SILVER AFFECTS WEREWOLVES–
BUT THE KEY IS THE DMSO.
"THERE'S AN OLD EXPERIMENT. MIX DMSO WITH SOME PEPPERMINT AND DIP IN YOUR FINGER."
"YOU'LL BE ABLE TO TASTE IT–"
BECAUSE DMSO CAN CROSS CELL MEMBRANES, AND TAKE OTHER SUBSTANCES WITH IT.
SO MIX SILVER NITRATE WITH DMSO...
AND IT CARRIES THE SILVER THROUGHOUT A WEREWOLVES' BODY!

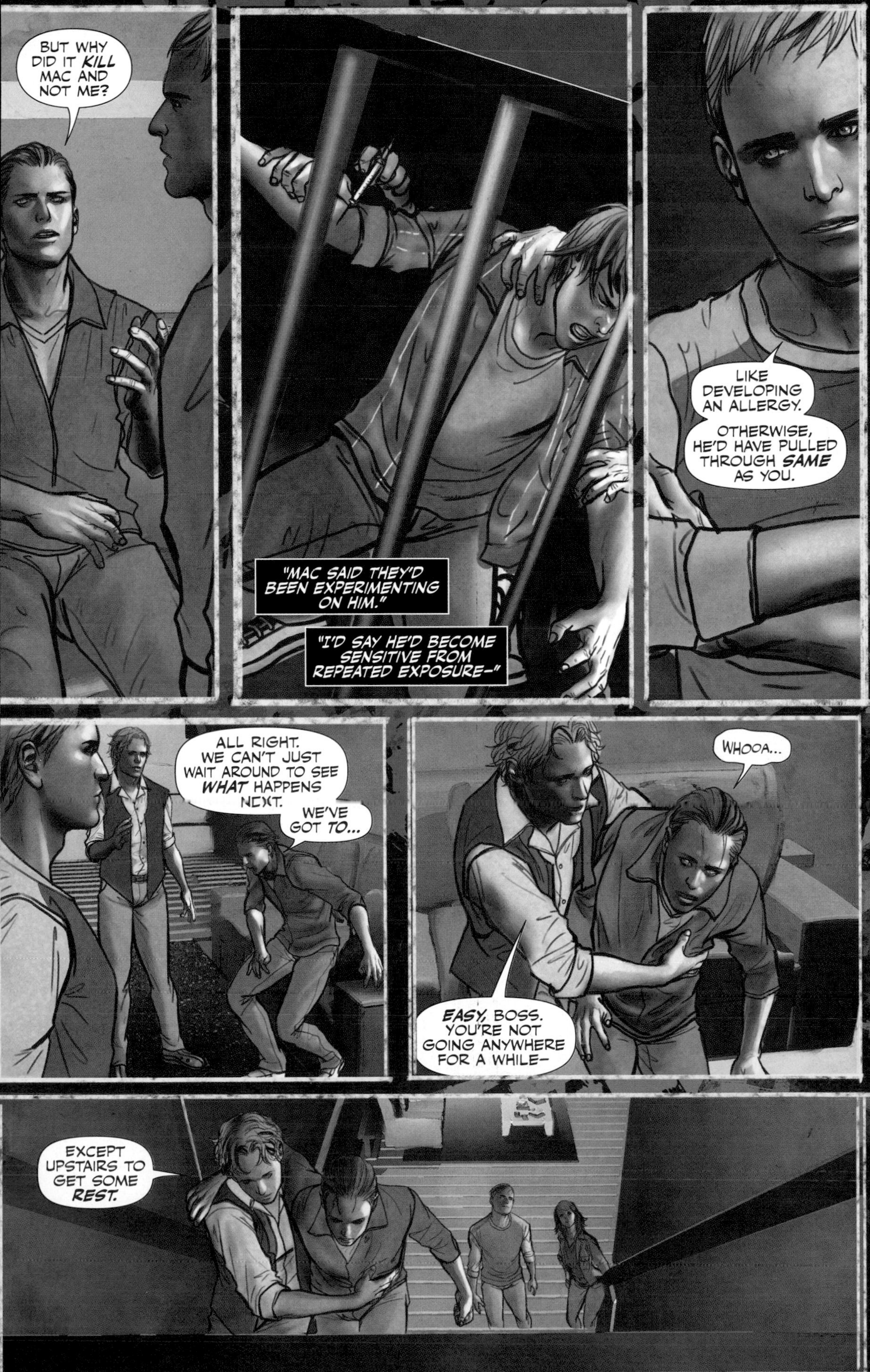
BUT WHY DID IT KILL MAC AND NOT ME?
"MAC SAID THEY'D BEEN EXPERIMENTING ON HIM."
"I'D SAY HE'D BECOME SENSITIVE FROM REPEATED EXPOSURE–"
LIKE DEVELOPING AN ALLERGY.
OTHERWISE, HE'D HAVE PULLED THROUGH SAME AS YOU.
ALL RIGHT. WE CAN'T JUST WAIT AROUND TO SEE WHAT HAPPENS NEXT.
WE'VE GOT TO...
WHOOA...
EASY, BOSS. YOU'RE NOT GOING ANYWHERE FOR A WHILE–
EXCEPT UPSTAIRS TO GET SOME REST.

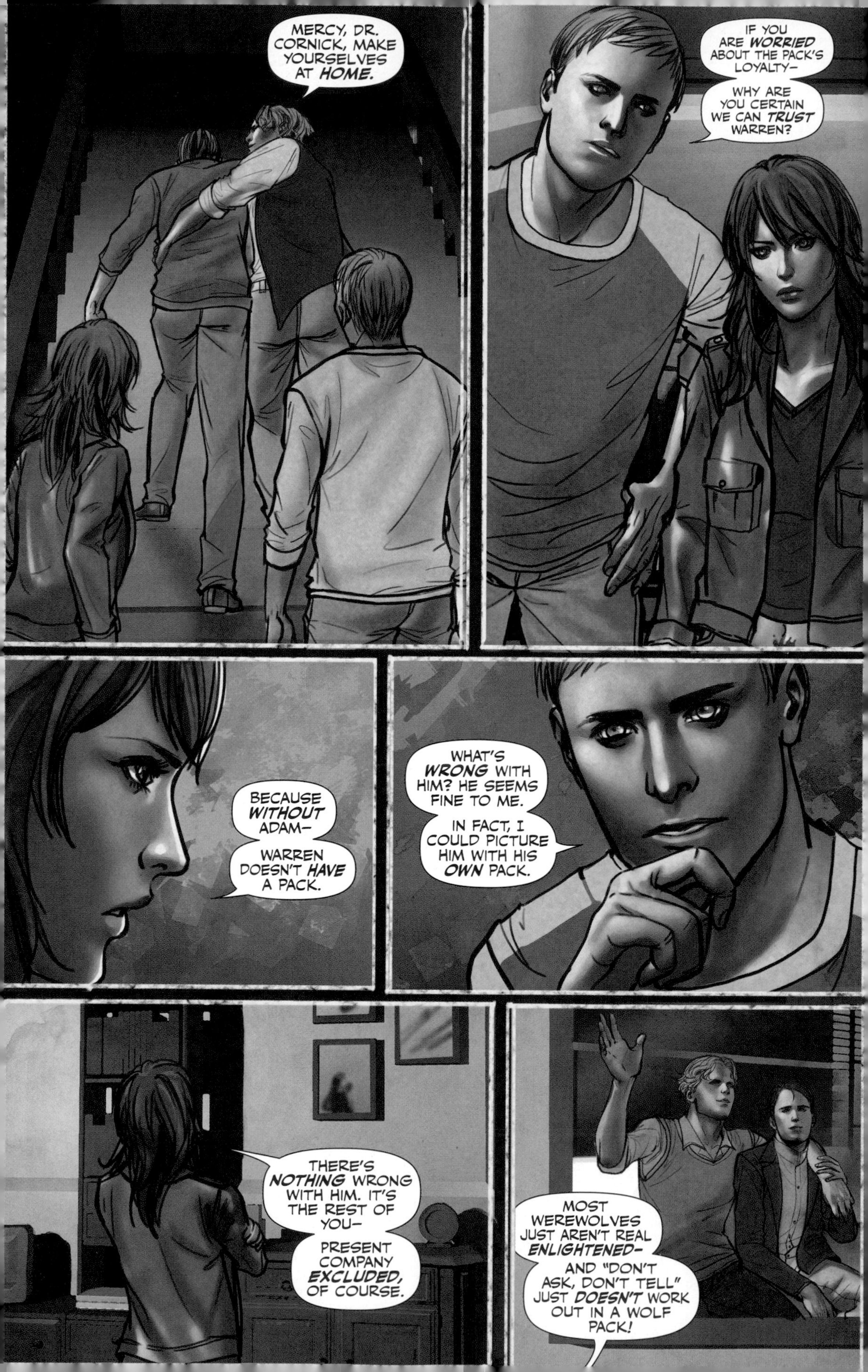
MERCY, DR. CORNICK, MAKE YOURSELVES AT HOME.
IF YOU ARE WORRIED ABOUT THE PACK'S LOYALTY—
WHY ARE YOU CERTAIN WE CAN TRUST WARREN?
BECAUSE WITHOUT ADAM—
WARREN DOESN'T HAVE A PACK.
WHAT'S WRONG WITH HIM? HE SEEMS FINE TO ME.
IN FACT, I COULD PICTURE HIM WITH HIS OWN PACK.
THERE'S NOTHING WRONG WITH HIM. IT'S THE REST OF YOU—
PRESENT COMPANY EXCLUDED, OF COURSE.
MOST WEREWOLVES JUST AREN'T REAL ENLIGHTENED—
AND "DON'T ASK, DON'T TELL" JUST DOESN'T WORK OUT IN A WOLF PACK!

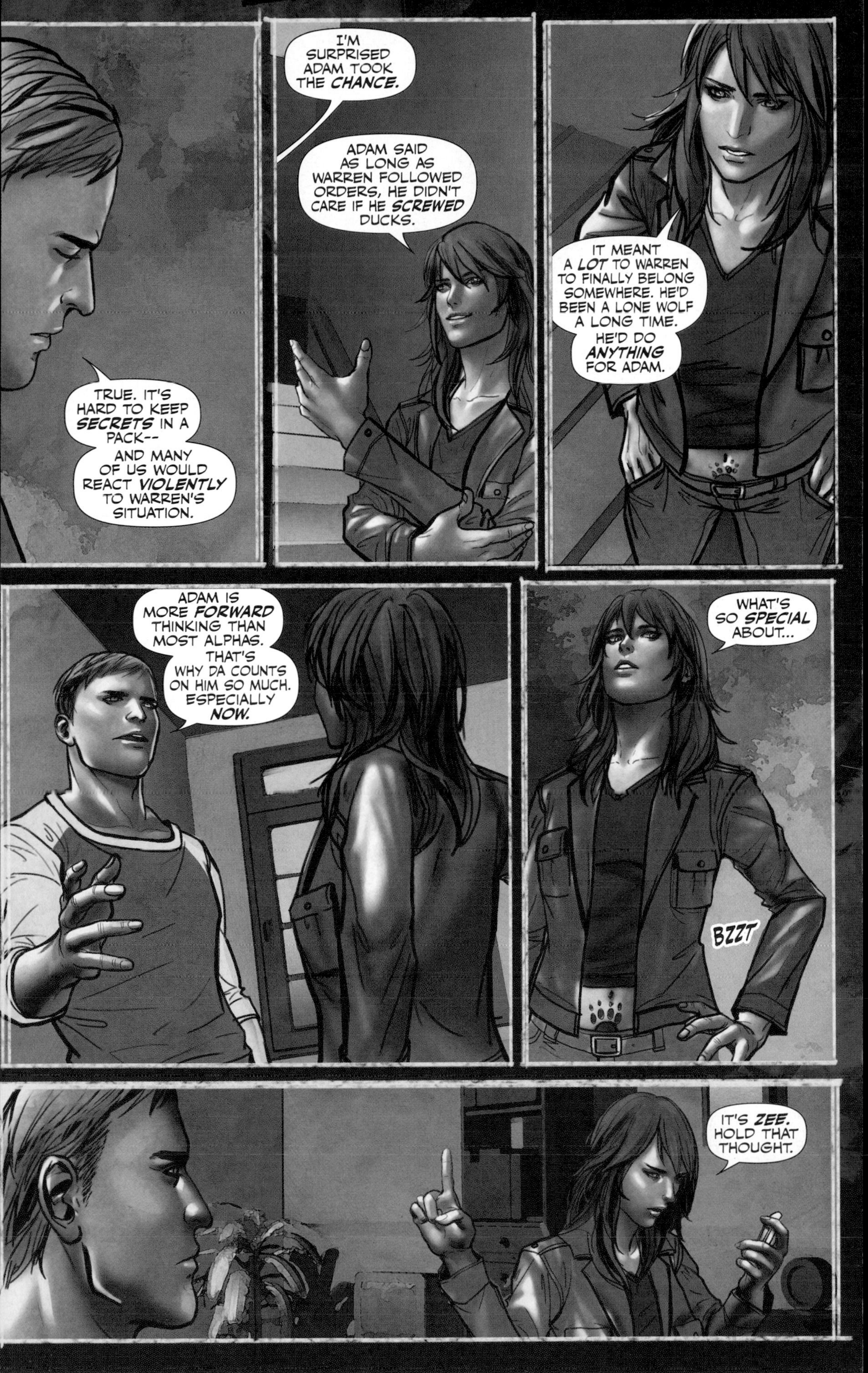
TRUE. IT'S HARD TO KEEP SECRETS IN A PACK--
AND MANY OF US WOULD REACT VIOLENTLY TO WARREN'S SITUATION.
I'M SURPRISED ADAM TOOK THE CHANCE.
ADAM SAID AS LONG AS WARREN FOLLOWED ORDERS, HE DIDN'T CARE IF HE SCREWED DUCKS.
IT MEANT A LOT TO WARREN TO FINALLY BELONG SOMEWHERE. HE'D BEEN A LONE WOLF A LONG TIME.
HE'D DO ANYTHING FOR ADAM.
ADAM IS MORE FORWARD THINKING THAN MOST ALPHAS.
THAT'S WHY DA COUNTS ON HIM SO MUCH. ESPECIALLY NOW.
WHAT'S SO SPECIAL ABOUT...
BZZT
IT'S ZEE. HOLD THAT THOUGHT.

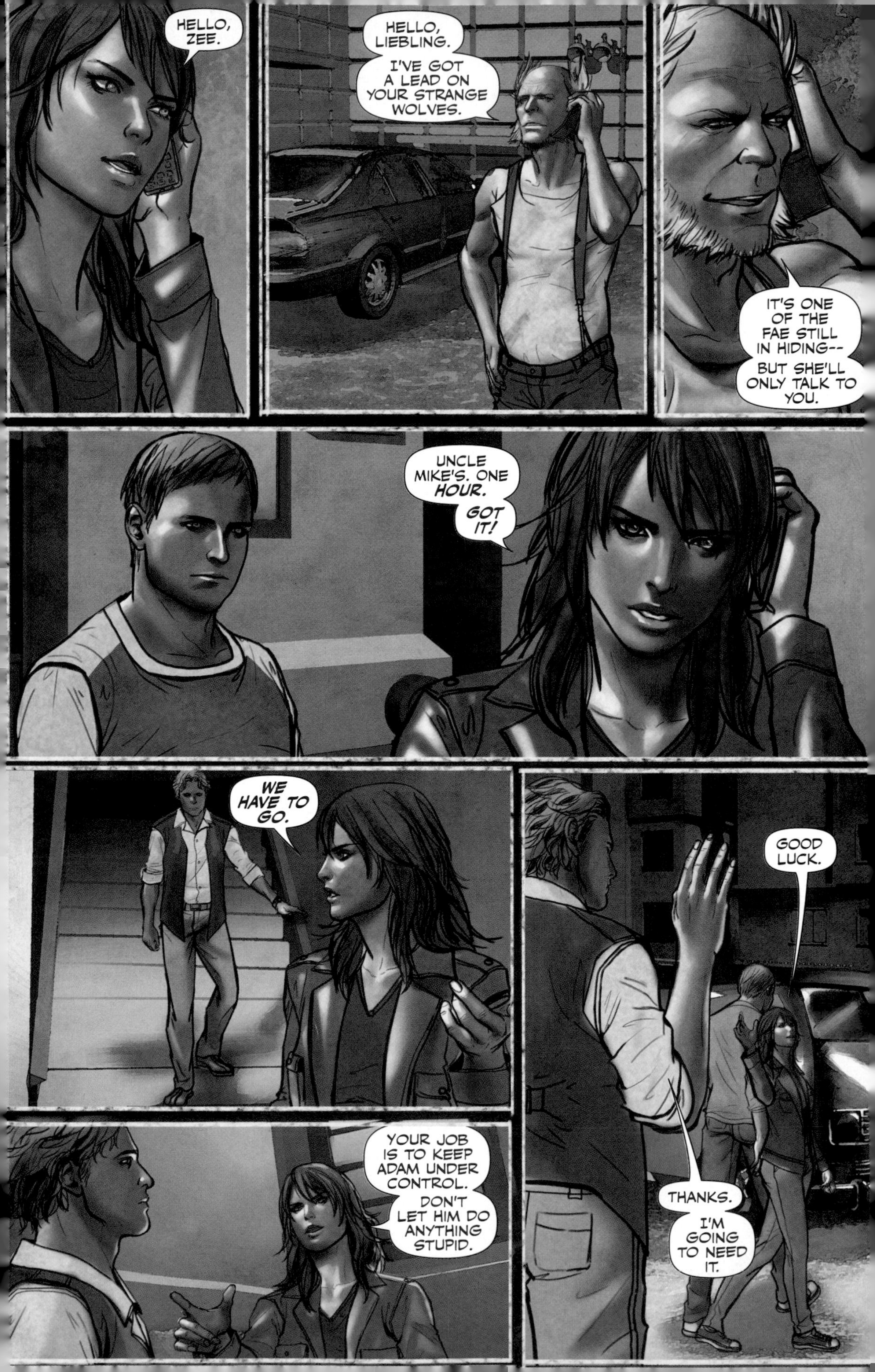
HELLO, ZEE.
HELLO, LIEBLING.
I'VE GOT A LEAD ON YOUR STRANGE WOLVES.
IT'S ONE OF THE FAE STILL IN HIDING--
BUT SHE'LL ONLY TALK TO YOU.
UNCLE MIKE'S. ONE *HOUR.*
*GOT IT!*
*WE HAVE TO GO.*
YOUR JOB IS TO KEEP ADAM UNDER CONTROL.
DON'T LET HIM DO ANYTHING STUPID.
GOOD LUCK.
THANKS.
I'M GOING TO NEED IT.

ESPECIALLY NOW?

WHAT DOES *THAT* MEAN?

I LEARNED SOMETHING IN MED SCHOOL.

SCIENCE IS CATCHING UP WITH US.

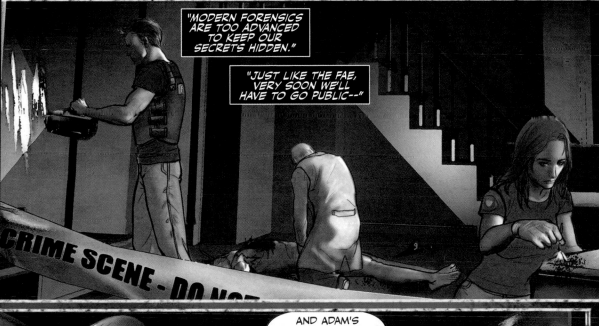

"MODERN FORENSICS ARE TOO ADVANCED TO KEEP OUR SECRETS HIDDEN."

"JUST LIKE THE FAE, VERY SOON WE'LL HAVE TO GO PUBLIC--"

CRIME SCENE - DO NOT

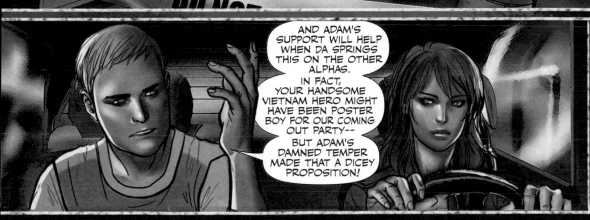

AND ADAM'S SUPPORT WILL HELP WHEN DA SPRINGS THIS ON THE OTHER ALPHAS.

IN FACT, YOUR HANDSOME VIETNAM HERO MIGHT HAVE BEEN POSTER BOY FOR OUR COMING OUT PARTY--

BUT ADAM'S DAMNED TEMPER MADE THAT A DICEY PROPOSITION!

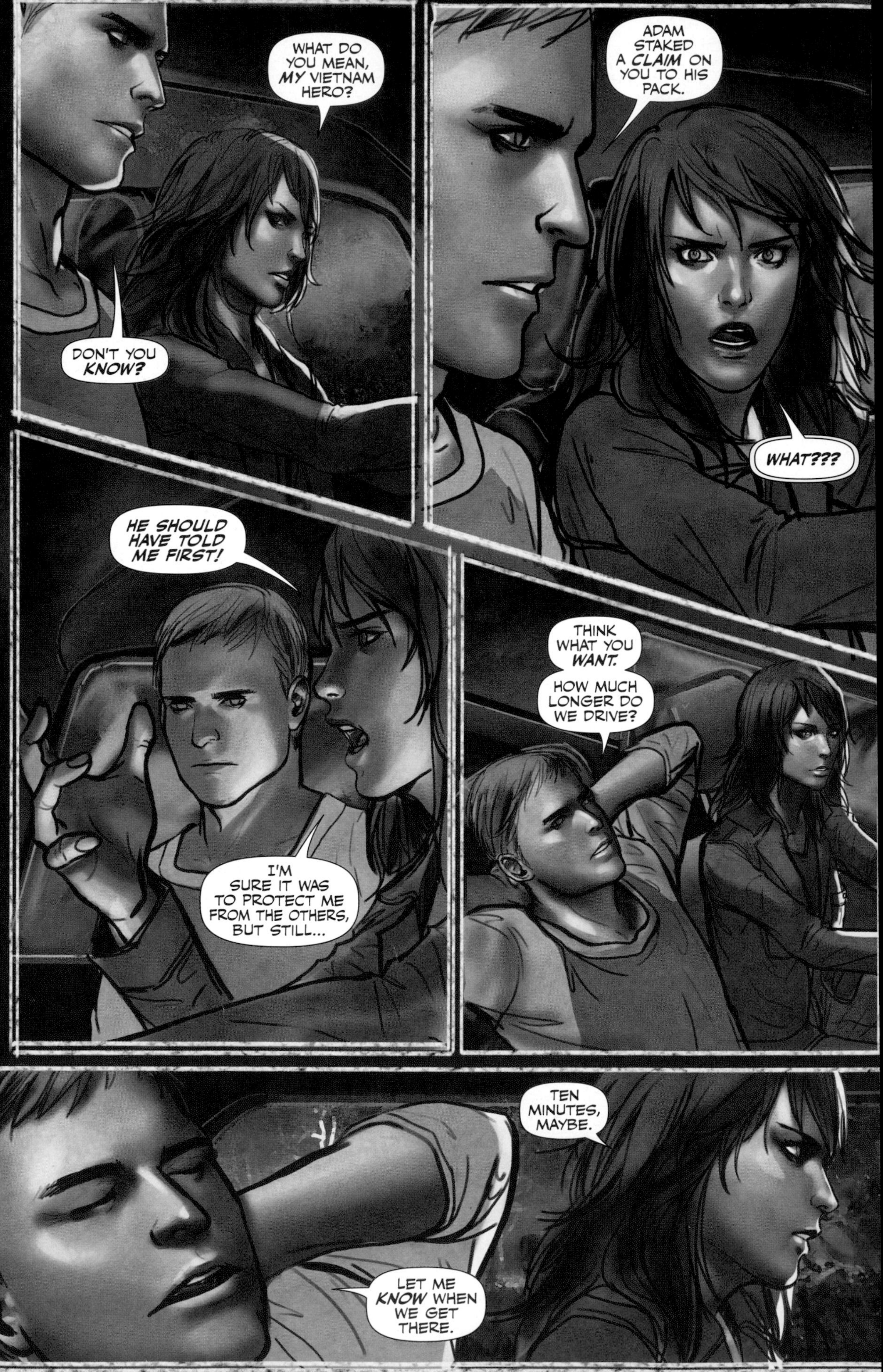
WHAT DO YOU MEAN, MY VIETNAM HERO?
DON'T YOU KNOW?
ADAM STAKED A CLAIM ON YOU TO HIS PACK.
WHAT???
HE SHOULD HAVE TOLD ME FIRST!
I'M SURE IT WAS TO PROTECT ME FROM THE OTHERS, BUT STILL...
THINK WHAT YOU WANT.
HOW MUCH LONGER DO WE DRIVE?
TEN MINUTES, MAYBE.
LET ME KNOW WHEN WE GET THERE.

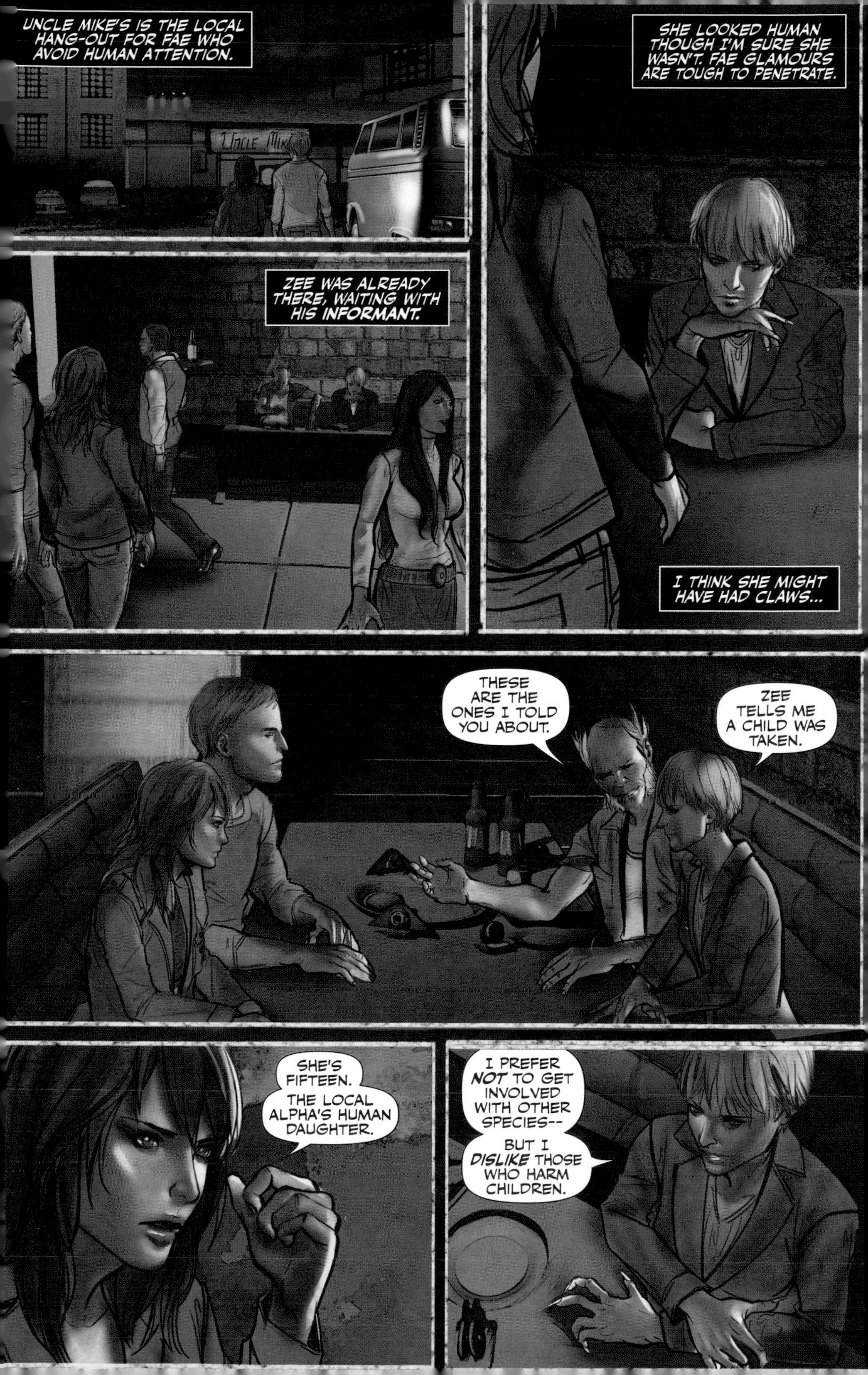
UNCLE MIKE'S IS THE LOCAL HANG-OUT FOR FAE WHO AVOID HUMAN ATTENTION.
SHE LOOKED HUMAN THOUGH I'M SURE SHE WASN'T. FAE GLAMOURS ARE TOUGH TO PENETRATE.
ZEE WAS ALREADY THERE, WAITING WITH HIS INFORMANT.
I THINK SHE MIGHT HAVE HAD CLAWS...
THESE ARE THE ONES I TOLD YOU ABOUT.
ZEE TELLS ME A CHILD WAS TAKEN.
SHE'S FIFTEEN.
THE LOCAL ALPHA'S HUMAN DAUGHTER.
I PREFER NOT TO GET INVOLVED WITH OTHER SPECIES--
BUT I DISLIKE THOSE WHO HARM CHILDREN.

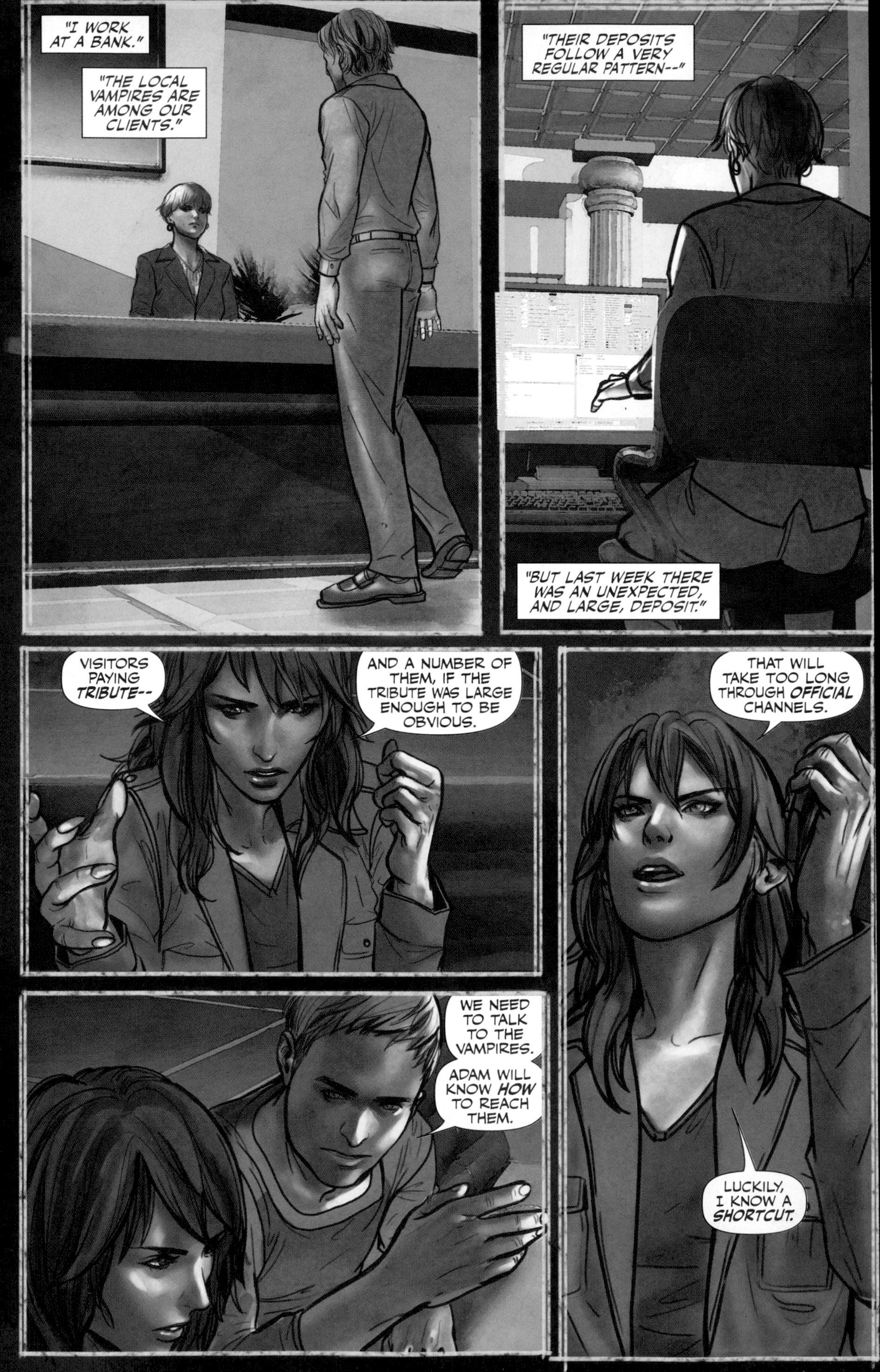
"I WORK AT A BANK."
"THE LOCAL VAMPIRES ARE AMONG OUR CLIENTS."
"THEIR DEPOSITS FOLLOW A VERY REGULAR PATTERN--"
"BUT LAST WEEK THERE WAS AN UNEXPECTED, AND LARGE, DEPOSIT."
VISITORS PAYING TRIBUTE--
AND A NUMBER OF THEM, IF THE TRIBUTE WAS LARGE ENOUGH TO BE OBVIOUS.
THAT WILL TAKE TOO LONG THROUGH OFFICIAL CHANNELS.
WE NEED TO TALK TO THE VAMPIRES.
ADAM WILL KNOW HOW TO REACH THEM.
LUCKILY, I KNOW A SHORTCUT.

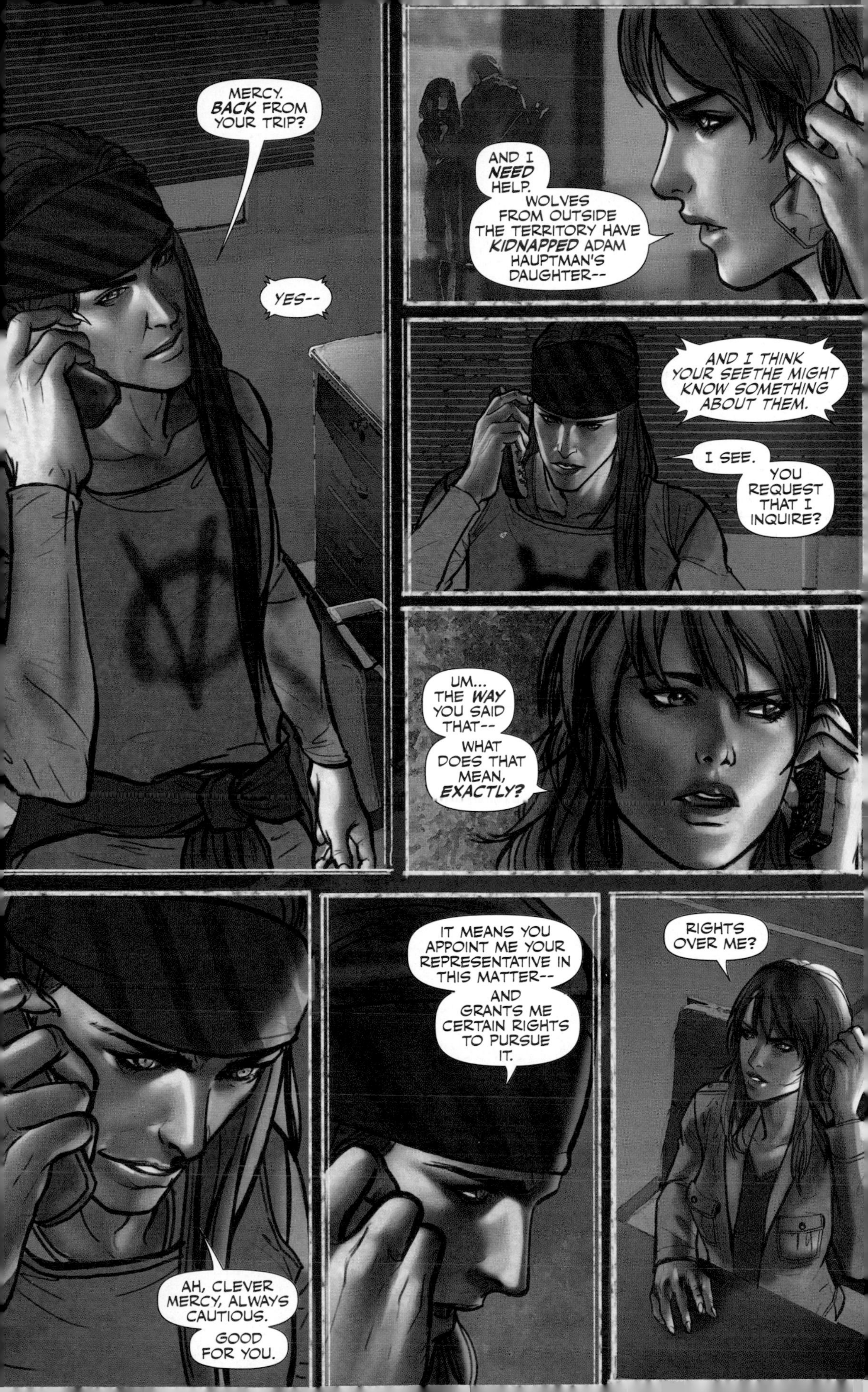
MERCY. BACK FROM YOUR TRIP?
YES--
AND I NEED HELP.
WOLVES FROM OUTSIDE THE TERRITORY HAVE KIDNAPPED ADAM HAUPTMAN'S DAUGHTER--
AND I THINK YOUR SEETHE MIGHT KNOW SOMETHING ABOUT THEM.
I SEE.
YOU REQUEST THAT I INQUIRE?
UM... THE WAY YOU SAID THAT--
WHAT DOES THAT MEAN, EXACTLY?
AH, CLEVER MERCY, ALWAYS CAUTIOUS.
GOOD FOR YOU.
IT MEANS YOU APPOINT ME YOUR REPRESENTATIVE IN THIS MATTER--
AND GRANTS ME CERTAIN RIGHTS TO PURSUE IT.
RIGHTS OVER ME?

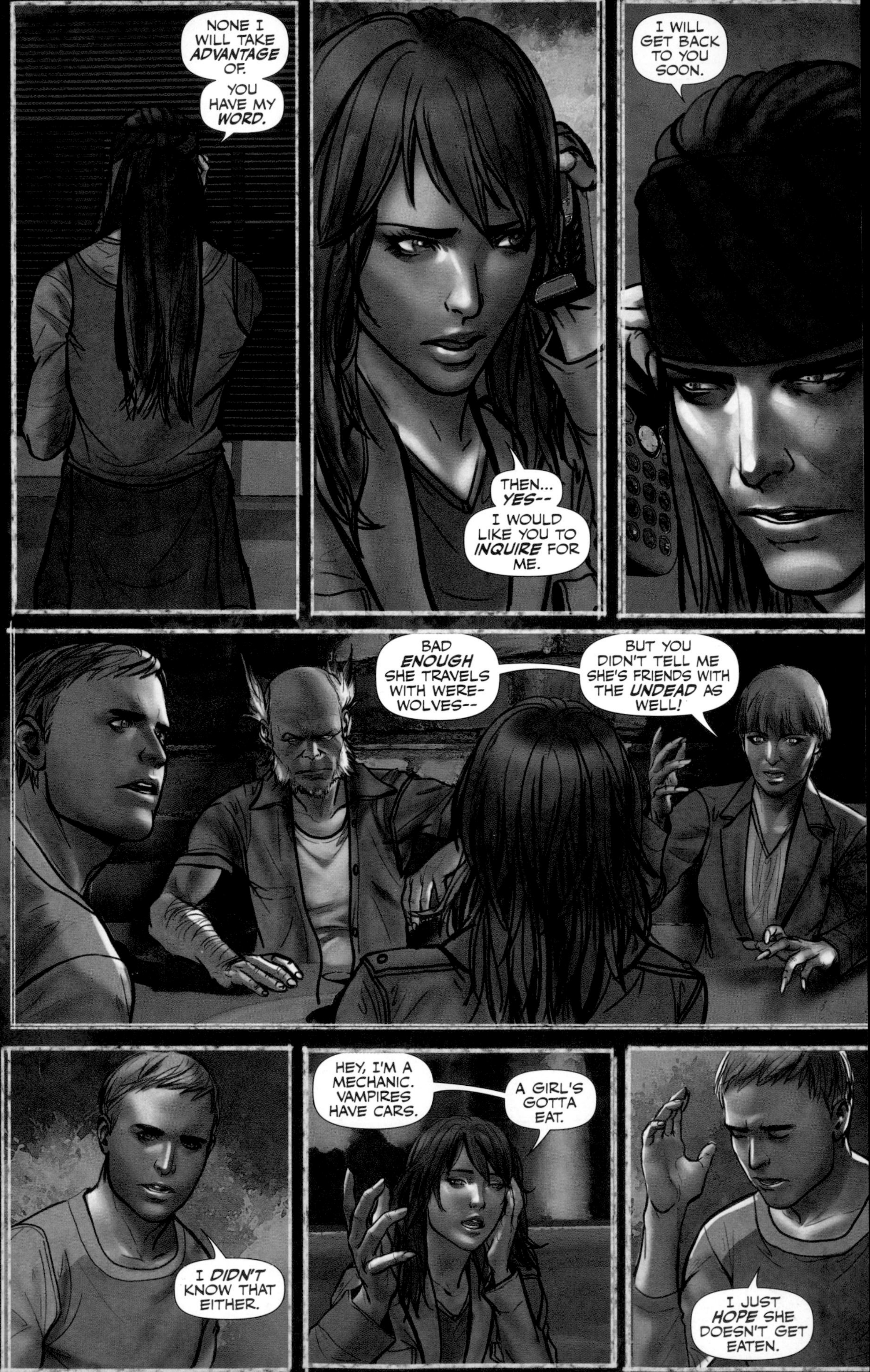

NONE I WILL TAKE *ADVANTAGE* OF.
YOU HAVE MY *WORD.*
THEN... *YES--*
I WOULD LIKE YOU TO *INQUIRE* FOR ME.
I WILL GET BACK TO YOU SOON.
BAD *ENOUGH* SHE TRAVELS WITH WERE-WOLVES--
BUT YOU DIDN'T TELL ME SHE'S FRIENDS WITH THE *UNDEAD* AS WELL!
I *DIDN'T* KNOW THAT EITHER.
HEY, I'M A MECHANIC. VAMPIRES HAVE CARS.
A GIRL'S GOTTA EAT.
I JUST *HOPE* SHE DOESN'T GET EATEN.

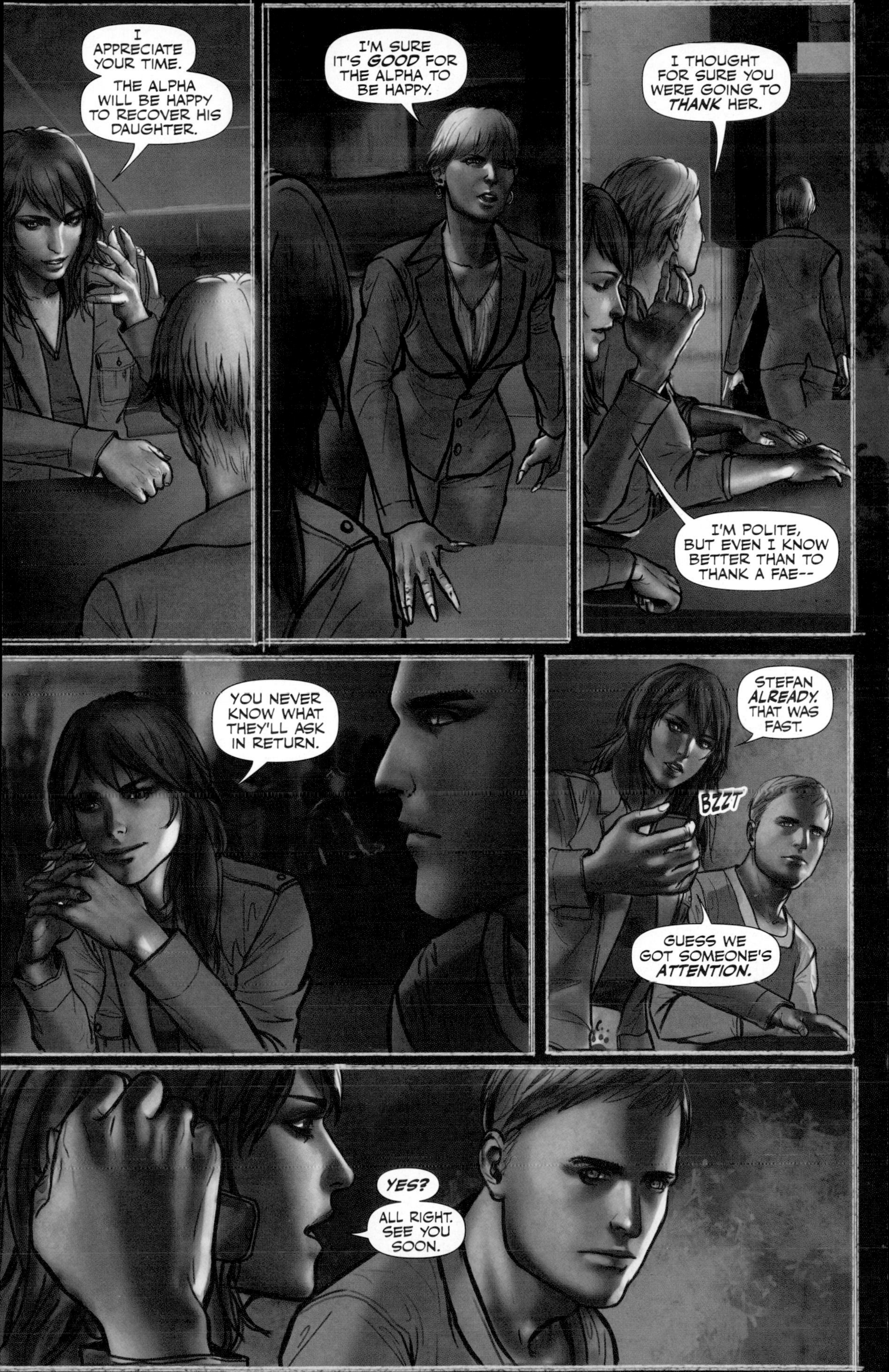
I APPRECIATE YOUR TIME.
THE ALPHA WILL BE HAPPY TO RECOVER HIS DAUGHTER.
I'M SURE IT'S *GOOD* FOR THE ALPHA TO BE HAPPY.
I THOUGHT FOR SURE YOU WERE GOING TO *THANK* HER.
I'M POLITE, BUT EVEN I KNOW BETTER THAN TO THANK A FAE--
YOU NEVER KNOW WHAT THEY'LL ASK IN RETURN.
STEFAN *ALREADY*. THAT WAS FAST.
BZZT
GUESS WE GOT SOMEONE'S *ATTENTION.*
*YES?*
ALL RIGHT. SEE YOU SOON.

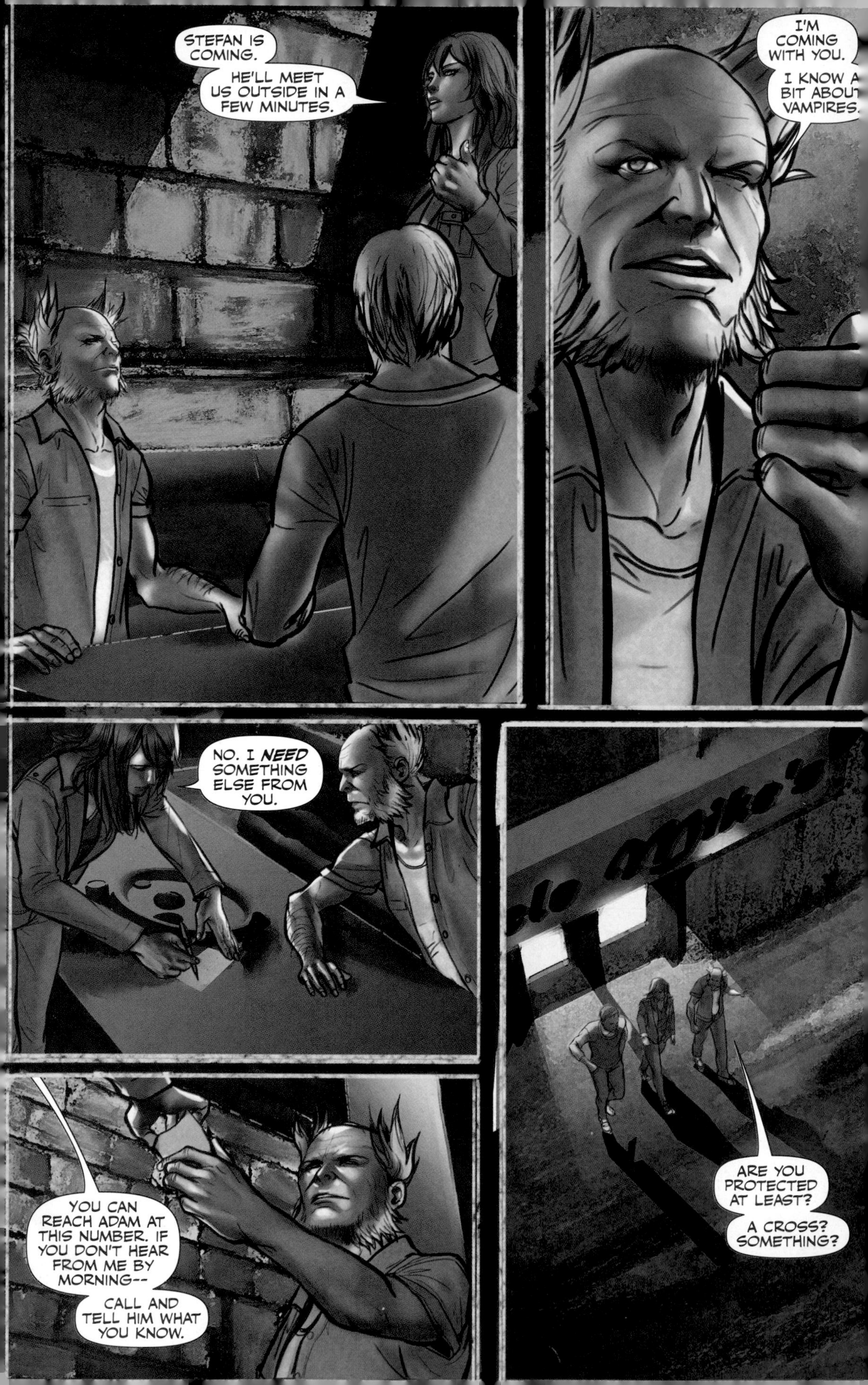
STEFAN IS COMING.
HE'LL MEET US OUTSIDE IN A FEW MINUTES.
I'M COMING WITH YOU.
I KNOW A BIT ABOUT VAMPIRES.
NO. I *NEED* SOMETHING ELSE FROM YOU.
YOU CAN REACH ADAM AT THIS NUMBER. IF YOU DON'T HEAR FROM ME BY MORNING--
CALL AND TELL HIM WHAT YOU KNOW.
ARE YOU PROTECTED AT LEAST?
A CROSS? SOMETHING?

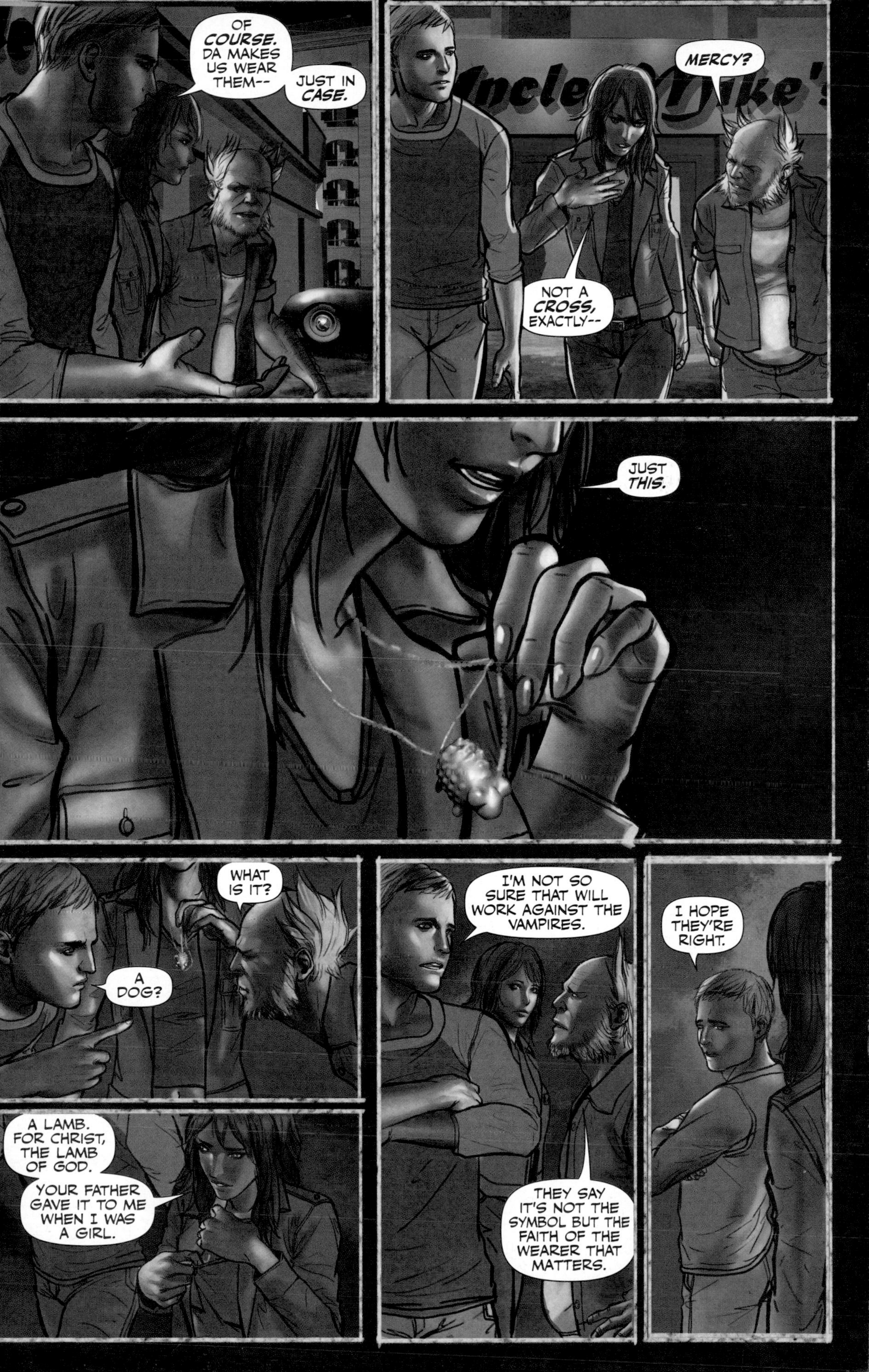
OF COURSE. DA MAKES US WEAR THEM--
JUST IN CASE.
Uncle Mike's
MERCY?
NOT A CROSS, EXACTLY--
JUST THIS.
WHAT IS IT?
A DOG?
A LAMB. FOR CHRIST, THE LAMB OF GOD.
YOUR FATHER GAVE IT TO ME WHEN I WAS A GIRL.
I'M NOT SO SURE THAT WILL WORK AGAINST THE VAMPIRES.
THEY SAY IT'S NOT THE SYMBOL BUT THE FAITH OF THE WEARER THAT MATTERS.
I HOPE THEY'RE RIGHT.

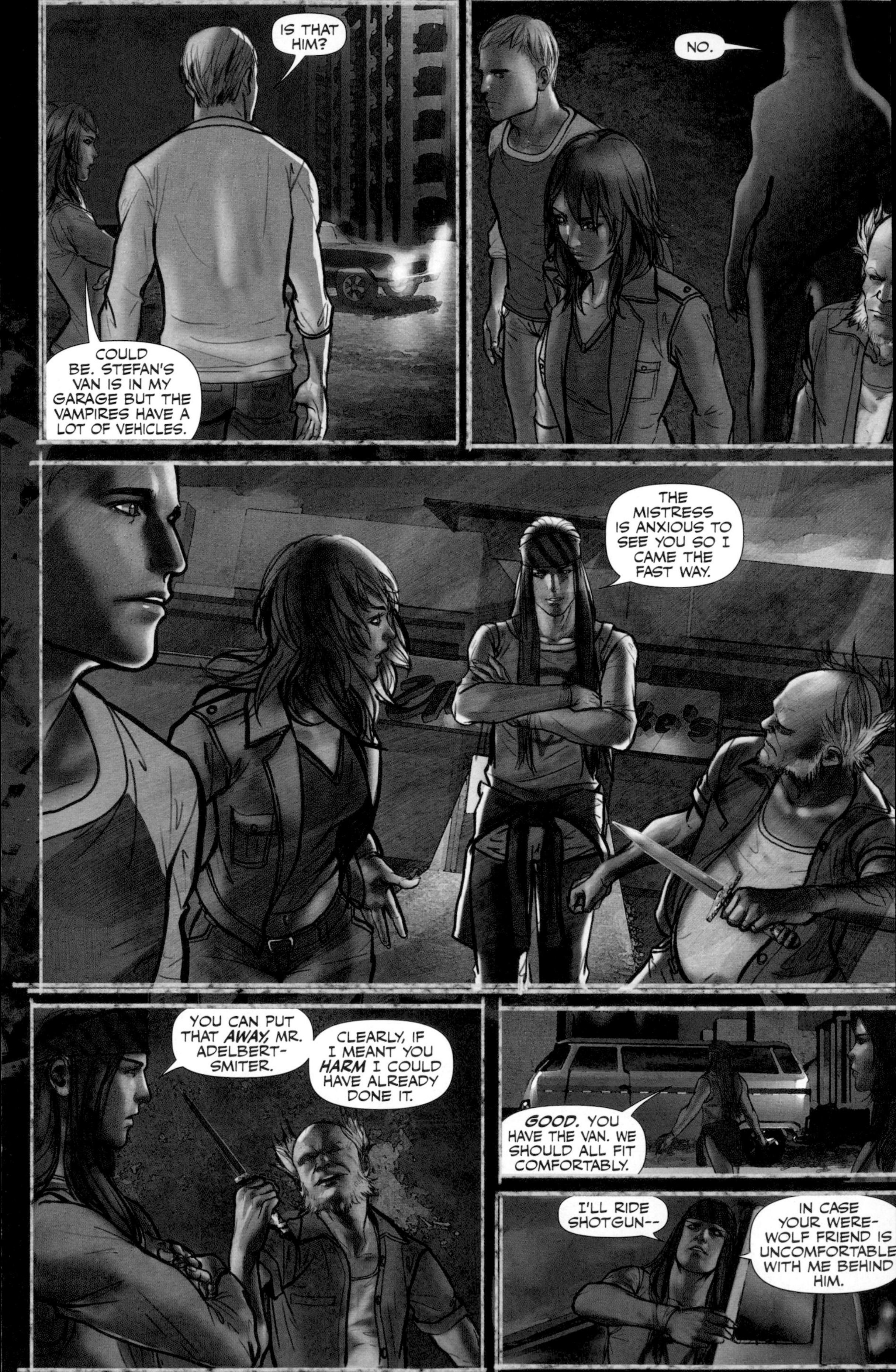
IS THAT HIM?
COULD BE. STEFAN'S VAN IS IN MY GARAGE BUT THE VAMPIRES HAVE A LOT OF VEHICLES.
NO.
THE MISTRESS IS ANXIOUS TO SEE YOU SO I CAME THE FAST WAY.
YOU CAN PUT THAT AWAY, MR. ADELBERT-SMITER.
CLEARLY, IF I MEANT YOU HARM I COULD HAVE ALREADY DONE IT.
GOOD. YOU HAVE THE VAN. WE SHOULD ALL FIT COMFORTABLY.
I'LL RIDE SHOTGUN--
IN CASE YOUR WERE-WOLF FRIEND IS UNCOMFORTABLE WITH ME BEHIND HIM.

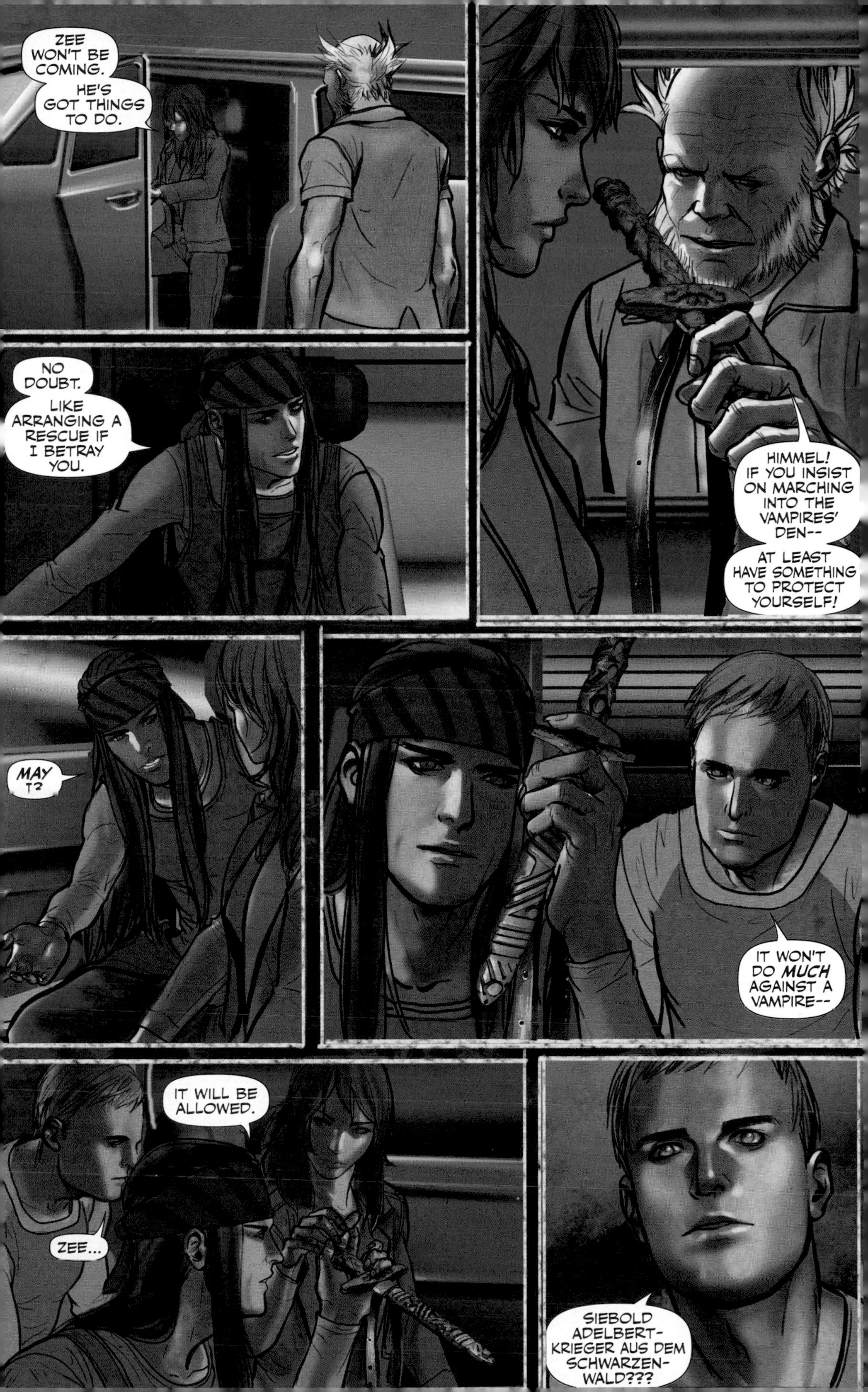
ZEE WON'T BE COMING.
HE'S GOT THINGS TO DO.
HIMMEL! IF YOU INSIST ON MARCHING INTO THE VAMPIRES' DEN--
AT LEAST HAVE SOMETHING TO PROTECT YOURSELF!
NO DOUBT.
LIKE ARRANGING A RESCUE IF I BETRAY YOU.
MAY I?
IT WON'T DO MUCH AGAINST A VAMPIRE--
IT WILL BE ALLOWED.
ZEE...
SIEBOLD ADELBERT-KRIEGER AUS DEM SCHWARZEN-WALD???

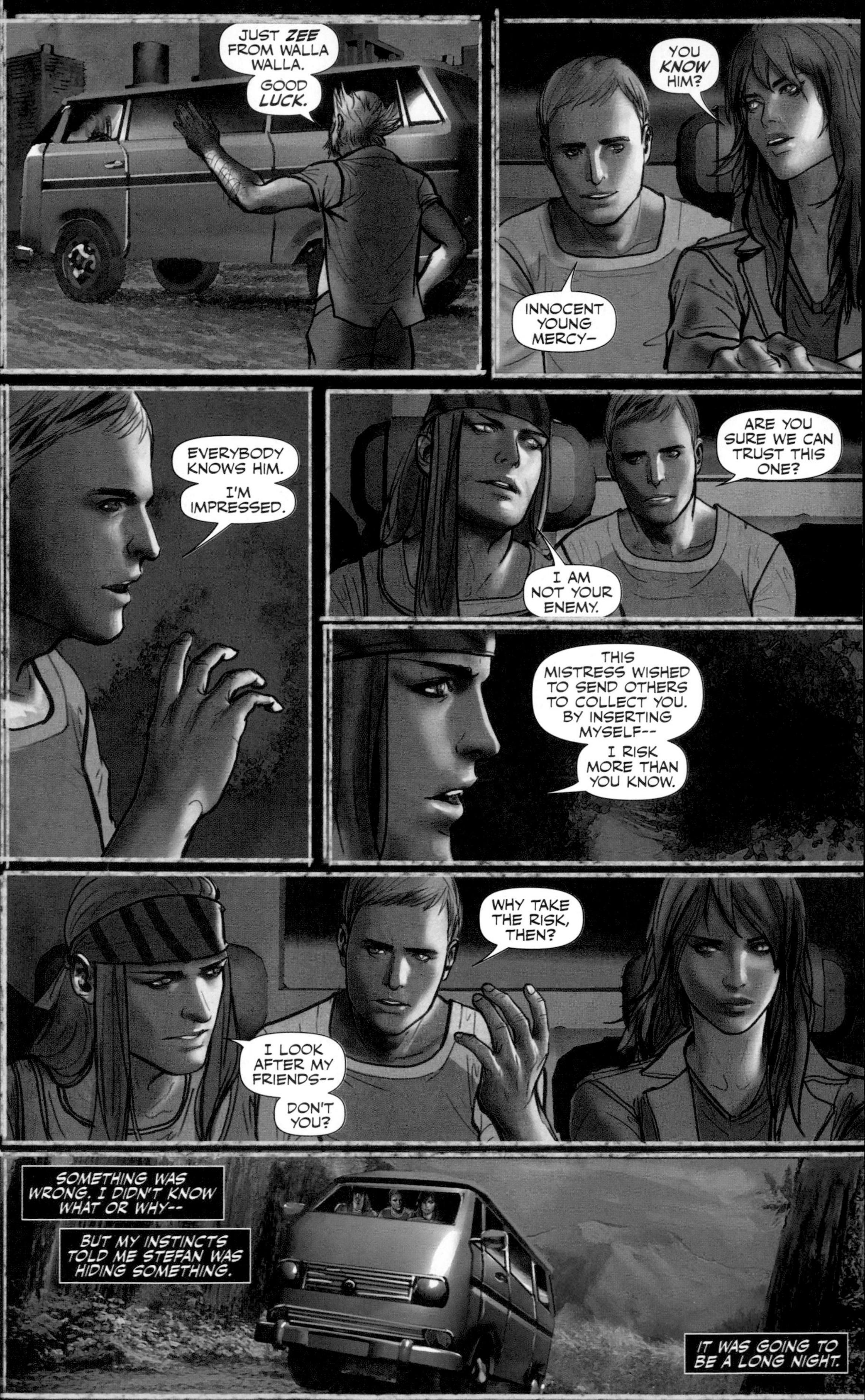
JUST ZEE FROM WALLA WALLA.
GOOD LUCK.
YOU KNOW HIM?
INNOCENT YOUNG MERCY–
EVERYBODY KNOWS HIM.
I'M IMPRESSED.
ARE YOU SURE WE CAN TRUST THIS ONE?
I AM NOT YOUR ENEMY.
THIS MISTRESS WISHED TO SEND OTHERS TO COLLECT YOU. BY INSERTING MYSELF--
I RISK MORE THAN YOU KNOW.
WHY TAKE THE RISK, THEN?
I LOOK AFTER MY FRIENDS--
DON'T YOU?
SOMETHING WAS WRONG. I DIDN'T KNOW WHAT OR WHY--
BUT MY INSTINCTS TOLD ME STEFAN WAS HIDING SOMETHING.
IT WAS GOING TO BE A LONG NIGHT.

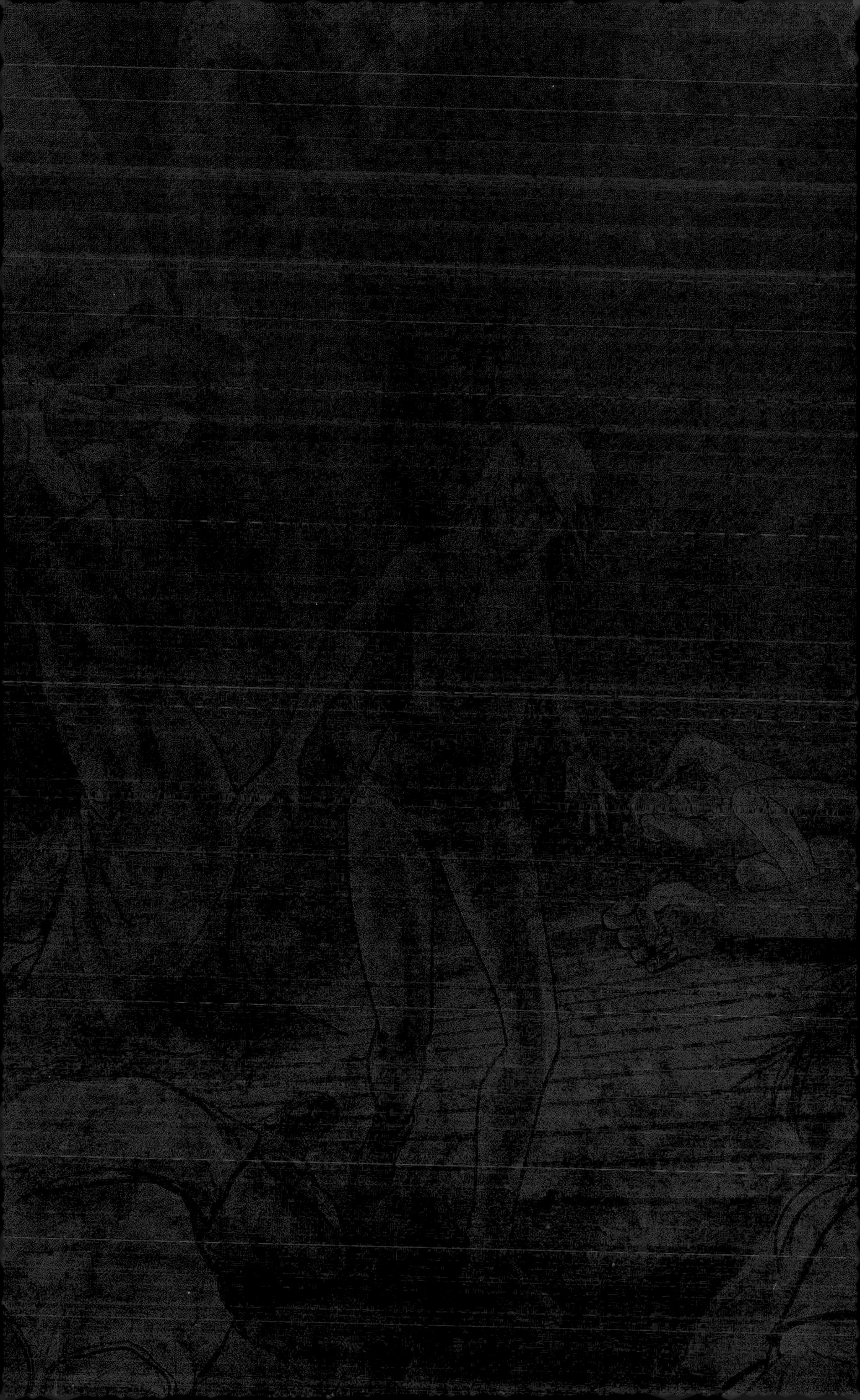

ISSUE SIX COVER BY:
**TYLER WALPOLE**

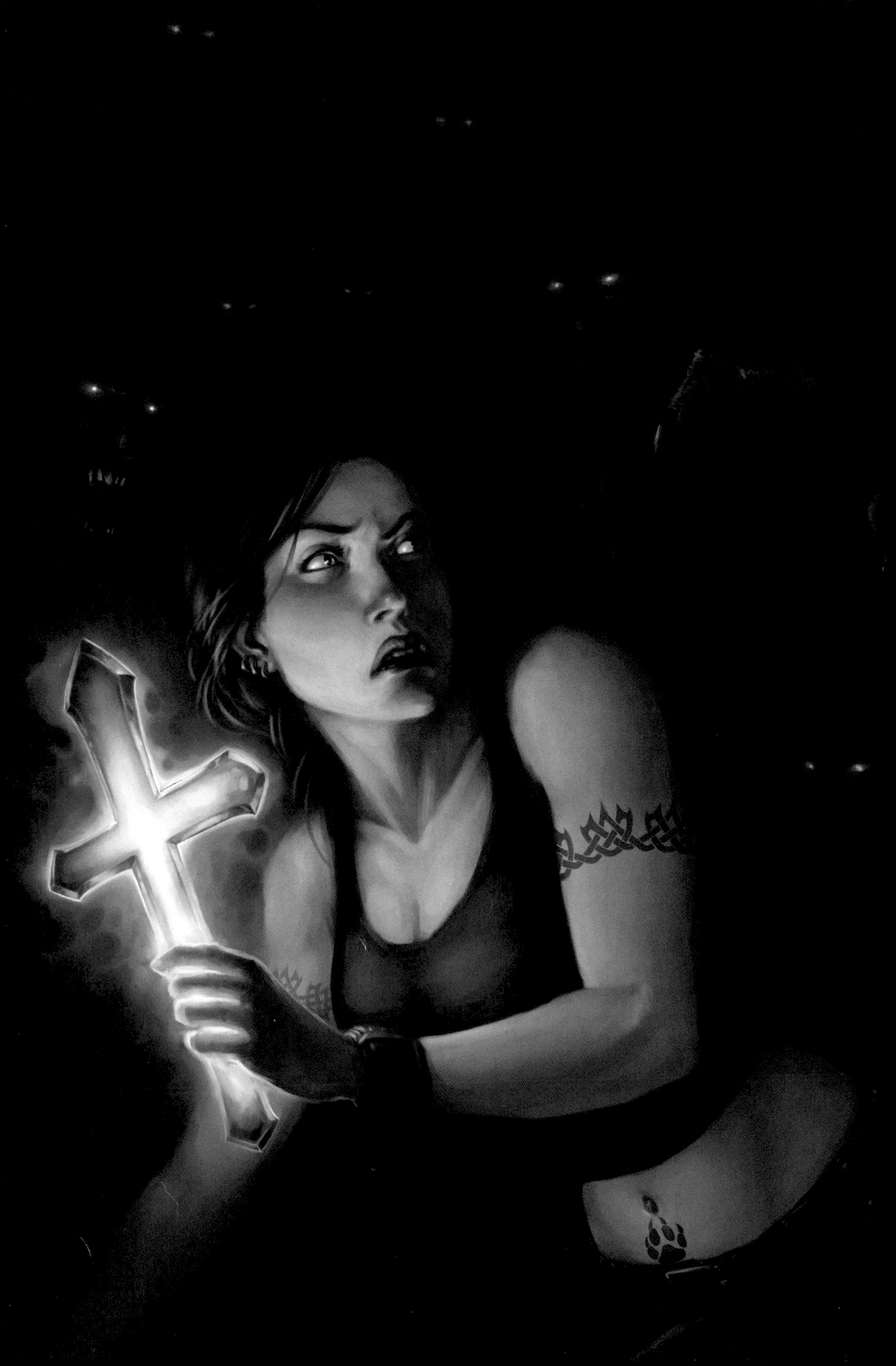

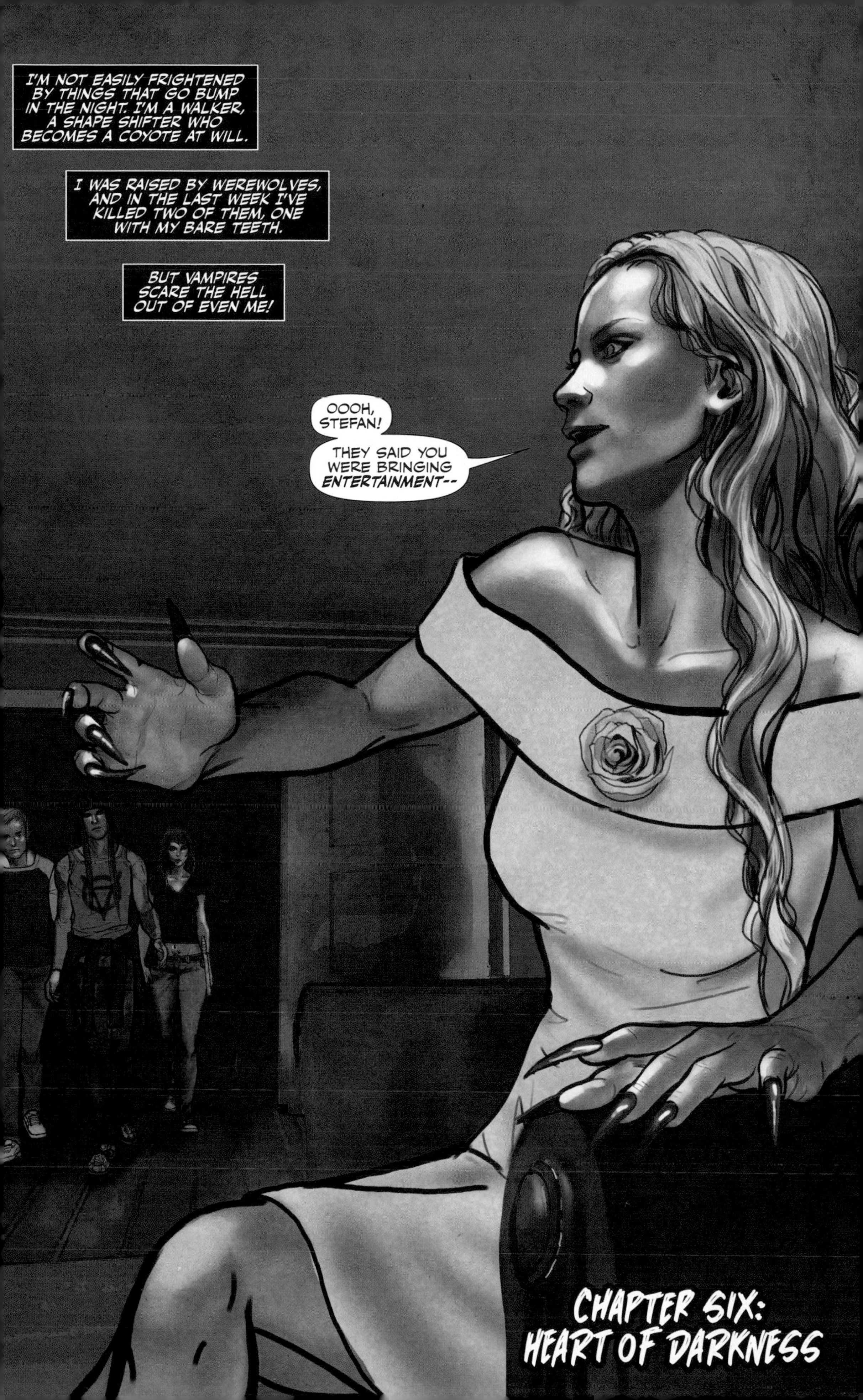
I'M NOT EASILY FRIGHTENED BY THINGS THAT GO BUMP IN THE NIGHT. I'M A WALKER, A SHAPE SHIFTER WHO BECOMES A COYOTE AT WILL.
I WAS RAISED BY WEREWOLVES, AND IN THE LAST WEEK I'VE KILLED TWO OF THEM, ONE WITH MY BARE TEETH.
BUT VAMPIRES SCARE THE HELL OUT OF EVEN ME!
OOOH, STEFAN!
THEY SAID YOU WERE BRINGING ENTERTAINMENT--
CHAPTER SIX: HEART OF DARKNESS

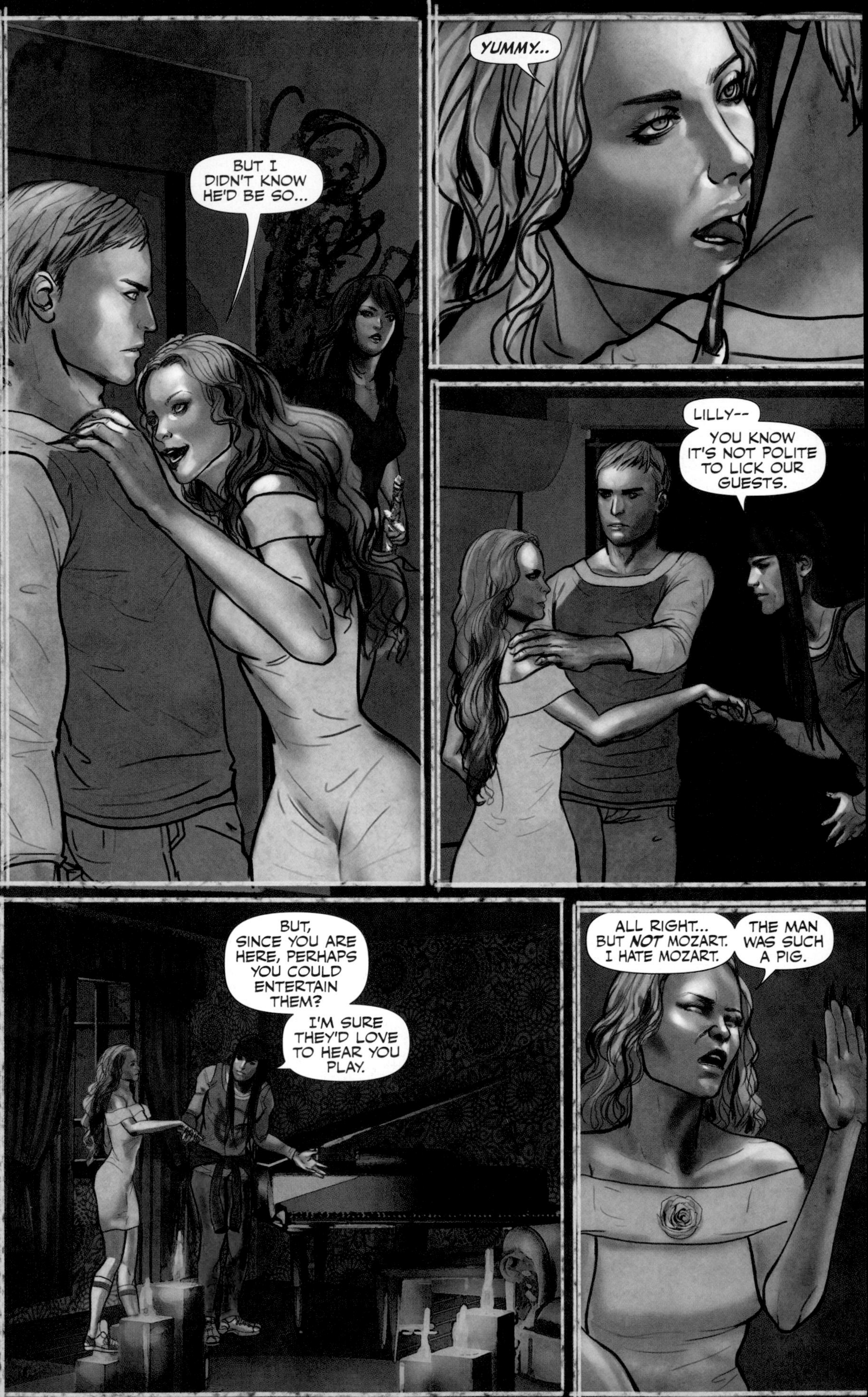
BUT I DIDN'T KNOW HE'D BE SO...
YUMMY...
LILLY--
YOU KNOW IT'S NOT POLITE TO LICK OUR GUESTS.
BUT, SINCE YOU ARE HERE, PERHAPS YOU COULD ENTERTAIN THEM?
I'M SURE THEY'D LOVE TO HEAR YOU PLAY.
ALL RIGHT... BUT NOT MOZART. I HATE MOZART.
THE MAN WAS SUCH A PIG.

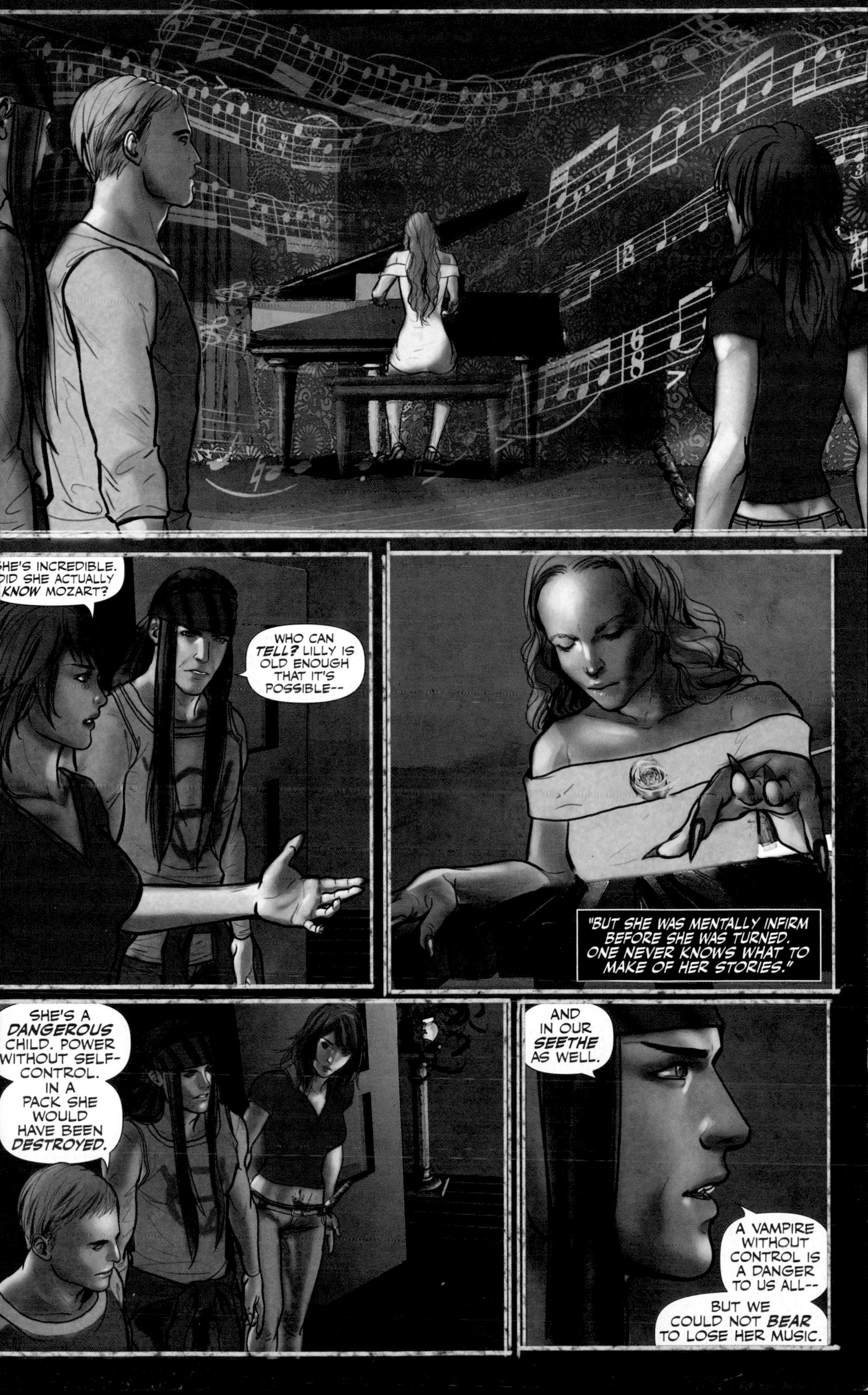

SHE'S INCREDIBLE. DID SHE ACTUALLY KNOW MOZART?
WHO CAN TELL? LILLY IS OLD ENOUGH THAT IT'S POSSIBLE--
"BUT SHE WAS MENTALLY INFIRM BEFORE SHE WAS TURNED. ONE NEVER KNOWS WHAT TO MAKE OF HER STORIES."
SHE'S A DANGEROUS CHILD. POWER WITHOUT SELF-CONTROL. IN A PACK SHE WOULD HAVE BEEN DESTROYED.
AND IN OUR SEETHE AS WELL.
A VAMPIRE WITHOUT CONTROL IS A DANGER TO US ALL--
BUT WE COULD NOT BEAR TO LOSE HER MUSIC.

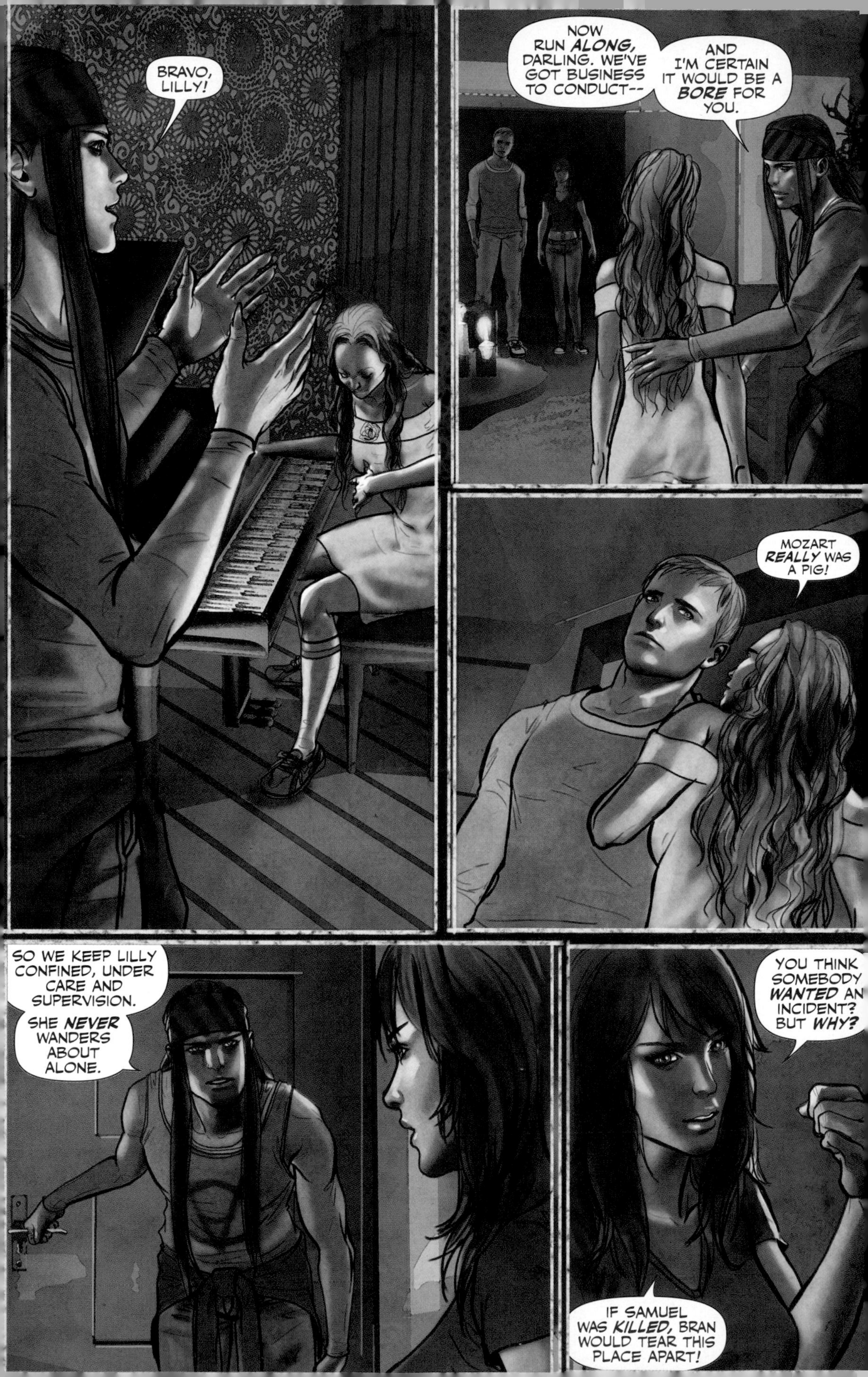
BRAVO, LILLY!
NOW RUN ALONG, DARLING. WE'VE GOT BUSINESS TO CONDUCT--
AND I'M CERTAIN IT WOULD BE A BORE FOR YOU.
MOZART REALLY WAS A PIG!
SO WE KEEP LILLY CONFINED, UNDER CARE AND SUPERVISION.
SHE NEVER WANDERS ABOUT ALONE.
YOU THINK SOMEBODY WANTED AN INCIDENT? BUT WHY?
IF SAMUEL WAS KILLED, BRAN WOULD TEAR THIS PLACE APART!

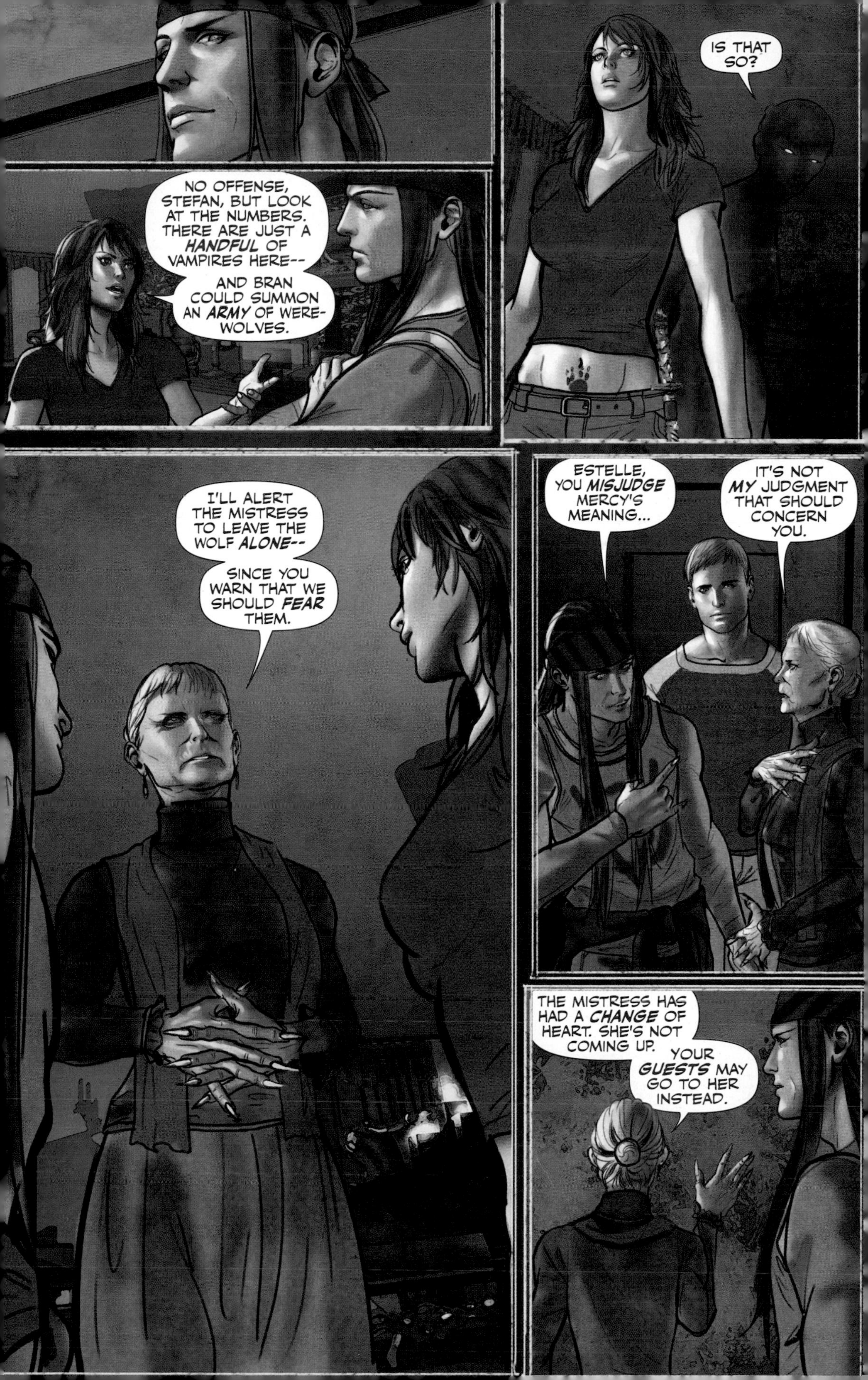
NO OFFENSE, STEFAN, BUT LOOK AT THE NUMBERS. THERE ARE JUST A HANDFUL OF VAMPIRES HERE--
AND BRAN COULD SUMMON AN ARMY OF WERE-WOLVES.
IS THAT SO?
I'LL ALERT THE MISTRESS TO LEAVE THE WOLF ALONE--
SINCE YOU WARN THAT WE SHOULD FEAR THEM.
ESTELLE, YOU MISJUDGE MERCY'S MEANING...
IT'S NOT MY JUDGMENT THAT SHOULD CONCERN YOU.
THE MISTRESS HAS HAD A CHANGE OF HEART. SHE'S NOT COMING UP.
YOUR GUESTS MAY GO TO HER INSTEAD.

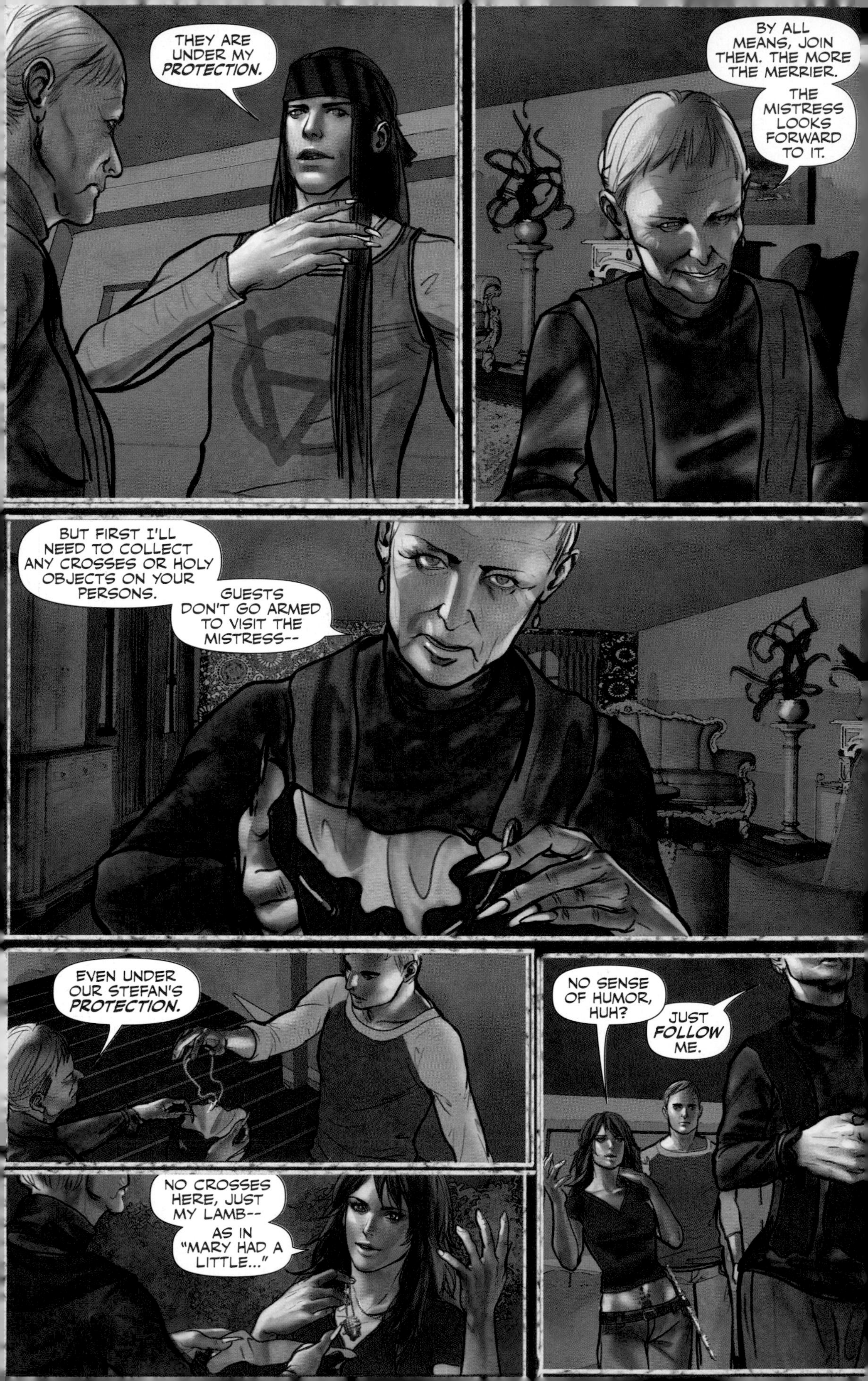
THEY ARE UNDER MY *PROTECTION.*
BY ALL MEANS, JOIN THEM. THE MORE THE MERRIER.
THE MISTRESS LOOKS FORWARD TO IT.
BUT FIRST I'LL NEED TO COLLECT ANY CROSSES OR HOLY OBJECTS ON YOUR PERSONS.
GUESTS DON'T GO ARMED TO VISIT THE MISTRESS--
EVEN UNDER OUR STEFAN'S *PROTECTION.*
NO CROSSES HERE, JUST MY LAMB--
AS IN "MARY HAD A LITTLE..."
NO SENSE OF HUMOR, HUH?
JUST *FOLLOW* ME.

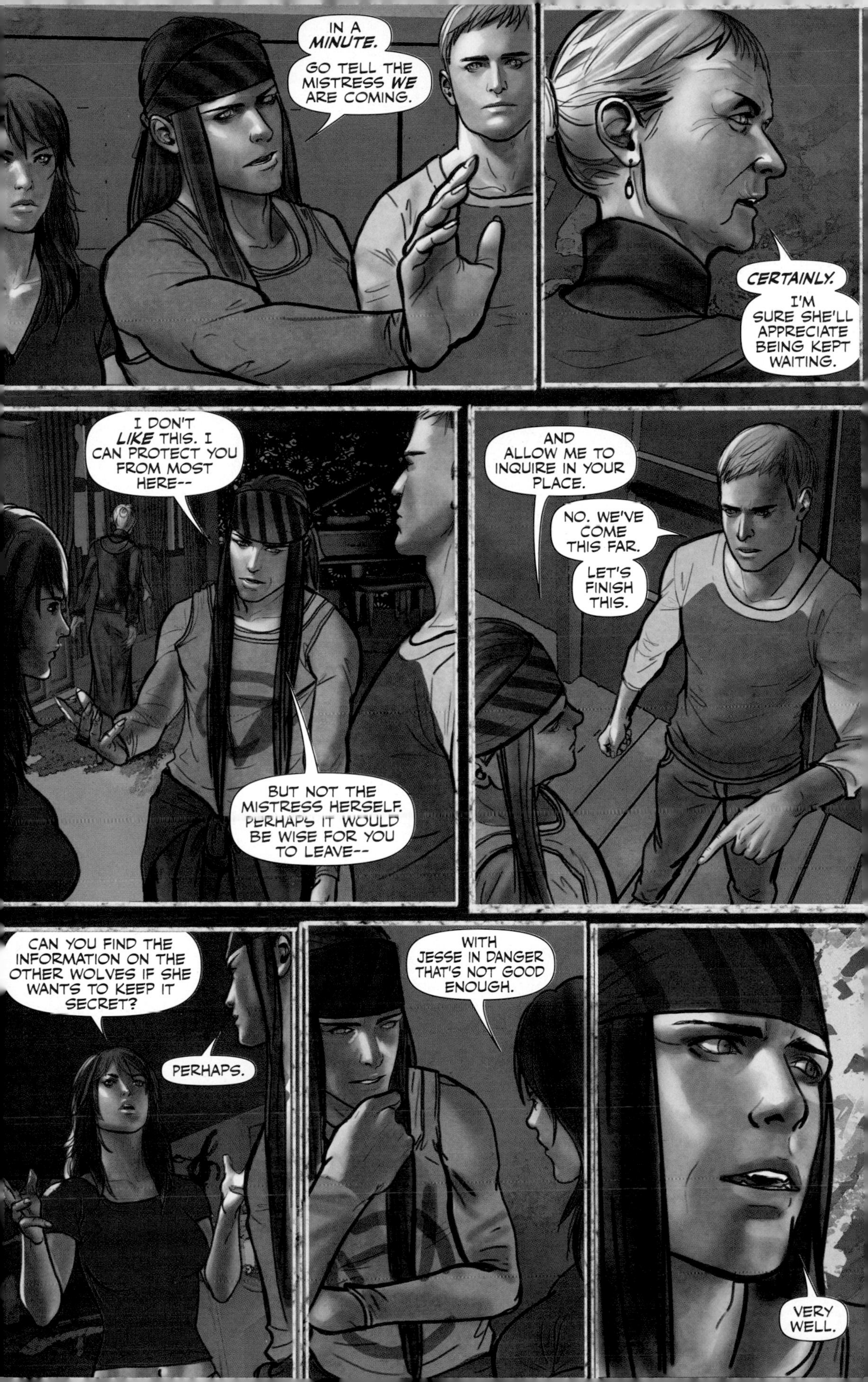
IN A MINUTE.
GO TELL THE MISTRESS WE ARE COMING.
CERTAINLY.
I'M SURE SHE'LL APPRECIATE BEING KEPT WAITING.
I DON'T LIKE THIS. I CAN PROTECT YOU FROM MOST HERE--
BUT NOT THE MISTRESS HERSELF. PERHAPS IT WOULD BE WISE FOR YOU TO LEAVE--
AND ALLOW ME TO INQUIRE IN YOUR PLACE.
NO. WE'VE COME THIS FAR.
LET'S FINISH THIS.
CAN YOU FIND THE INFORMATION ON THE OTHER WOLVES IF SHE WANTS TO KEEP IT SECRET?
PERHAPS.
WITH JESSE IN DANGER THAT'S NOT GOOD ENOUGH.
VERY WELL.

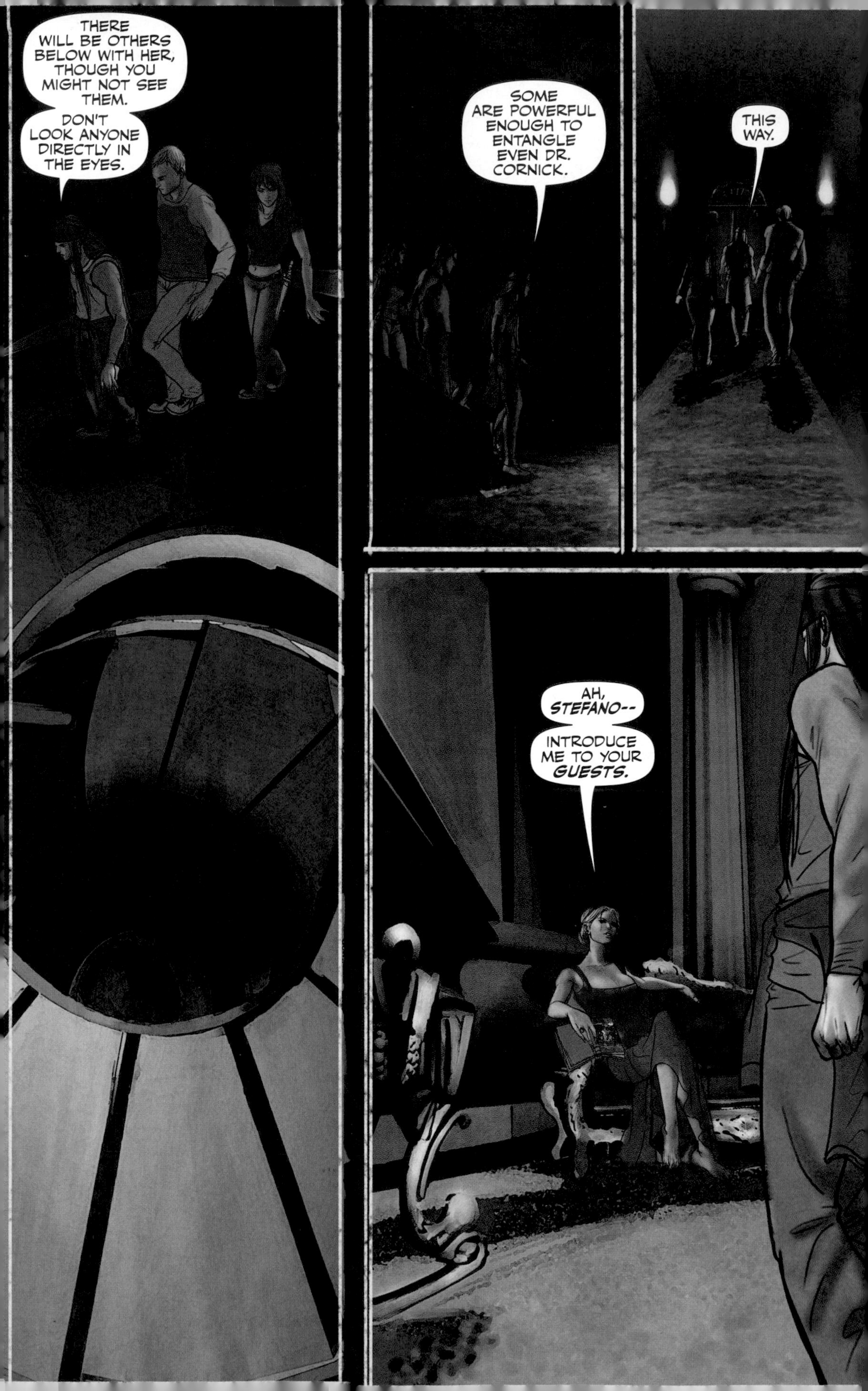
THERE WILL BE OTHERS BELOW WITH HER, THOUGH YOU MIGHT NOT SEE THEM.
DON'T LOOK ANYONE DIRECTLY IN THE EYES.
SOME ARE POWERFUL ENOUGH TO ENTANGLE EVEN DR. CORNICK.
THIS WAY.
AH, STEFANO--
INTRODUCE ME TO YOUR GUESTS.

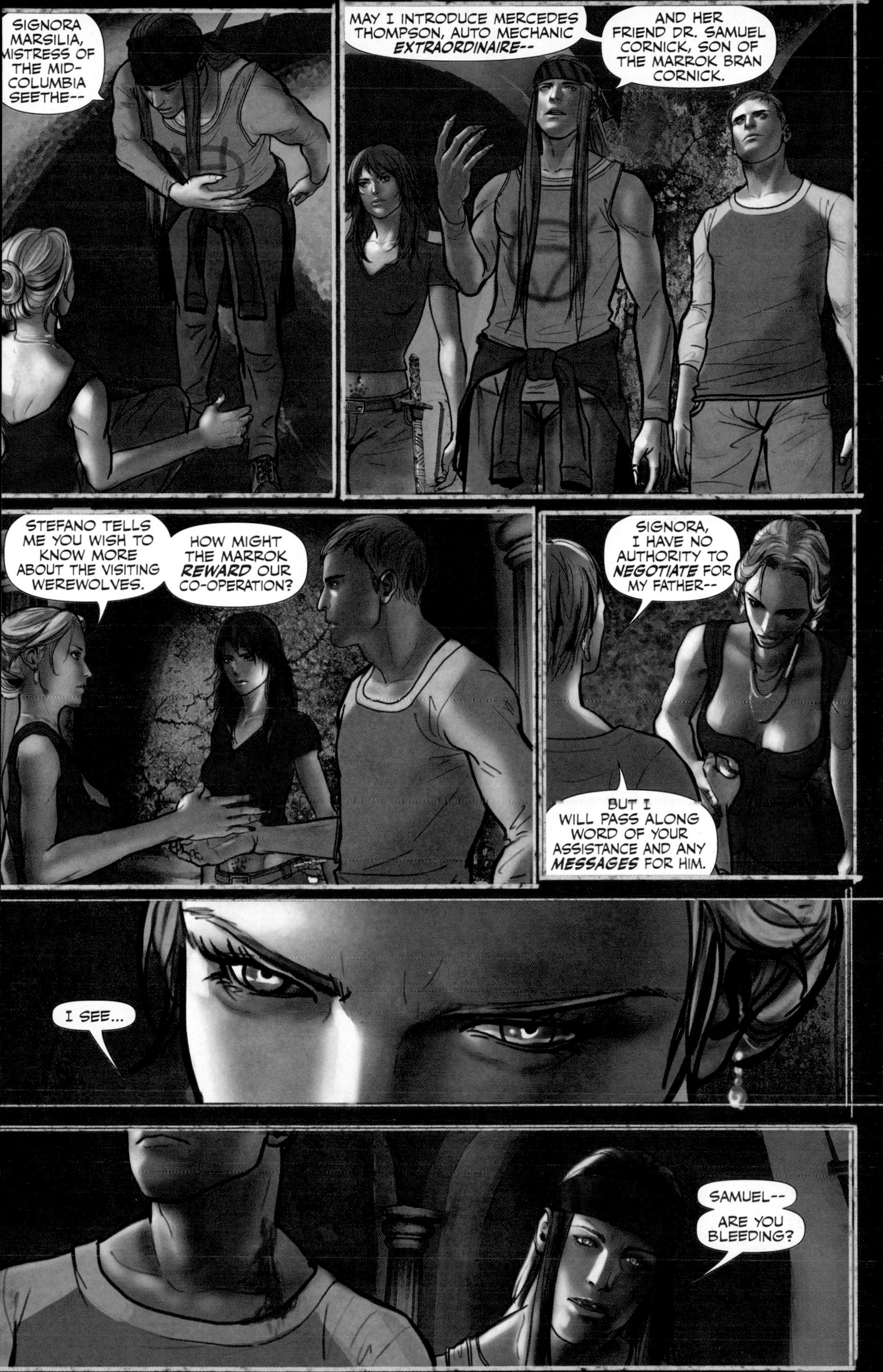
SIGNORA MARSILIA, MISTRESS OF THE MID-COLUMBIA SEETHE--
MAY I INTRODUCE MERCEDES THOMPSON, AUTO MECHANIC EXTRAORDINAIRE--
AND HER FRIEND DR. SAMUEL CORNICK, SON OF THE MARROK BRAN CORNICK.
STEFANO TELLS ME YOU WISH TO KNOW MORE ABOUT THE VISITING WEREWOLVES.
HOW MIGHT THE MARROK REWARD OUR CO-OPERATION?
SIGNORA, I HAVE NO AUTHORITY TO NEGOTIATE FOR MY FATHER--
BUT I WILL PASS ALONG WORD OF YOUR ASSISTANCE AND ANY MESSAGES FOR HIM.
I SEE...
SAMUEL--
ARE YOU BLEEDING?

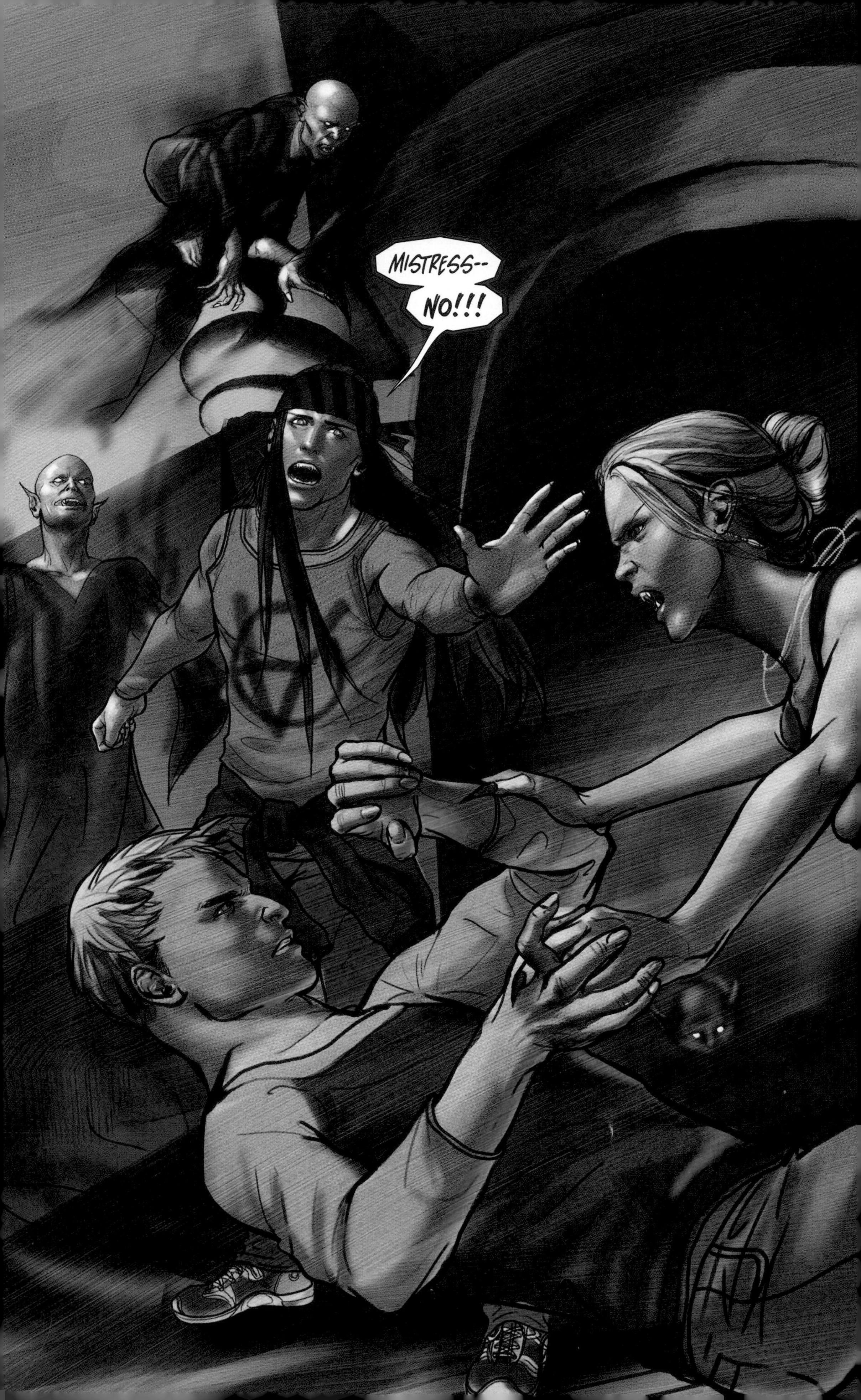
MISTRESS--
NO!!!

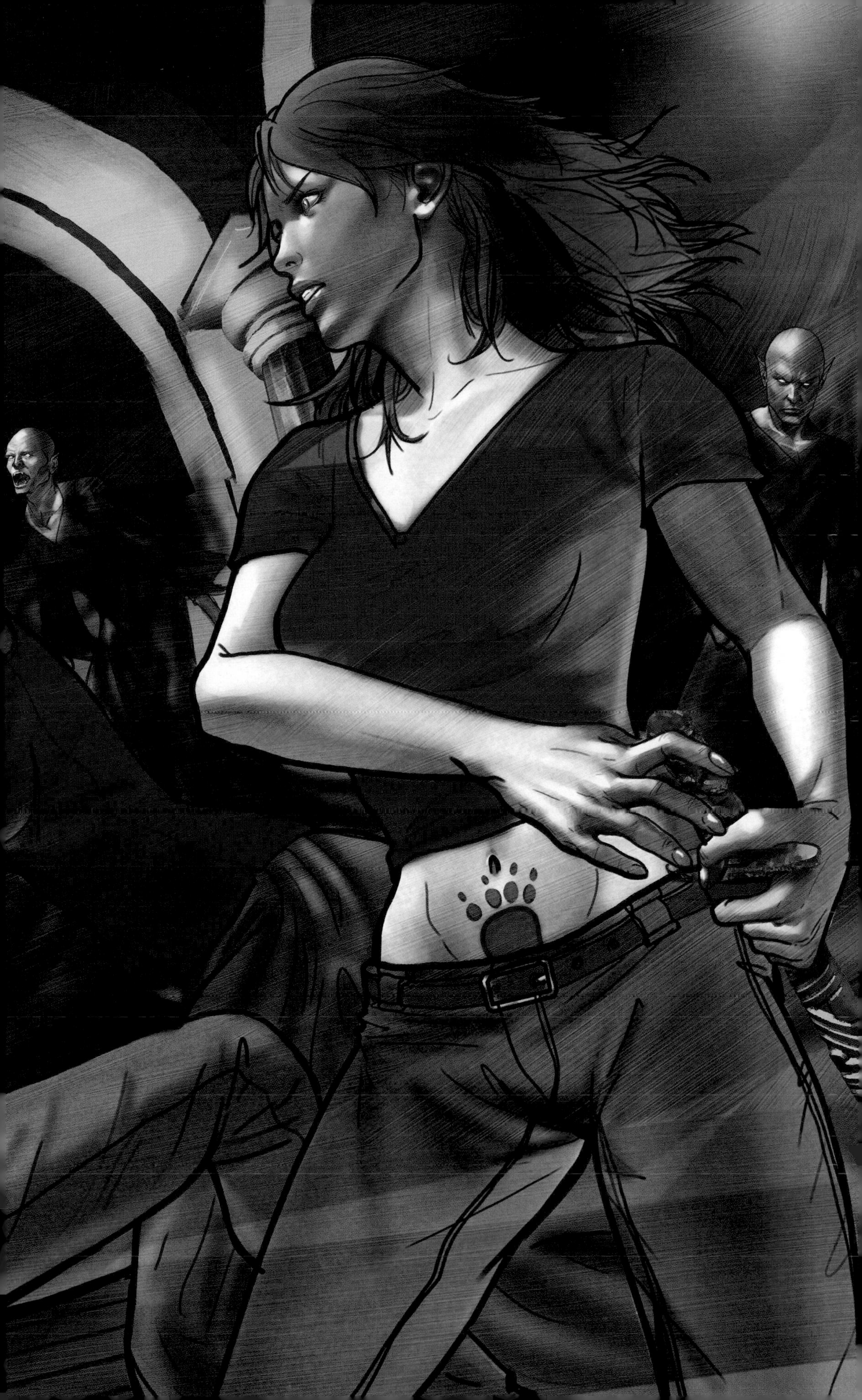

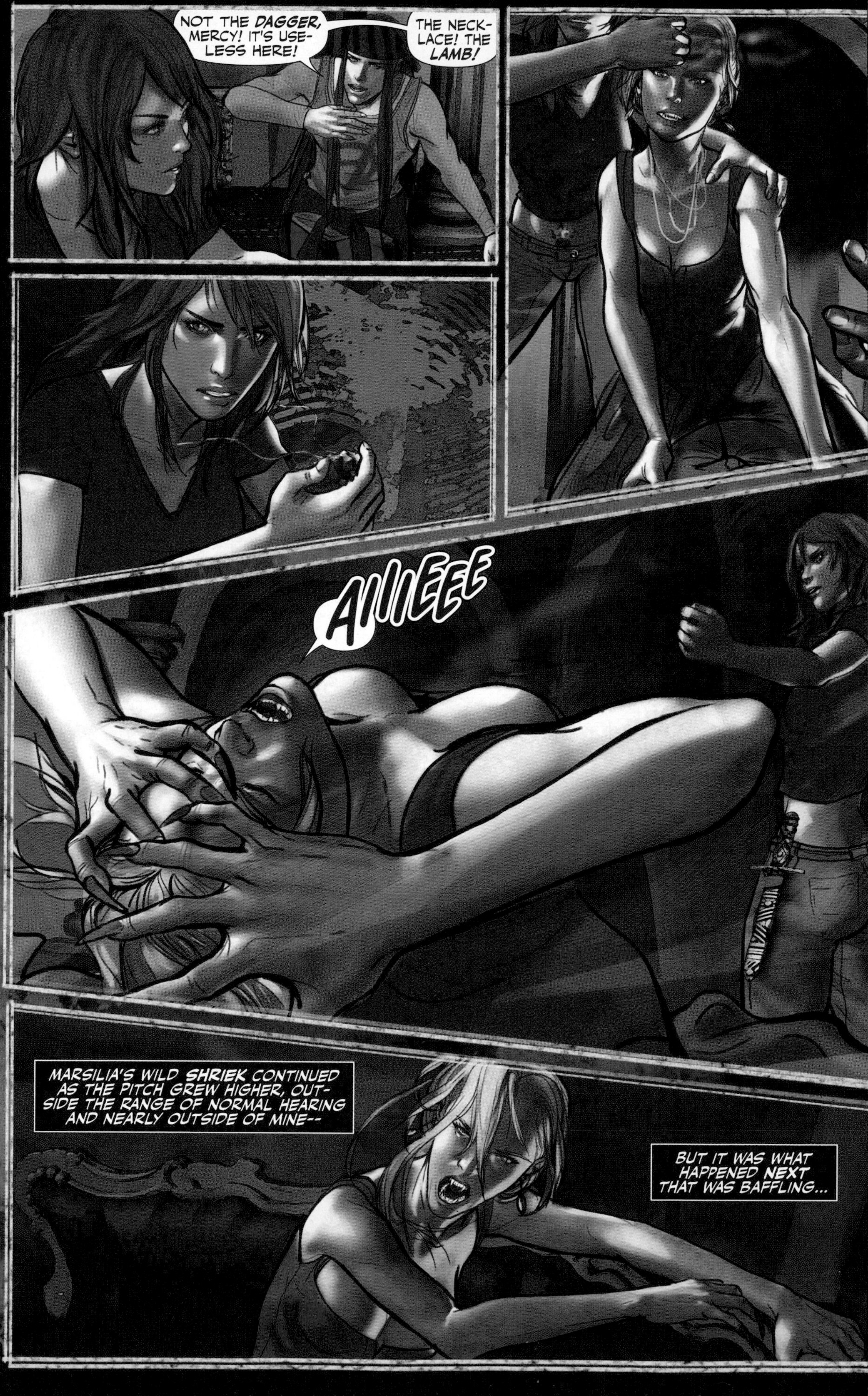
NOT THE DAGGER, MERCY! IT'S USELESS HERE!
THE NECKLACE! THE LAMB!
AIIIEEE
MARSILIA'S WILD SHRIEK CONTINUED AS THE PITCH GREW HIGHER, OUTSIDE THE RANGE OF NORMAL HEARING AND NEARLY OUTSIDE OF MINE--
BUT IT WAS WHAT HAPPENED NEXT THAT WAS BAFFLING...

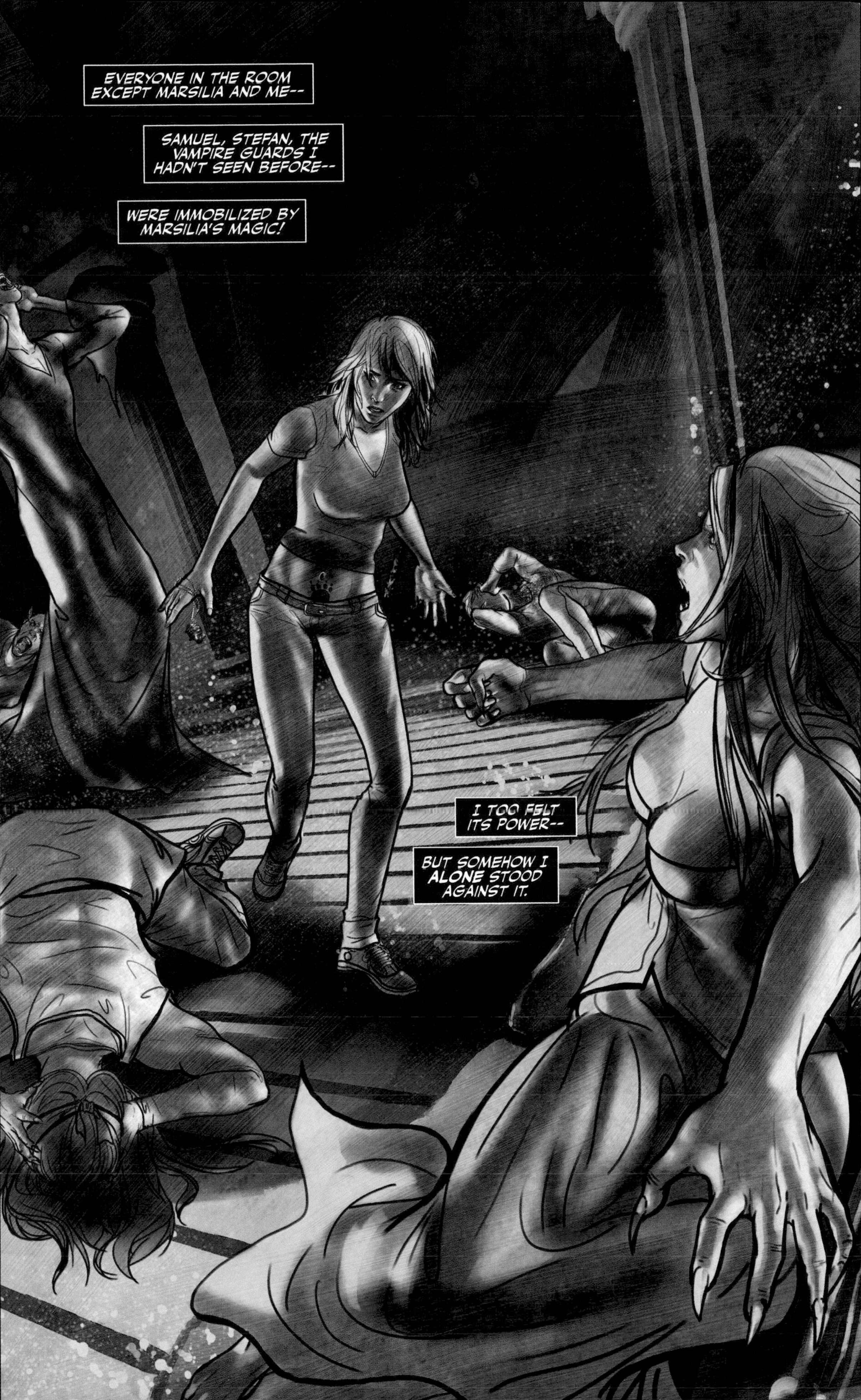
EVERYONE IN THE ROOM EXCEPT MARSILIA AND ME--
SAMUEL, STEFAN, THE VAMPIRE GUARDS I HADN'T SEEN BEFORE--
WERE IMMOBILIZED BY MARSILIA'S MAGIC!
I TOO FELT ITS POWER--
BUT SOMEHOW I **ALONE** STOOD AGAINST IT.

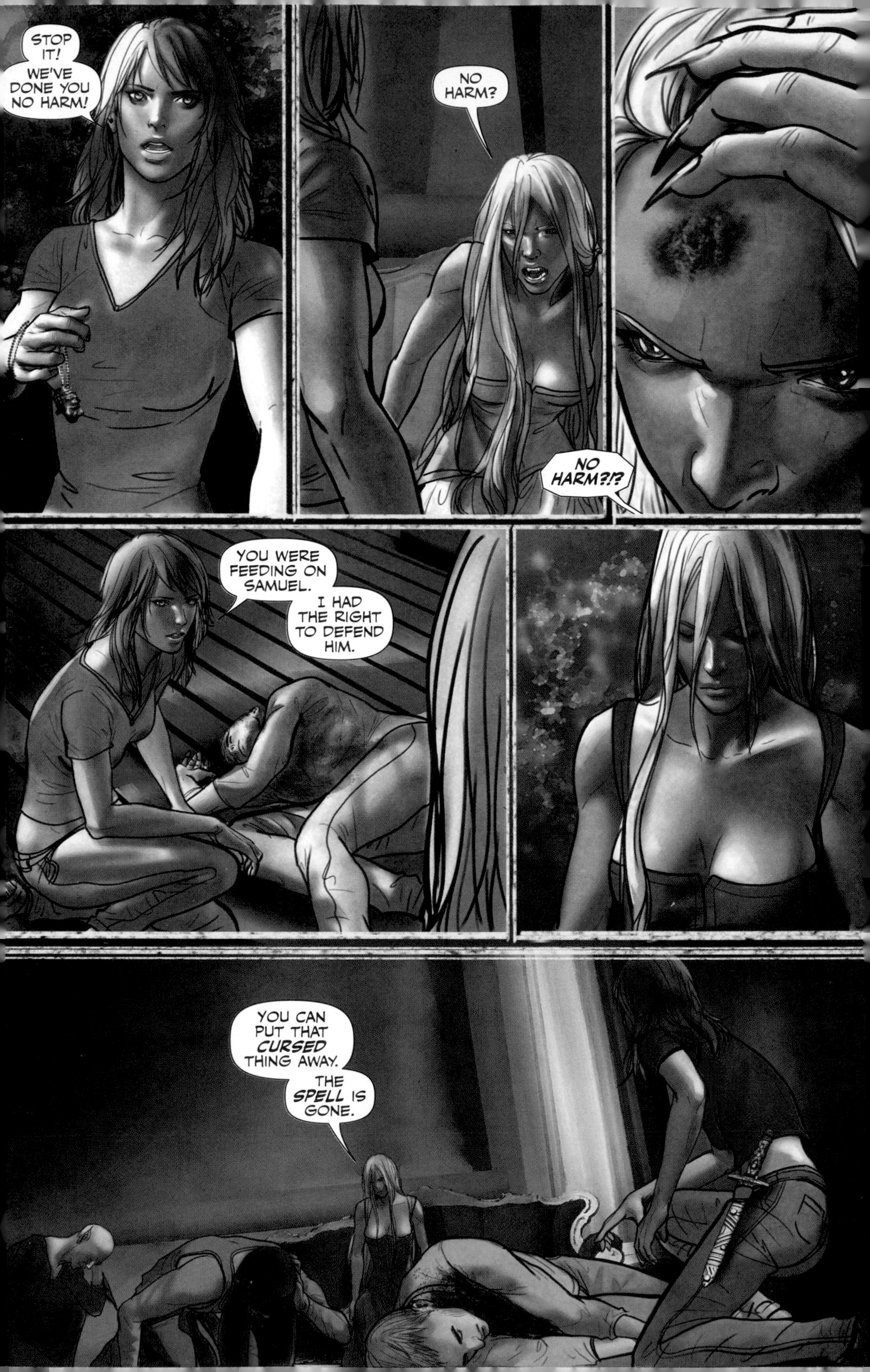
STOP IT!
WE'VE DONE YOU NO HARM!
NO HARM?
NO HARM?!?
YOU WERE FEEDING ON SAMUEL.
I HAD THE RIGHT TO DEFEND HIM.
YOU CAN PUT THAT CURSED THING AWAY.
THE SPELL IS GONE.

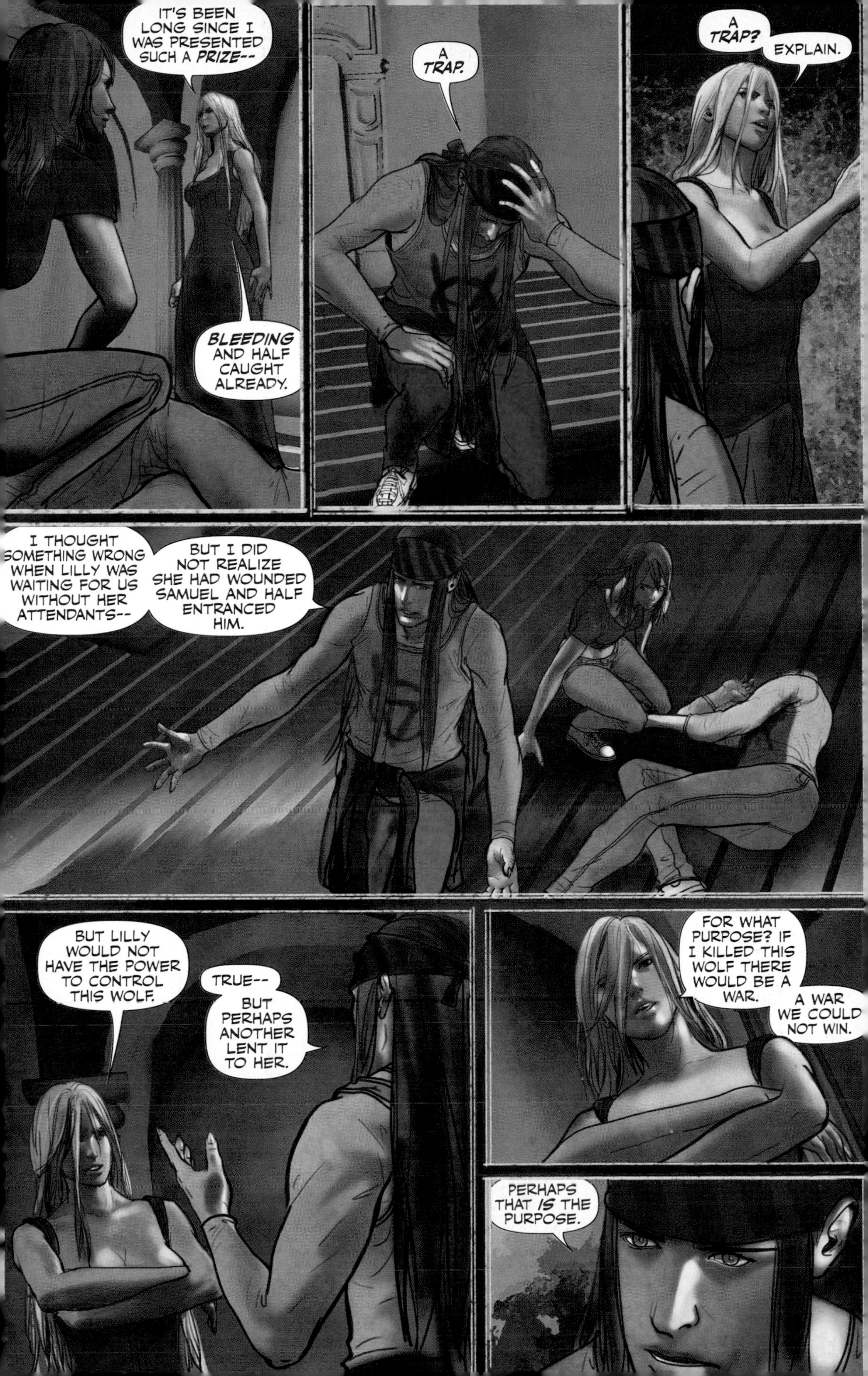
IT'S BEEN LONG SINCE I WAS PRESENTED SUCH A *PRIZE*--
*BLEEDING* AND HALF CAUGHT ALREADY.
A *TRAP.*
A *TRAP?*
EXPLAIN.
I THOUGHT SOMETHING WRONG WHEN LILLY WAS WAITING FOR US WITHOUT HER ATTENDANTS--
BUT I DID NOT REALIZE SHE HAD WOUNDED SAMUEL AND HALF ENTRANCED HIM.
BUT LILLY WOULD NOT HAVE THE POWER TO CONTROL THIS WOLF.
TRUE--
BUT PERHAPS ANOTHER LENT IT TO HER.
FOR WHAT PURPOSE? IF I KILLED THIS WOLF THERE WOULD BE A WAR.
A WAR WE COULD NOT WIN.
PERHAPS THAT *IS* THE PURPOSE.

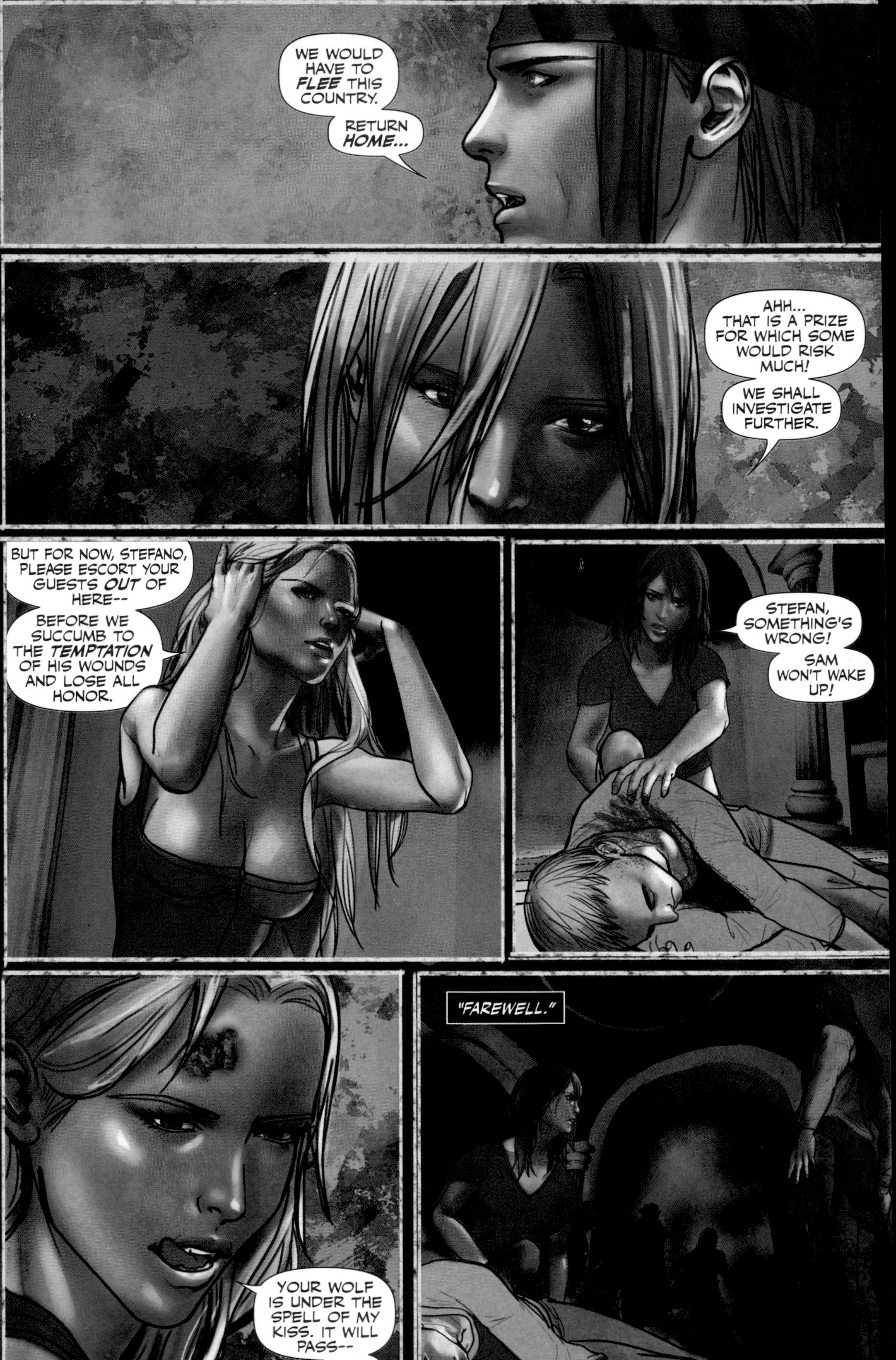
WE WOULD HAVE TO *FLEE* THIS COUNTRY.
RETURN *HOME*...
AHH... THAT IS A PRIZE FOR WHICH SOME WOULD RISK MUCH!
WE SHALL INVESTIGATE FURTHER.
BUT FOR NOW, STEFANO, PLEASE ESCORT YOUR GUESTS *OUT* OF HERE--
BEFORE WE SUCCUMB TO THE *TEMPTATION* OF HIS WOUNDS AND LOSE ALL HONOR.
STEFAN, SOMETHING'S WRONG!
SAM WON'T WAKE UP!
YOUR WOLF IS UNDER THE SPELL OF MY KISS. IT WILL PASS--
IN TIME.
"FAREWELL."

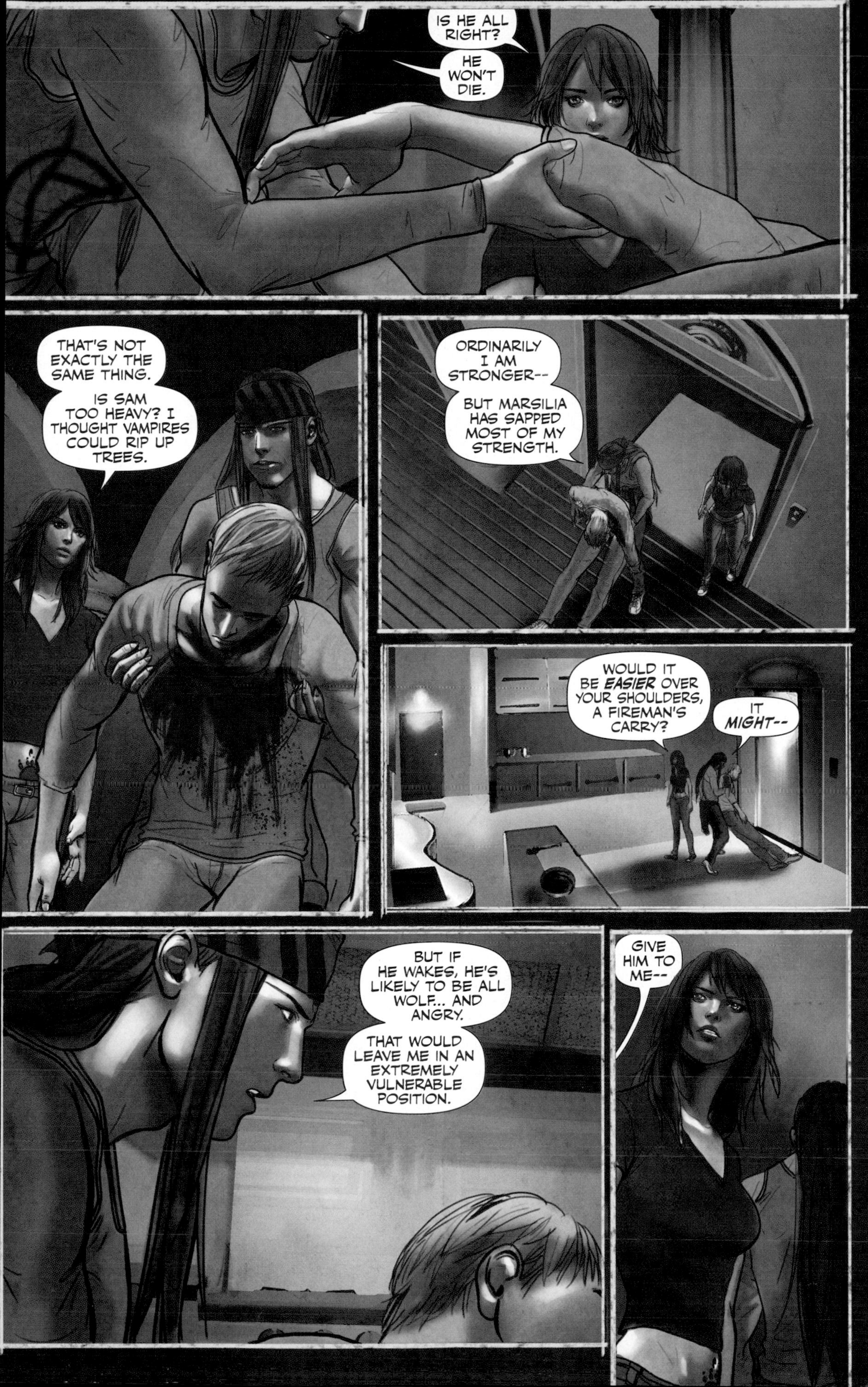
IS HE ALL RIGHT?
HE WON'T DIE.
THAT'S NOT EXACTLY THE SAME THING.
IS SAM TOO HEAVY? I THOUGHT VAMPIRES COULD RIP UP TREES.
ORDINARILY I AM STRONGER--
BUT MARSILIA HAS SAPPED MOST OF MY STRENGTH.
WOULD IT BE EASIER OVER YOUR SHOULDERS, A FIREMAN'S CARRY?
IT MIGHT--
BUT IF HE WAKES, HE'S LIKELY TO BE ALL WOLF... AND ANGRY.
THAT WOULD LEAVE ME IN AN EXTREMELY VULNERABLE POSITION.
GIVE HIM TO ME--

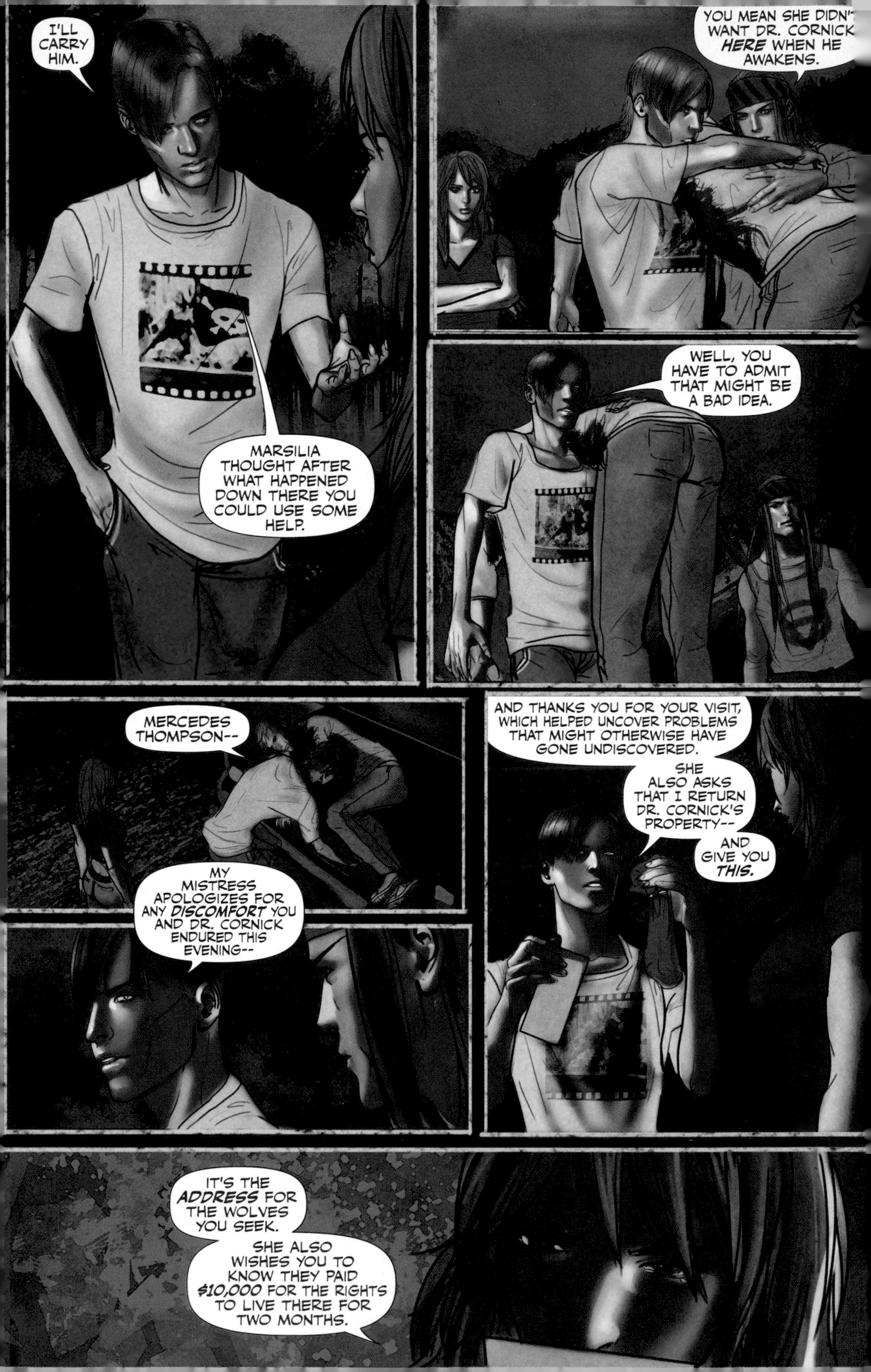
I'LL CARRY HIM.
MARSILIA THOUGHT AFTER WHAT HAPPENED DOWN THERE YOU COULD USE SOME HELP.
YOU MEAN SHE DIDN'T WANT DR. CORNICK *HERE* WHEN HE AWAKENS.
WELL, YOU HAVE TO ADMIT THAT MIGHT BE A BAD IDEA.
MERCEDES THOMPSON--
MY MISTRESS APOLOGIZES FOR ANY *DISCOMFORT* YOU AND DR. CORNICK ENDURED THIS EVENING--
AND THANKS YOU FOR YOUR VISIT, WHICH HELPED UNCOVER PROBLEMS THAT MIGHT OTHERWISE HAVE GONE UNDISCOVERED.
SHE ALSO ASKS THAT I RETURN DR. CORNICK'S PROPERTY--
AND GIVE YOU *THIS.*
IT'S THE *ADDRESS* FOR THE WOLVES YOU SEEK.
SHE ALSO WISHES YOU TO KNOW THEY PAID *$10,000* FOR THE RIGHTS TO LIVE THERE FOR TWO MONTHS.

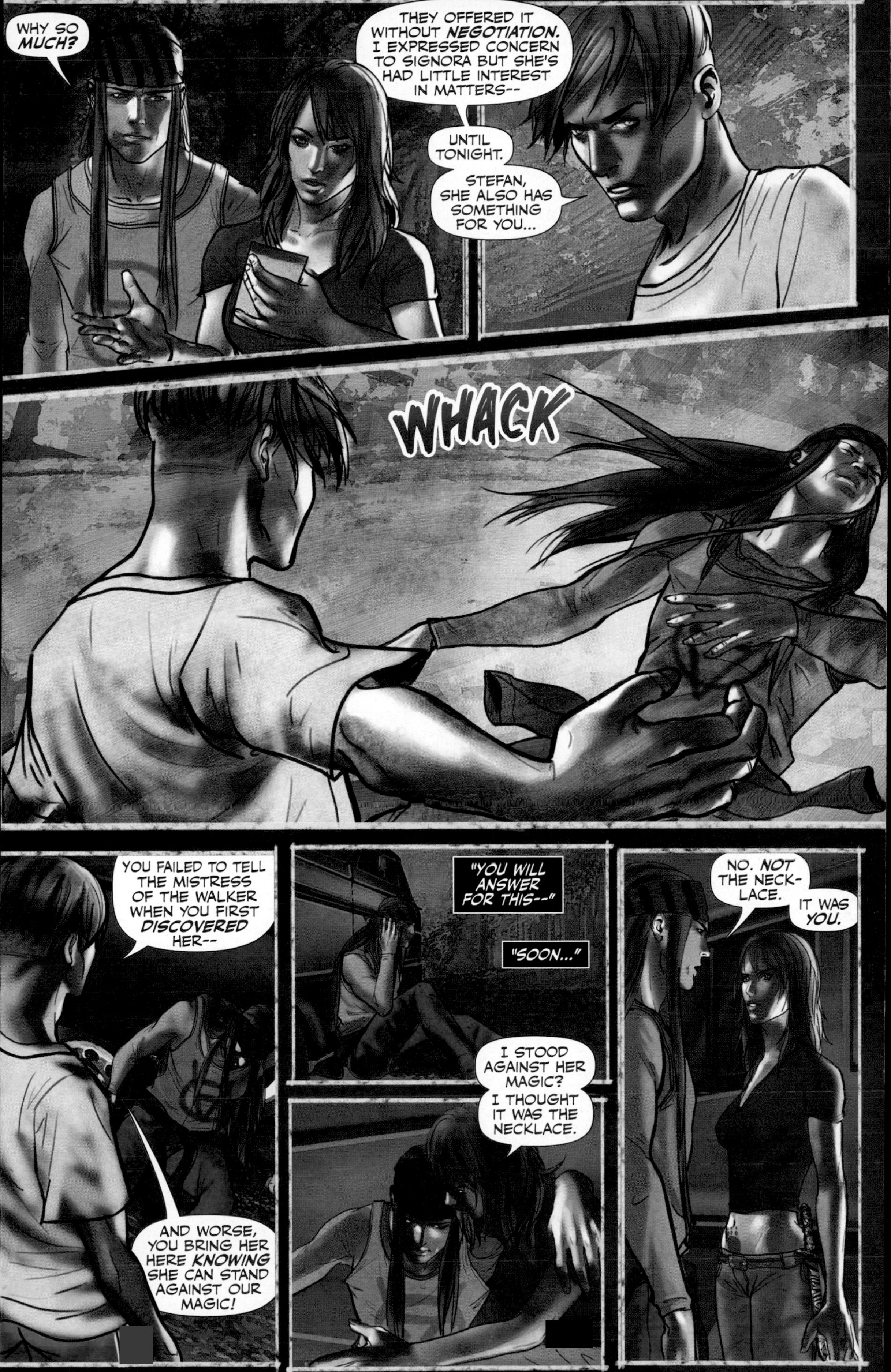

WHY SO *MUCH?*
THEY OFFERED IT WITHOUT *NEGOTIATION.* I EXPRESSED CONCERN TO SIGNORA BUT SHE'S HAD LITTLE INTEREST IN MATTERS--
UNTIL TONIGHT.
STEFAN, SHE ALSO HAS SOMETHING FOR YOU...
WHACK
YOU FAILED TO TELL THE MISTRESS OF THE WALKER WHEN YOU FIRST *DISCOVERED* HER--
AND WORSE, YOU BRING HER HERE *KNOWING* SHE CAN STAND AGAINST OUR MAGIC!
*"YOU WILL ANSWER FOR THIS--"*
*"SOON..."*
I STOOD AGAINST HER MAGIC? I THOUGHT IT WAS THE NECKLACE.
NO. *NOT* THE NECK-LACE.
IT WAS *YOU.*

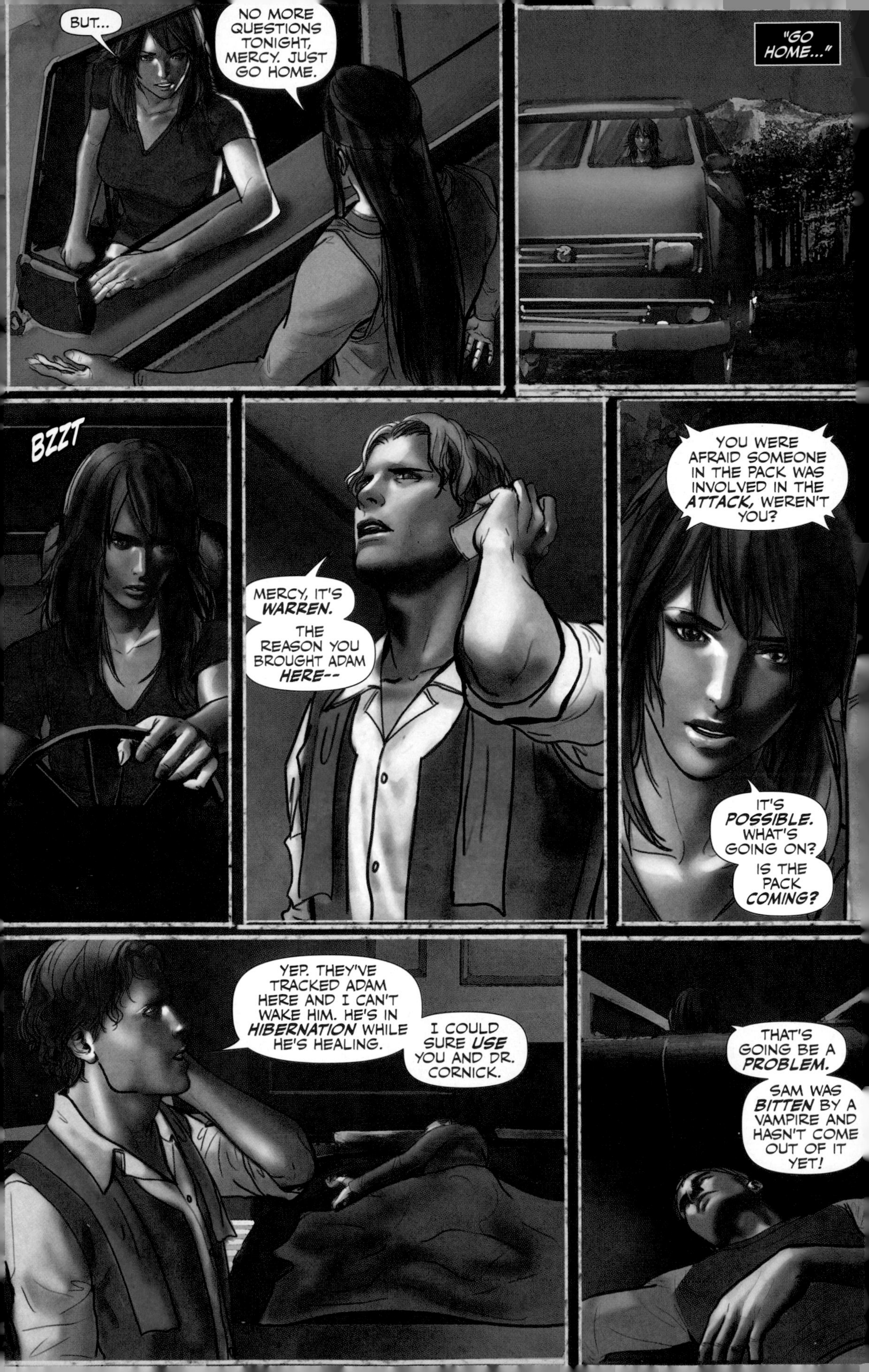
BUT...
NO MORE QUESTIONS TONIGHT, MERCY. JUST GO HOME.
"GO HOME..."
BZZT
MERCY, IT'S WARREN.
THE REASON YOU BROUGHT ADAM HERE--
YOU WERE AFRAID SOMEONE IN THE PACK WAS INVOLVED IN THE ATTACK, WEREN'T YOU?
IT'S POSSIBLE. WHAT'S GOING ON?
IS THE PACK COMING?
YEP. THEY'VE TRACKED ADAM HERE AND I CAN'T WAKE HIM. HE'S IN HIBERNATION WHILE HE'S HEALING.
I COULD SURE USE YOU AND DR. CORNICK.
THAT'S GOING BE A PROBLEM.
SAM WAS BITTEN BY A VAMPIRE AND HASN'T COME OUT OF IT YET!

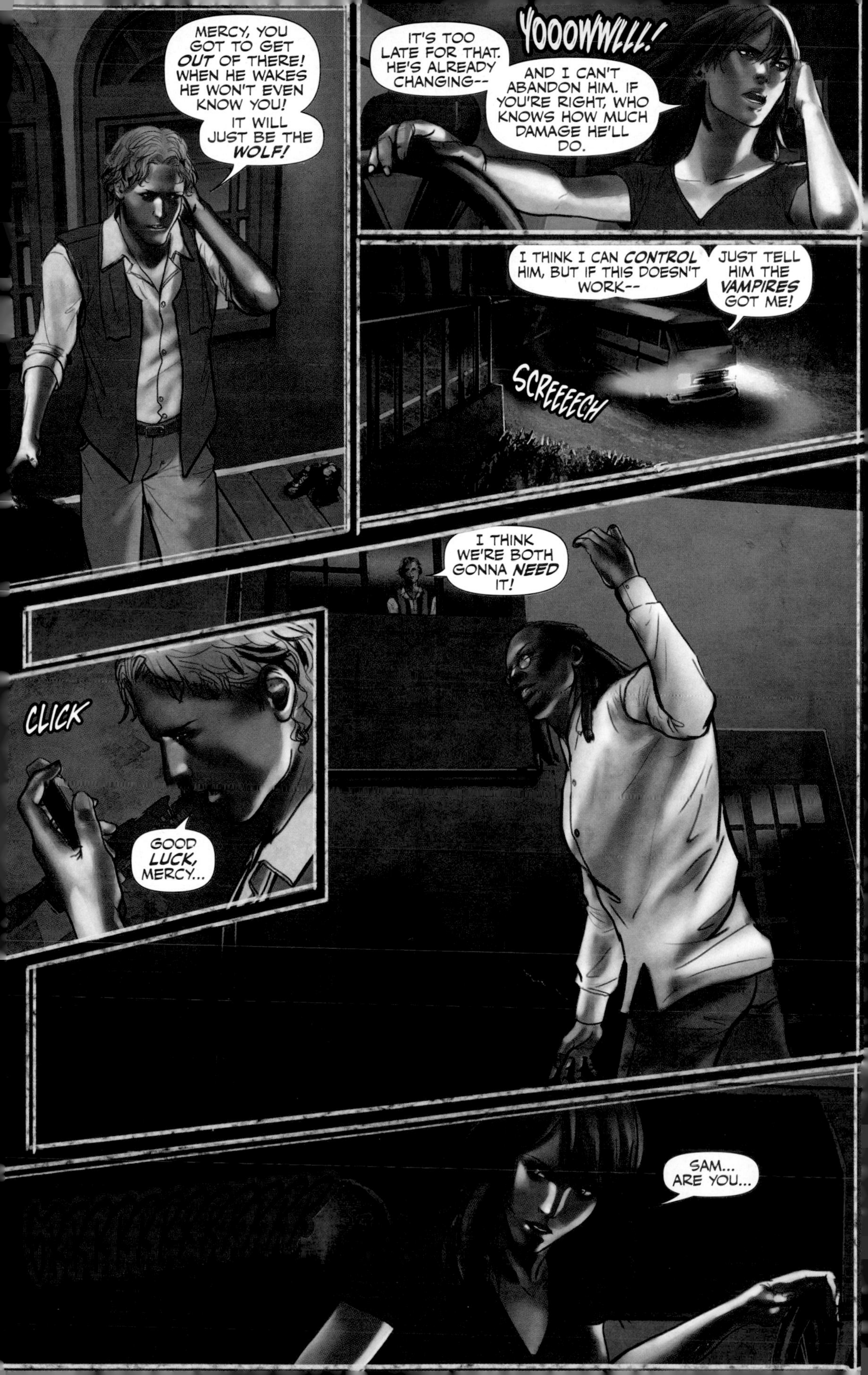
MERCY, YOU GOT TO GET OUT OF THERE! WHEN HE WAKES HE WON'T EVEN KNOW YOU!
IT WILL JUST BE THE WOLF!
YOOOWWLLL!
IT'S TOO LATE FOR THAT. HE'S ALREADY CHANGING--
AND I CAN'T ABANDON HIM. IF YOU'RE RIGHT, WHO KNOWS HOW MUCH DAMAGE HE'LL DO.
I THINK I CAN CONTROL HIM, BUT IF THIS DOESN'T WORK--
JUST TELL HIM THE VAMPIRES GOT ME!
SCREEEECH
I THINK WE'RE BOTH GONNA NEED IT!
CLICK
GOOD LUCK, MERCY...
SAM... ARE YOU...

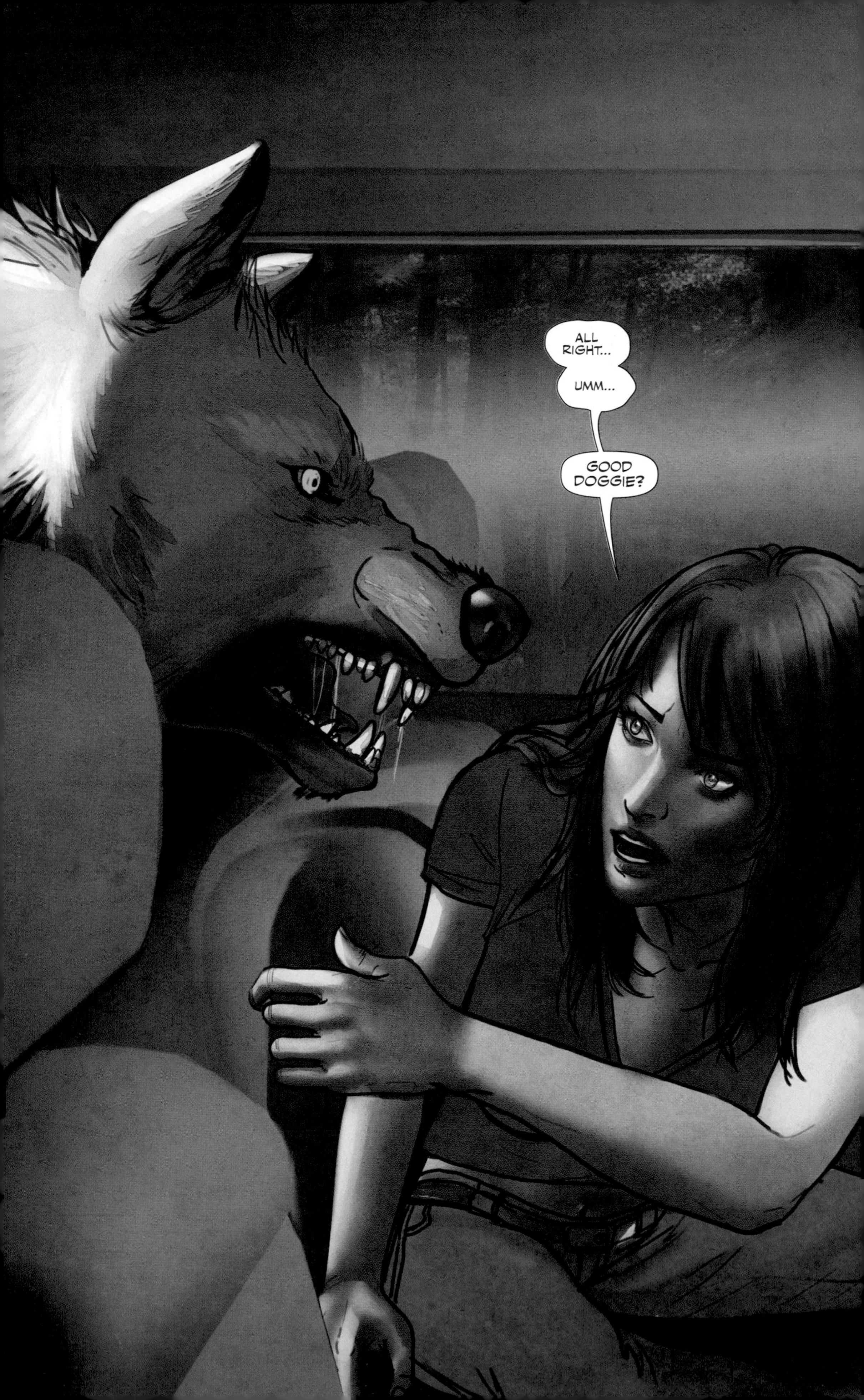
ALL RIGHT...
UMM...
GOOD DOGGIE?

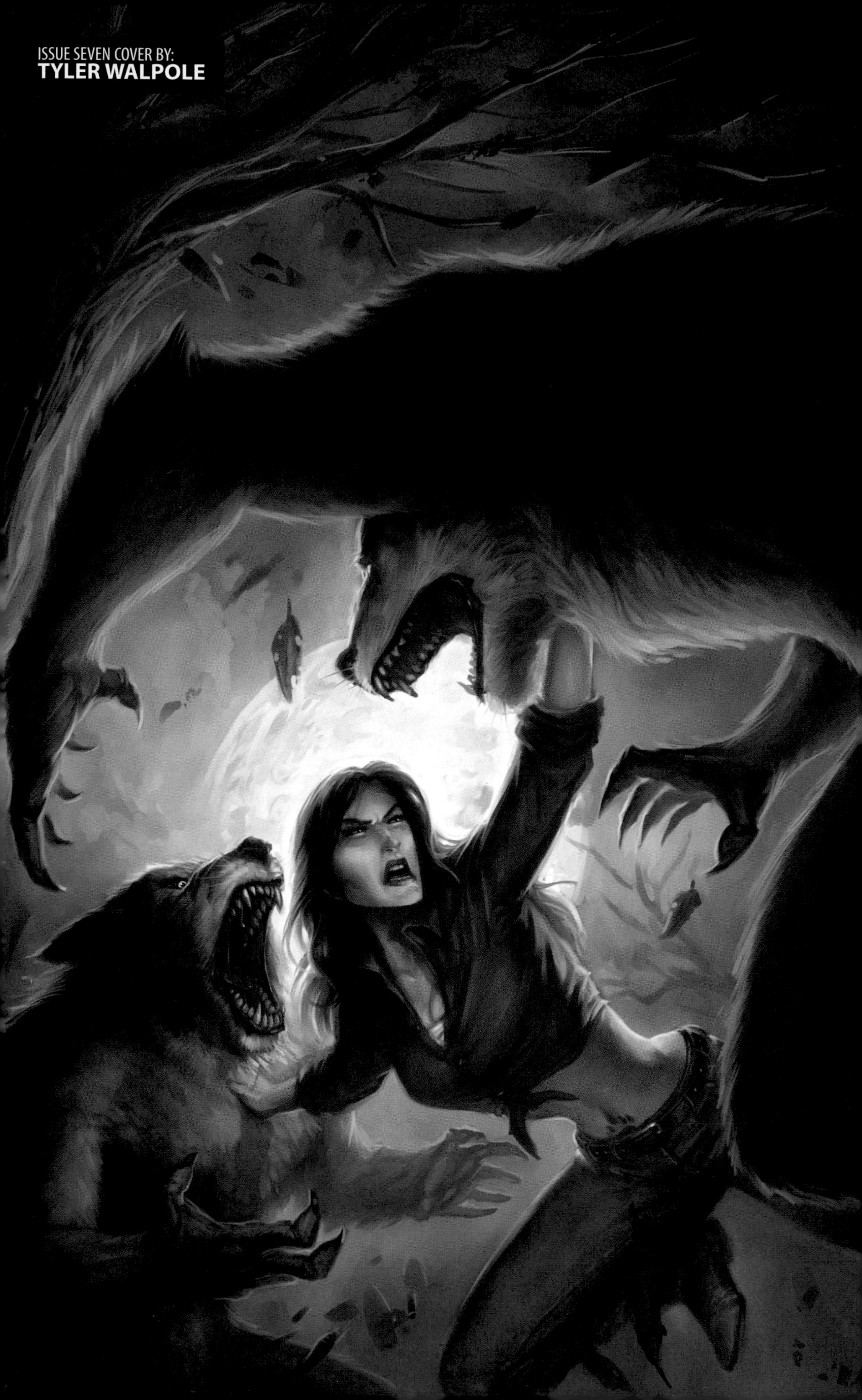

ISSUE SEVEN COVER BY:
**TYLER WALPOLE**

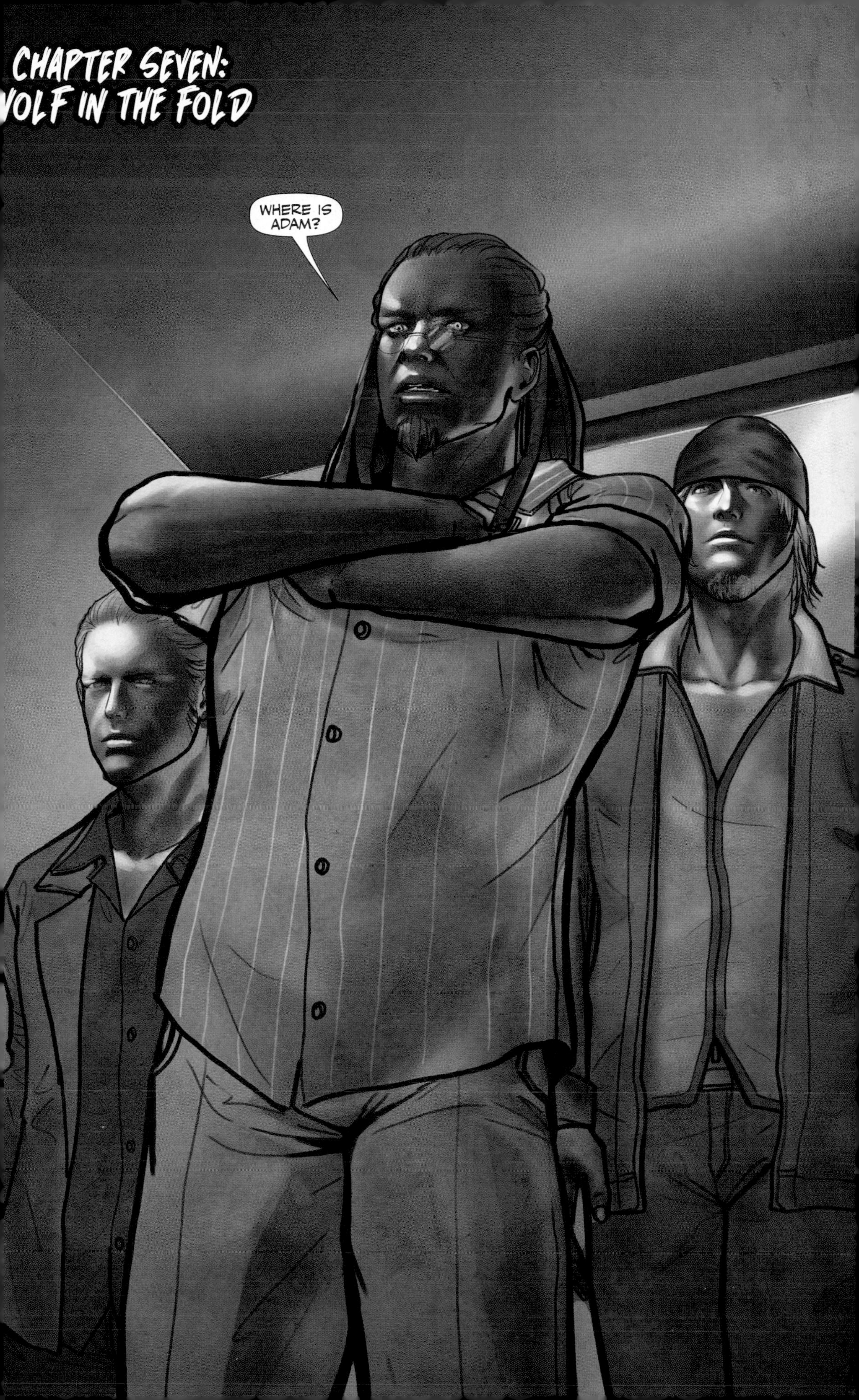
CHAPTER SEVEN:
WOLF IN THE FOLD
WHERE IS ADAM?

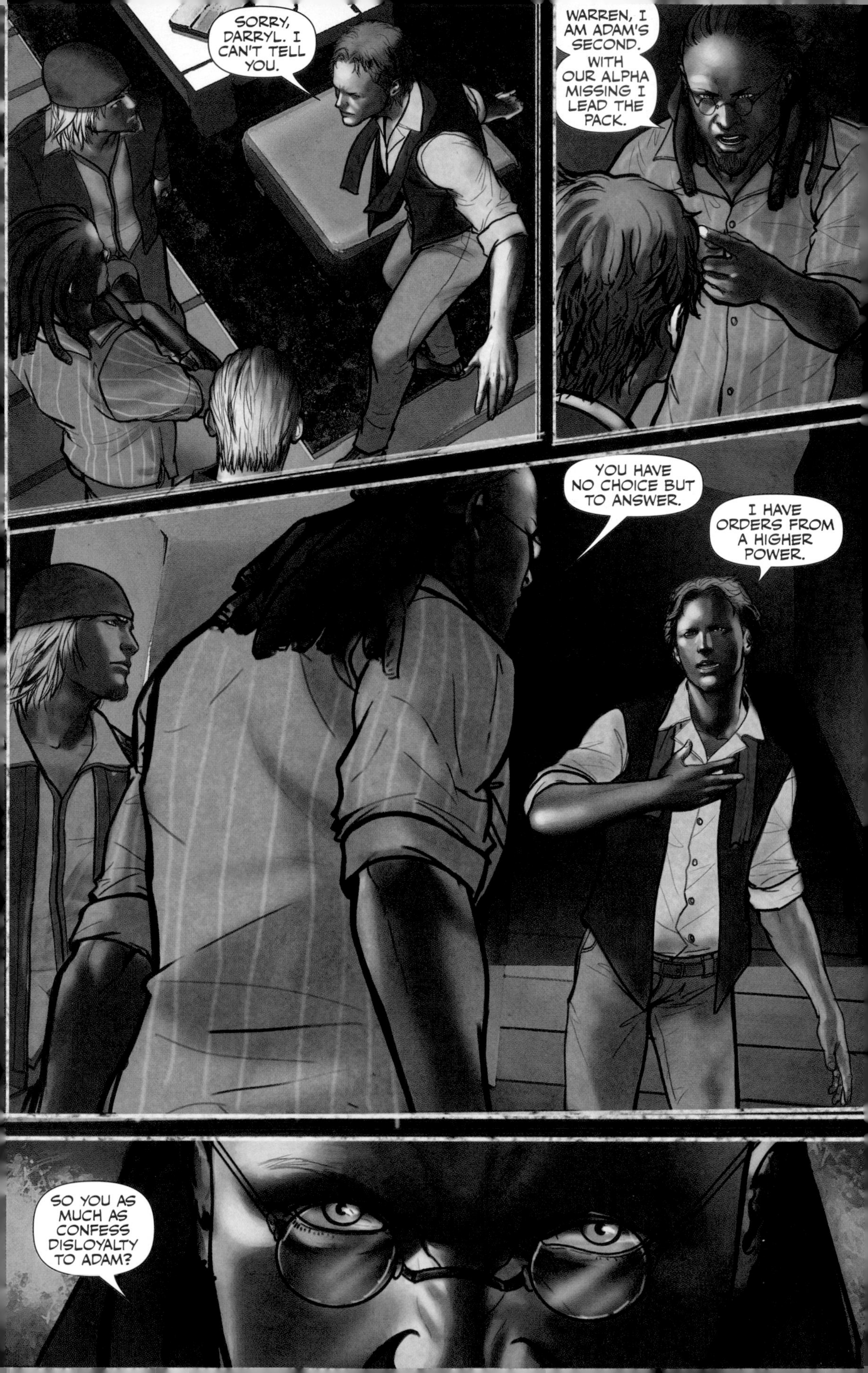
SORRY, DARRYL. I CAN'T TELL YOU.
WARREN, I AM ADAM'S SECOND. WITH OUR ALPHA MISSING I LEAD THE PACK.
YOU HAVE NO CHOICE BUT TO ANSWER.
I HAVE ORDERS FROM A HIGHER POWER.
SO YOU AS MUCH AS CONFESS DISLOYALTY TO ADAM?

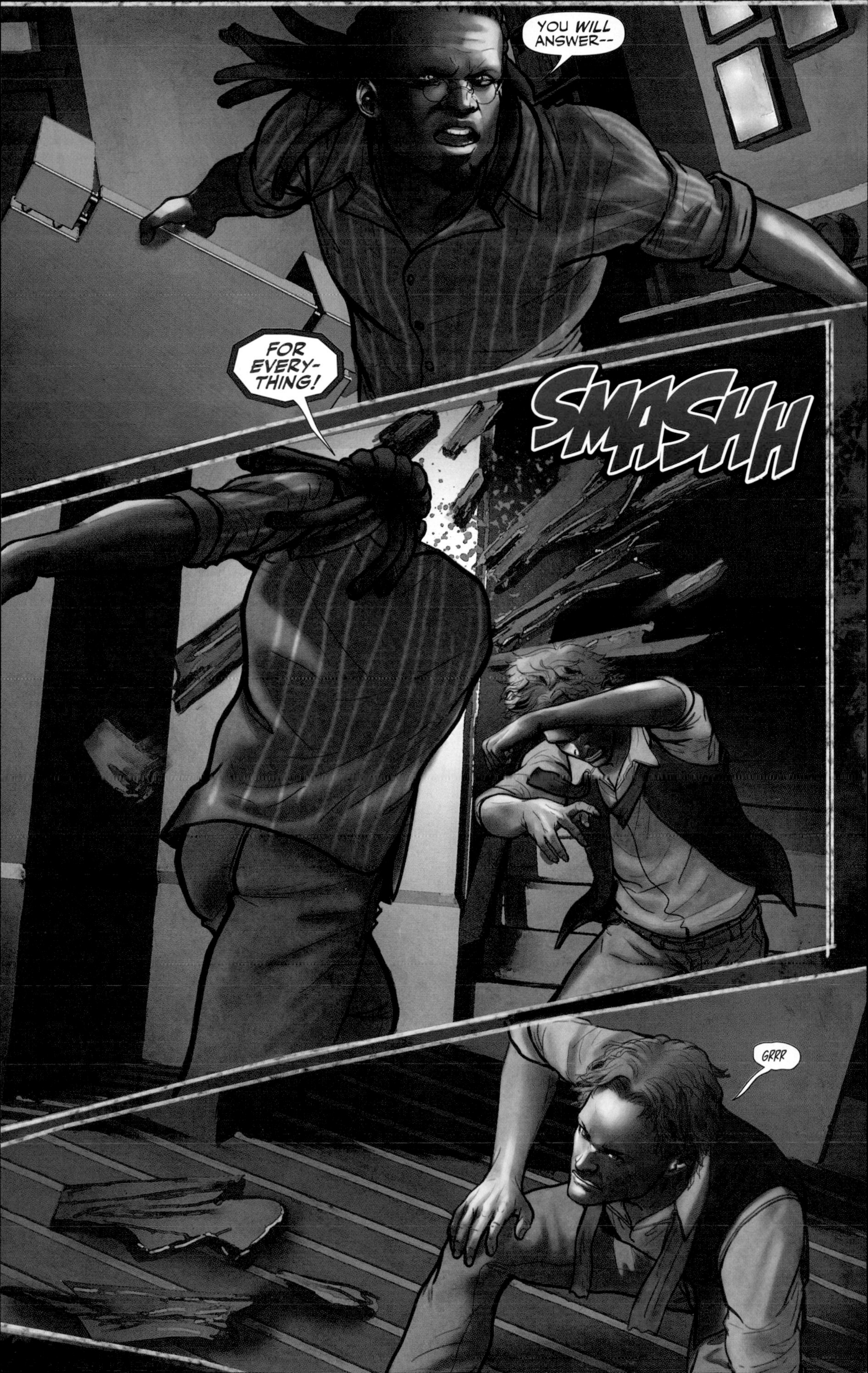
YOU WILL ANSWER--
FOR EVERY-THING!
SMASHH
GRRR

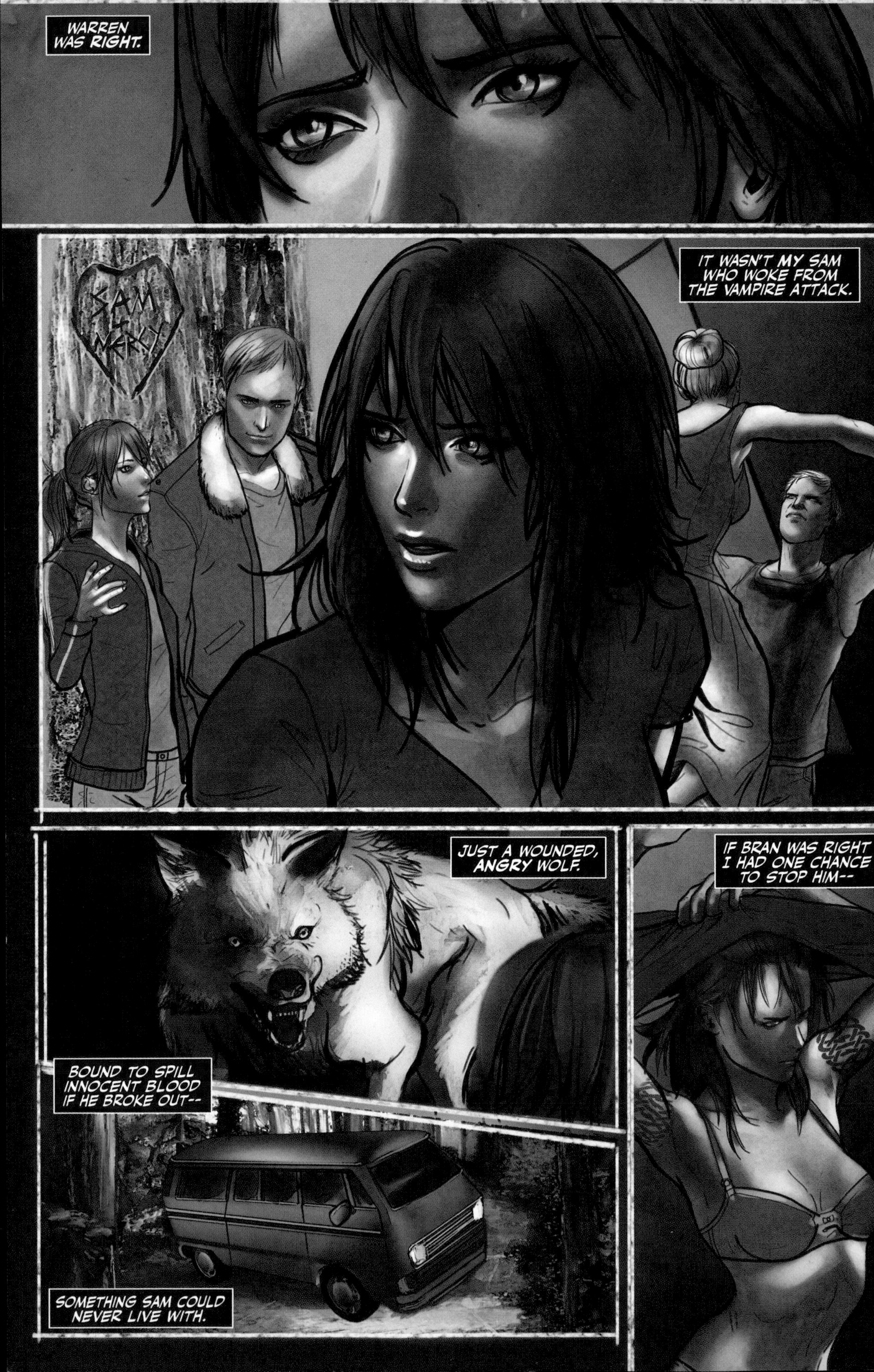
WARREN WAS RIGHT.
IT WASN'T MY SAM WHO WOKE FROM THE VAMPIRE ATTACK.
JUST A WOUNDED, ANGRY WOLF.
BOUND TO SPILL INNOCENT BLOOD IF HE BROKE OUT--
SOMETHING SAM COULD NEVER LIVE WITH.
IF BRAN WAS RIGHT I HAD ONE CHANCE TO STOP HIM--

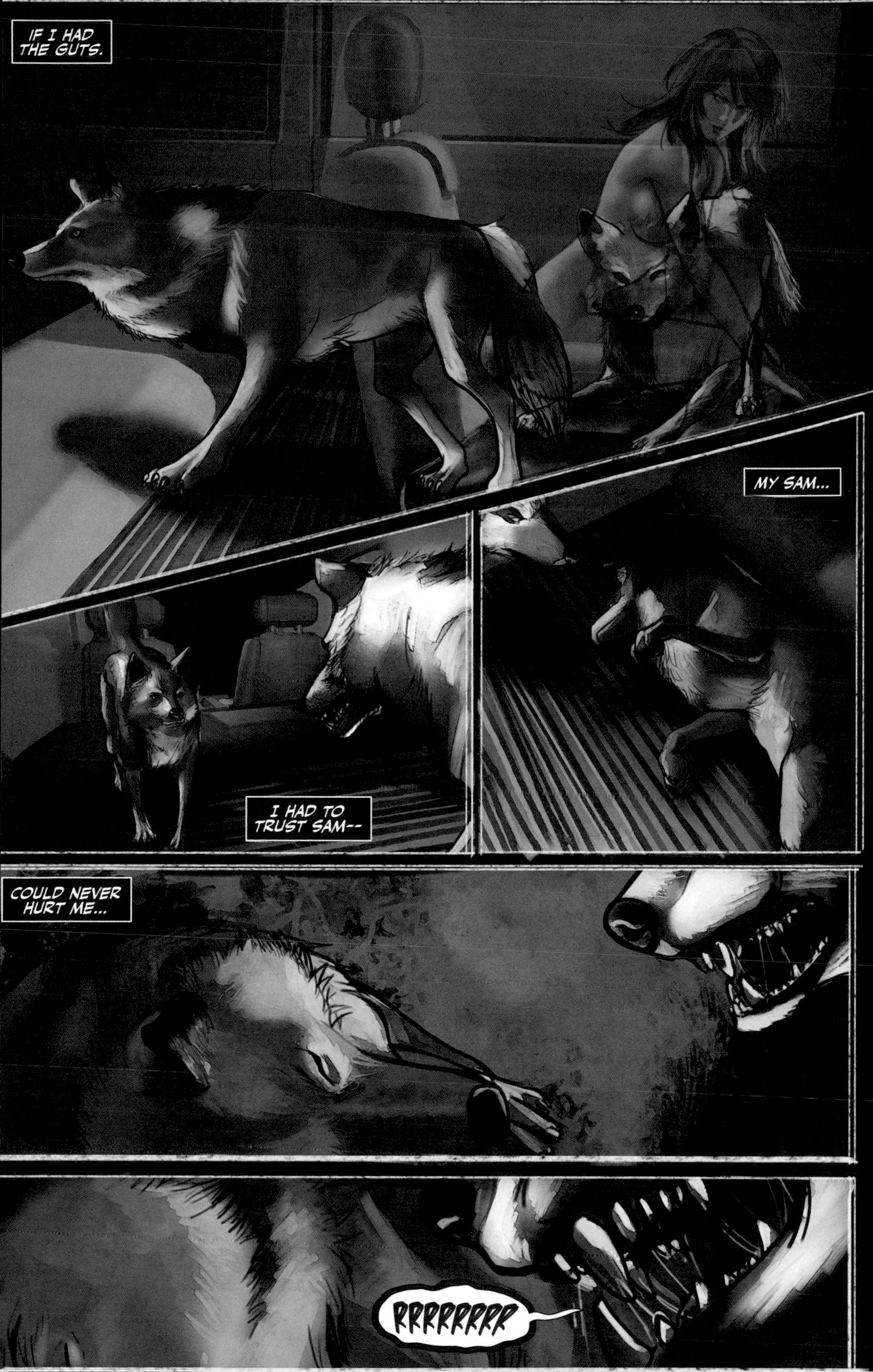
IF I HAD THE GUTS.
MY SAM...
I HAD TO TRUST SAM--
COULD NEVER HURT ME...
RRRRRRRR

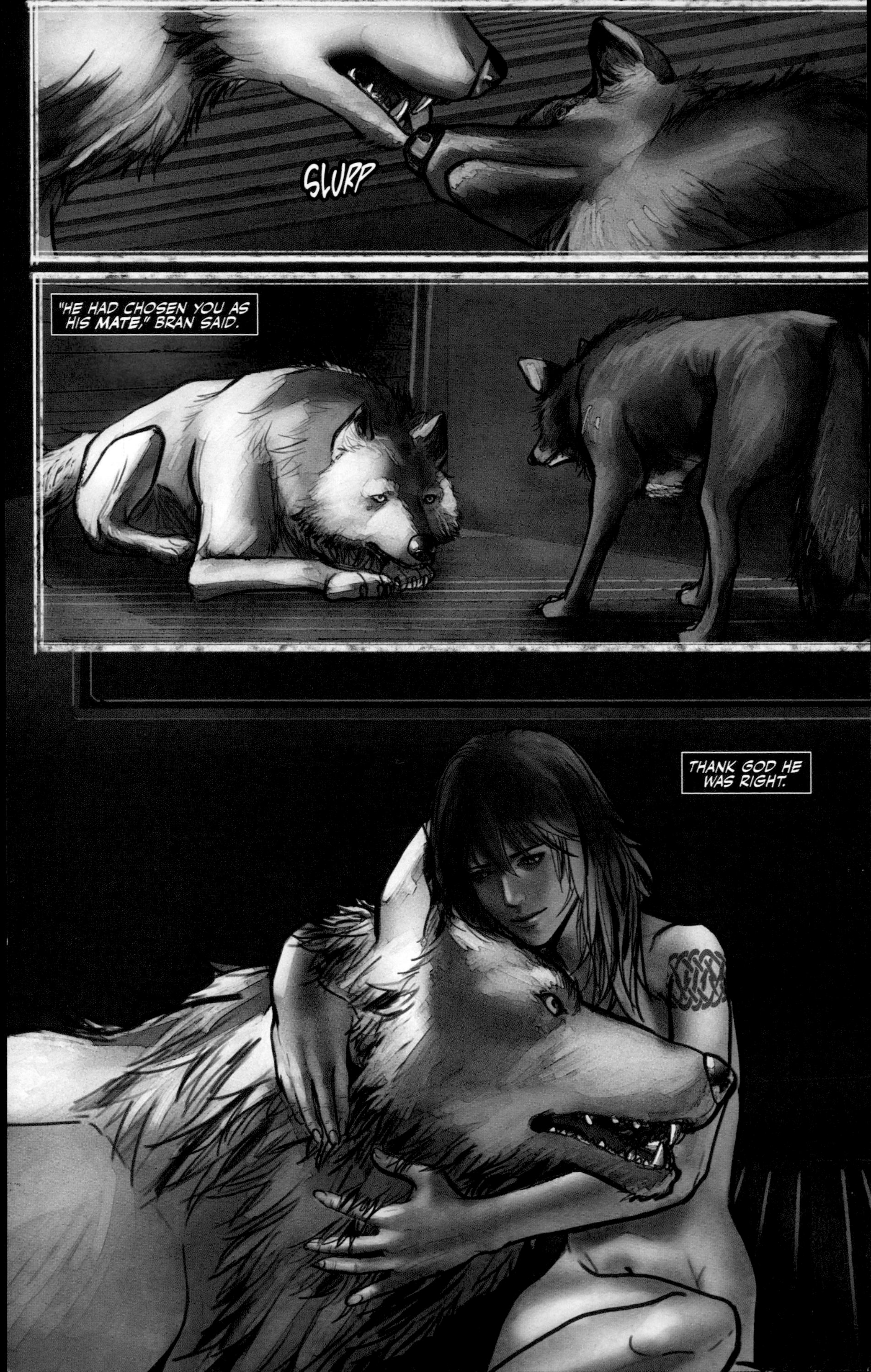
SLURP
"HE HAD CHOSEN YOU AS HIS MATE," BRAN SAID.
THANK GOD HE WAS RIGHT.

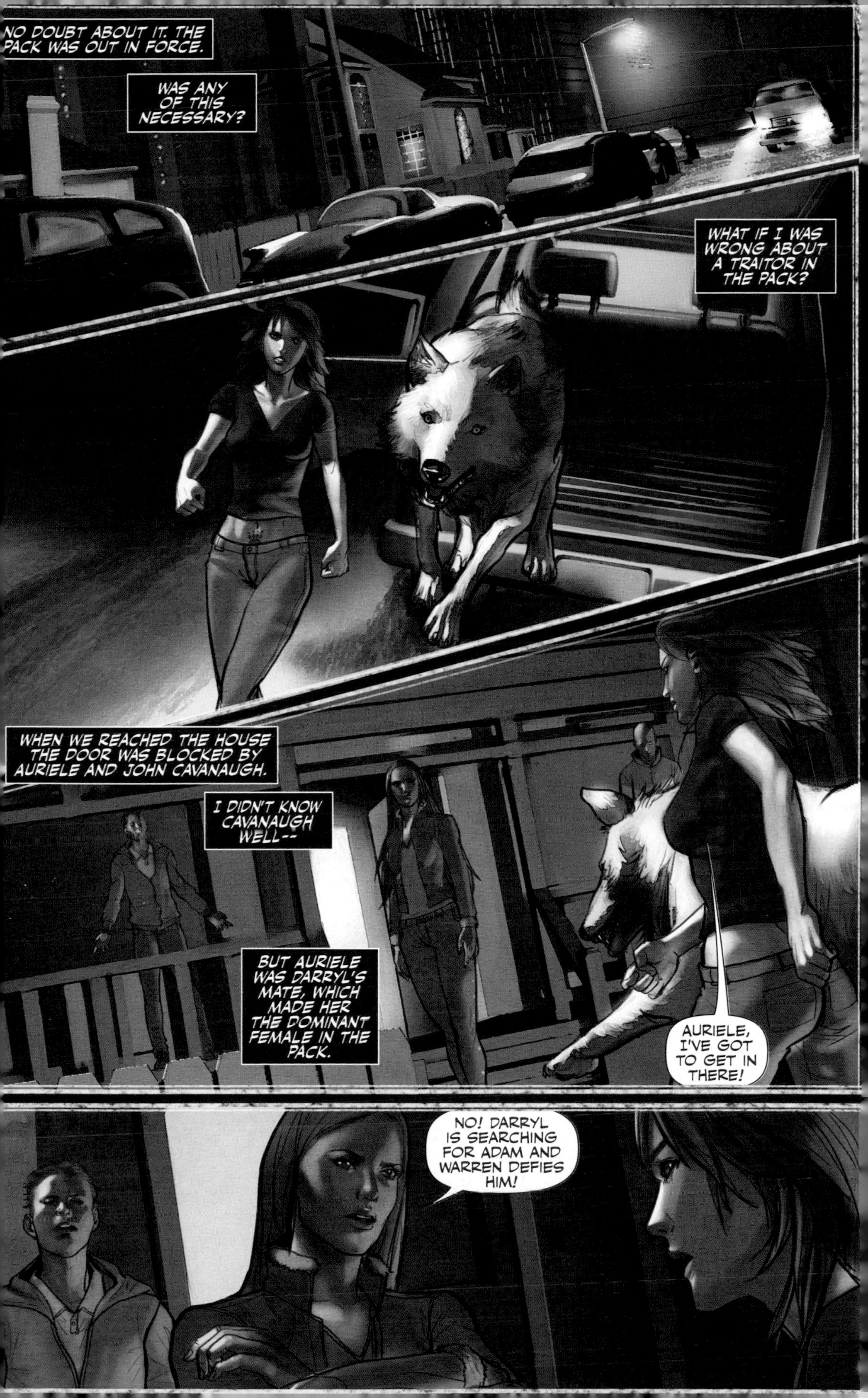

NO DOUBT ABOUT IT. THE PACK WAS OUT IN FORCE.
WAS ANY OF THIS NECESSARY?
WHAT IF I WAS WRONG ABOUT A TRAITOR IN THE PACK?
WHEN WE REACHED THE HOUSE THE DOOR WAS BLOCKED BY AURIELE AND JOHN CAVANAUGH.
I DIDN'T KNOW CAVANAUGH WELL--
BUT AURIELE WAS DARRYL'S MATE, WHICH MADE HER THE DOMINANT FEMALE IN THE PACK.
AURIELE, I'VE GOT TO GET IN THERE!
NO! DARRYL IS SEARCHING FOR ADAM AND WARREN DEFIES HIM!

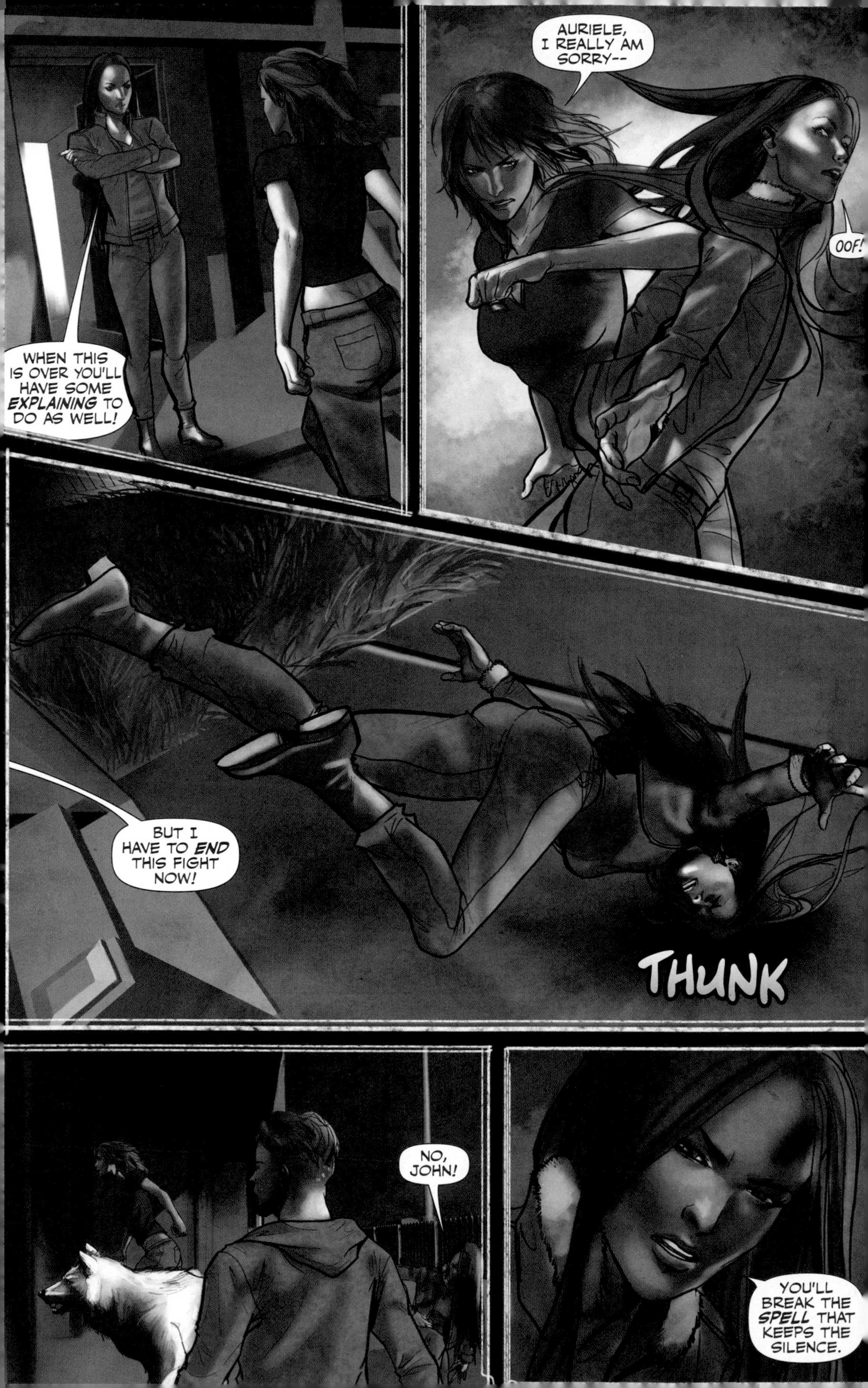
WHEN THIS IS OVER YOU'LL HAVE SOME EXPLAINING TO DO AS WELL!
AURIELE, I REALLY AM SORRY--
OOF!
BUT I HAVE TO END THIS FIGHT NOW!
THUNK
NO, JOHN!
YOU'LL BREAK THE SPELL THAT KEEPS THE SILENCE.

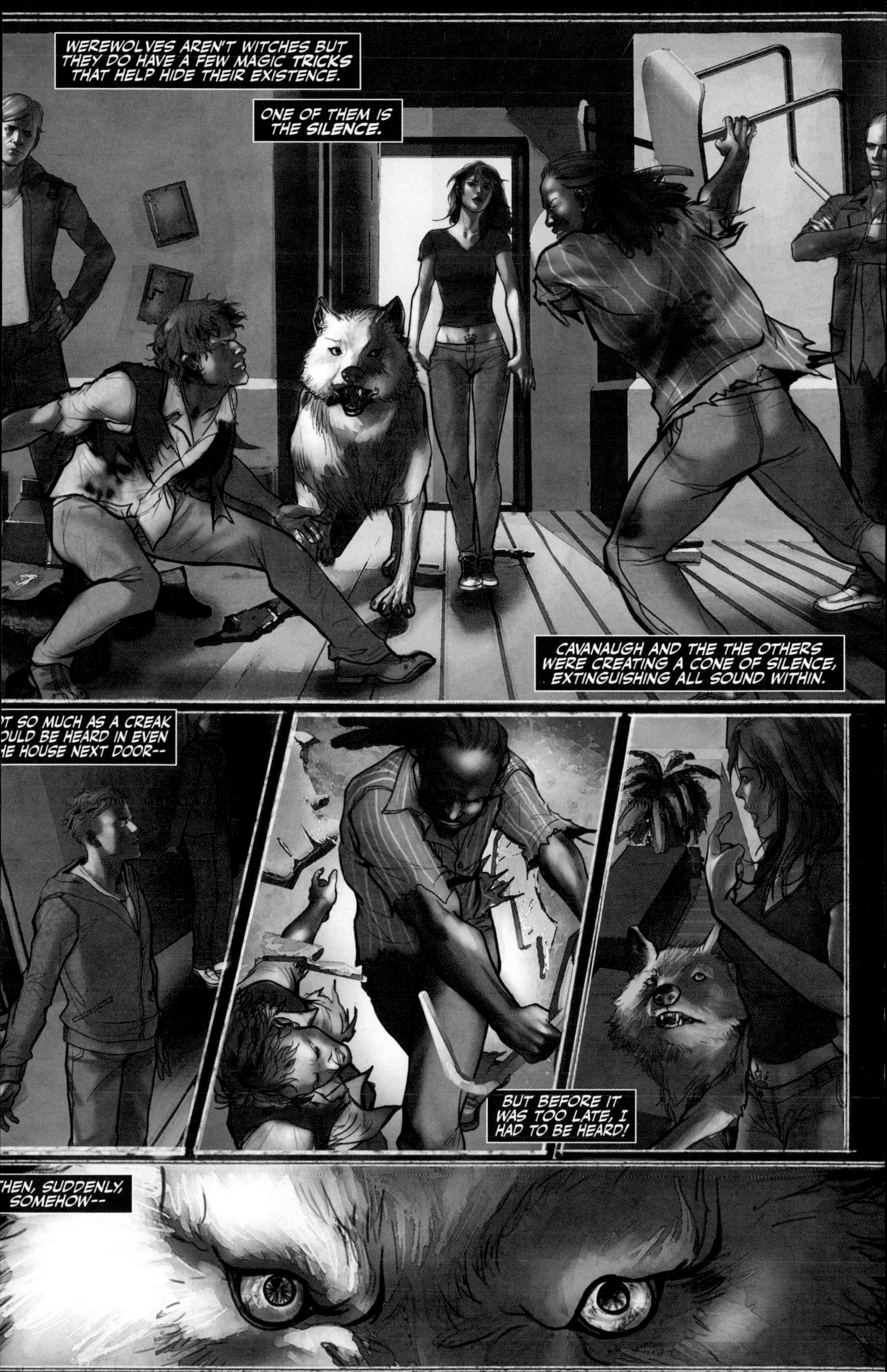
WEREWOLVES AREN'T WITCHES BUT THEY DO HAVE A FEW MAGIC TRICKS THAT HELP HIDE THEIR EXISTENCE.
ONE OF THEM IS THE SILENCE.
CAVANAUGH AND THE THE OTHERS WERE CREATING A CONE OF SILENCE, EXTINGUISHING ALL SOUND WITHIN.
OT SO MUCH AS A CREAK OULD BE HEARD IN EVEN HE HOUSE NEXT DOOR--
BUT BEFORE IT WAS TOO LATE, I HAD TO BE HEARD!
THEN, SUDDENLY, SOMEHOW--

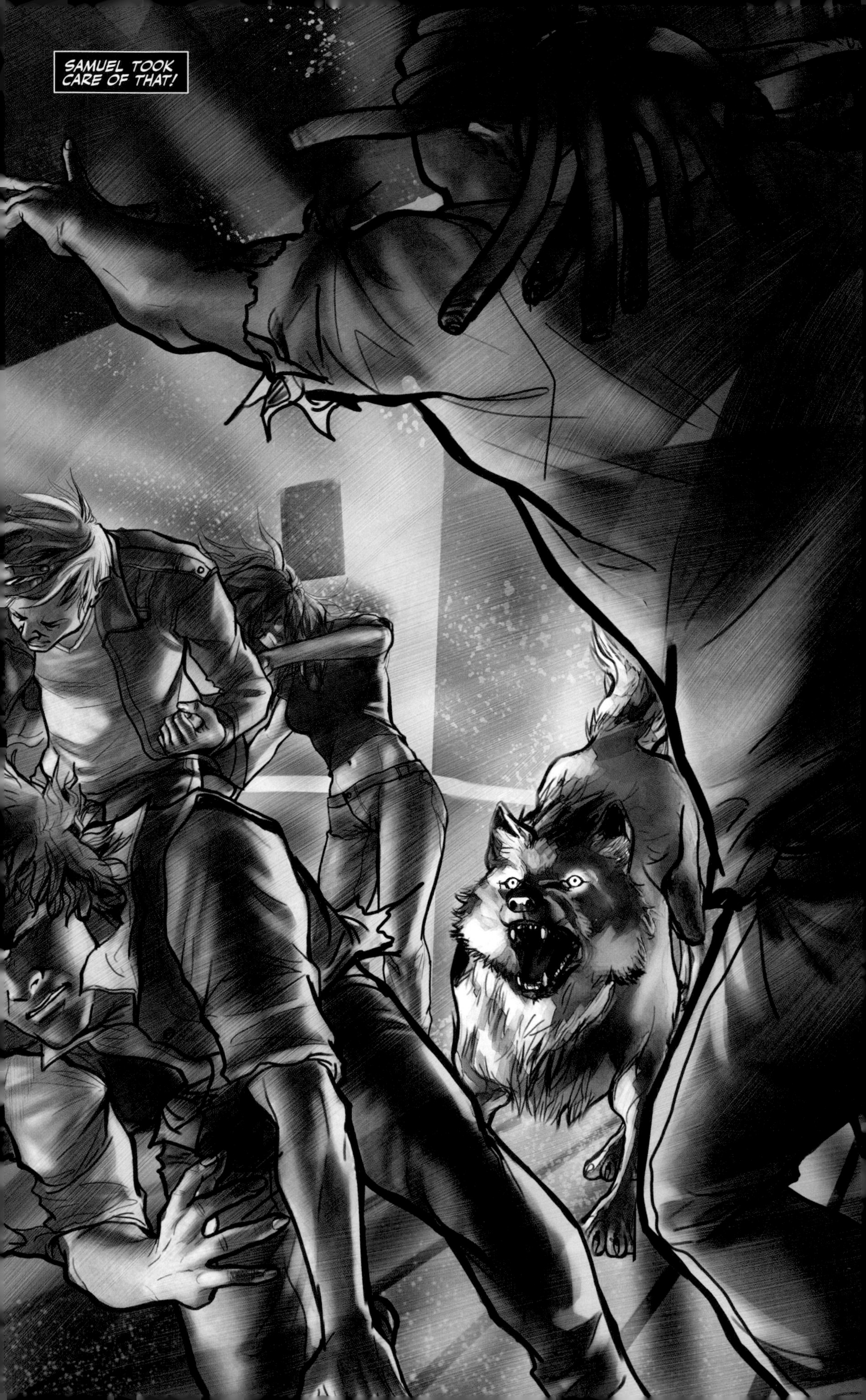
SAMUEL TOOK CARE OF THAT!

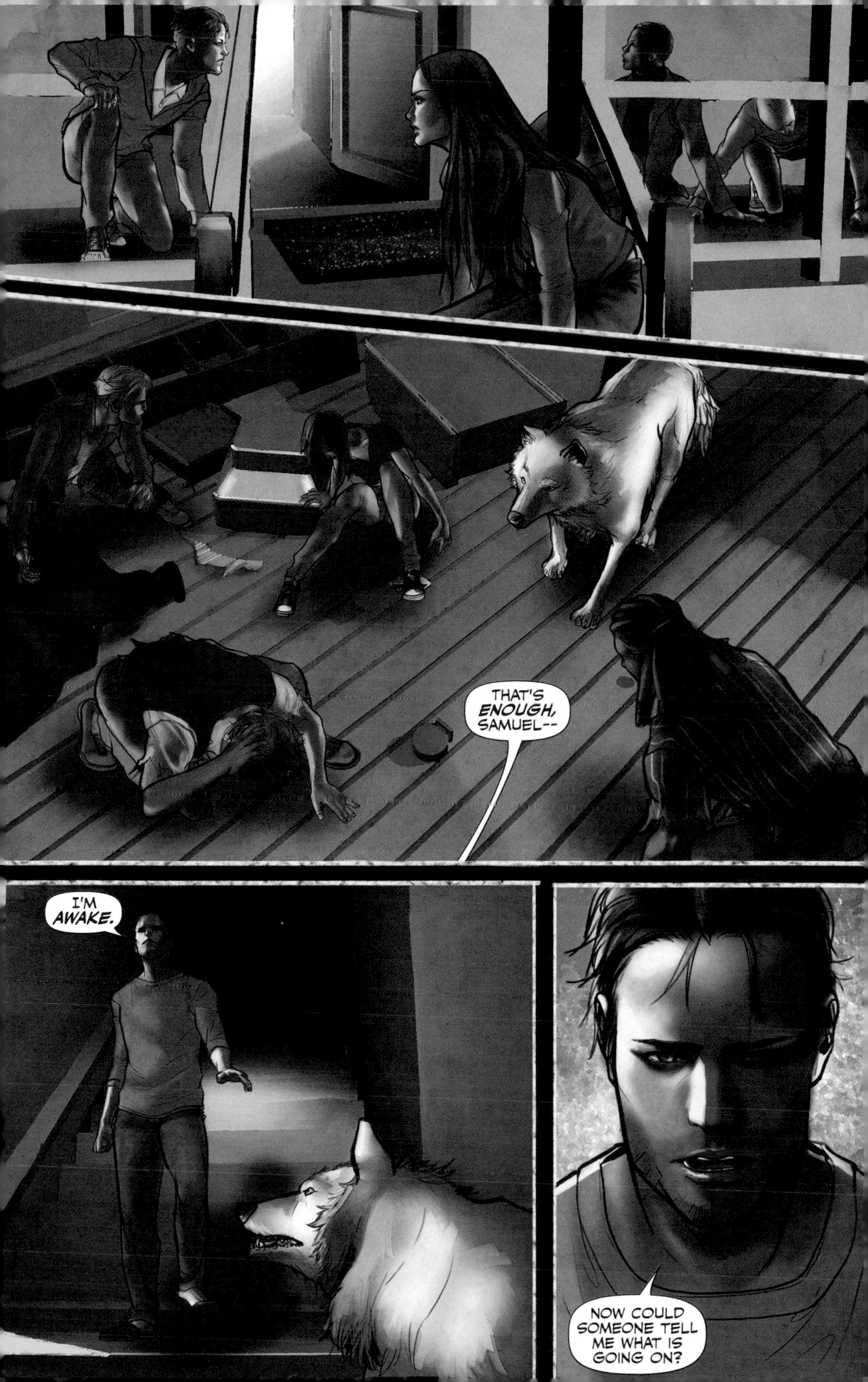
THAT'S ENOUGH, SAMUEL--
I'M AWAKE.
NOW COULD SOMEONE TELL ME WHAT IS GOING ON?

ADAM! YOU'RE HERE! WE'VE BEEN SEARCHING EVERYWHERE!

WHY DIDN'T WARREN JUST *TELL* US YOU WERE HERE?

WARREN WAS ACTING ON MY ORDERS.

I SEE...

IT WAS NOTHING PERSONAL. JUST TOO MANY THINGS DIDN'T ADD UP.

HOW DID YOU FIND ME?

LUCK.

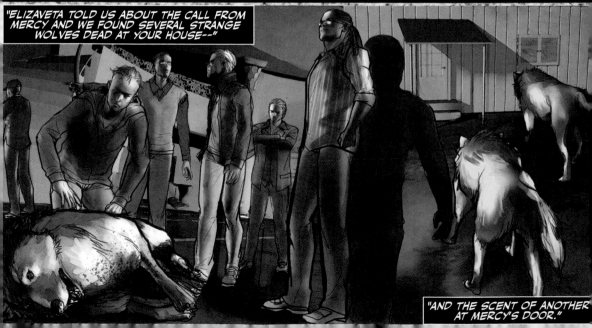

"ELIZAVETA TOLD US ABOUT THE CALL FROM MERCY AND WE FOUND SEVERAL STRANGE WOLVES DEAD AT YOUR HOUSE--"

"AND THE SCENT OF ANOTHER AT MERCY'S DOOR."

"BUT THERE WAS NO SIGN OF YOU OR MERCY, AND JESSE WAS MISSING TOO--"

"SO THE PACK FANNED OUT TO SEARCH."

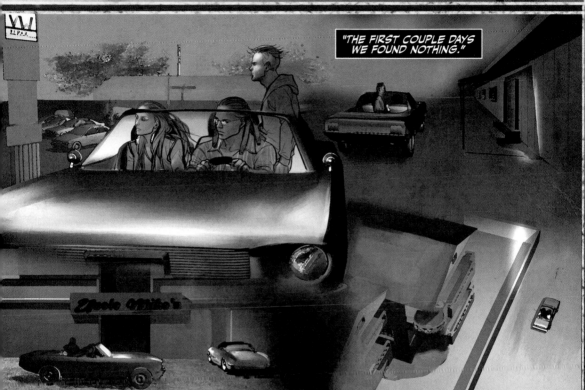

"THE FIRST COUPLE DAYS WE FOUND NOTHING."

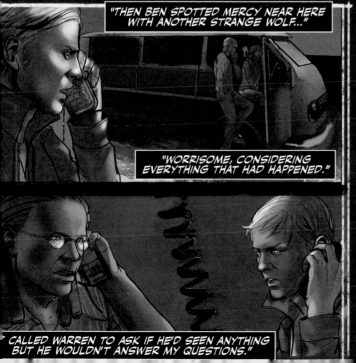

"THEN BEN SPOTTED MERCY NEAR HERE WITH ANOTHER STRANGE WOLF..."

"WORRISOME, CONSIDERING EVERYTHING THAT HAD HAPPENED."

"CALLED WARREN TO ASK IF HE'D SEEN ANYTHING BUT HE WOULDN'T ANSWER MY QUESTIONS."

I DIDN'T KNOW WARREN WAS ACTING ON YOUR ORDERS-- BUT WHY?

IT WAS ALL TOO CONVENIENT...

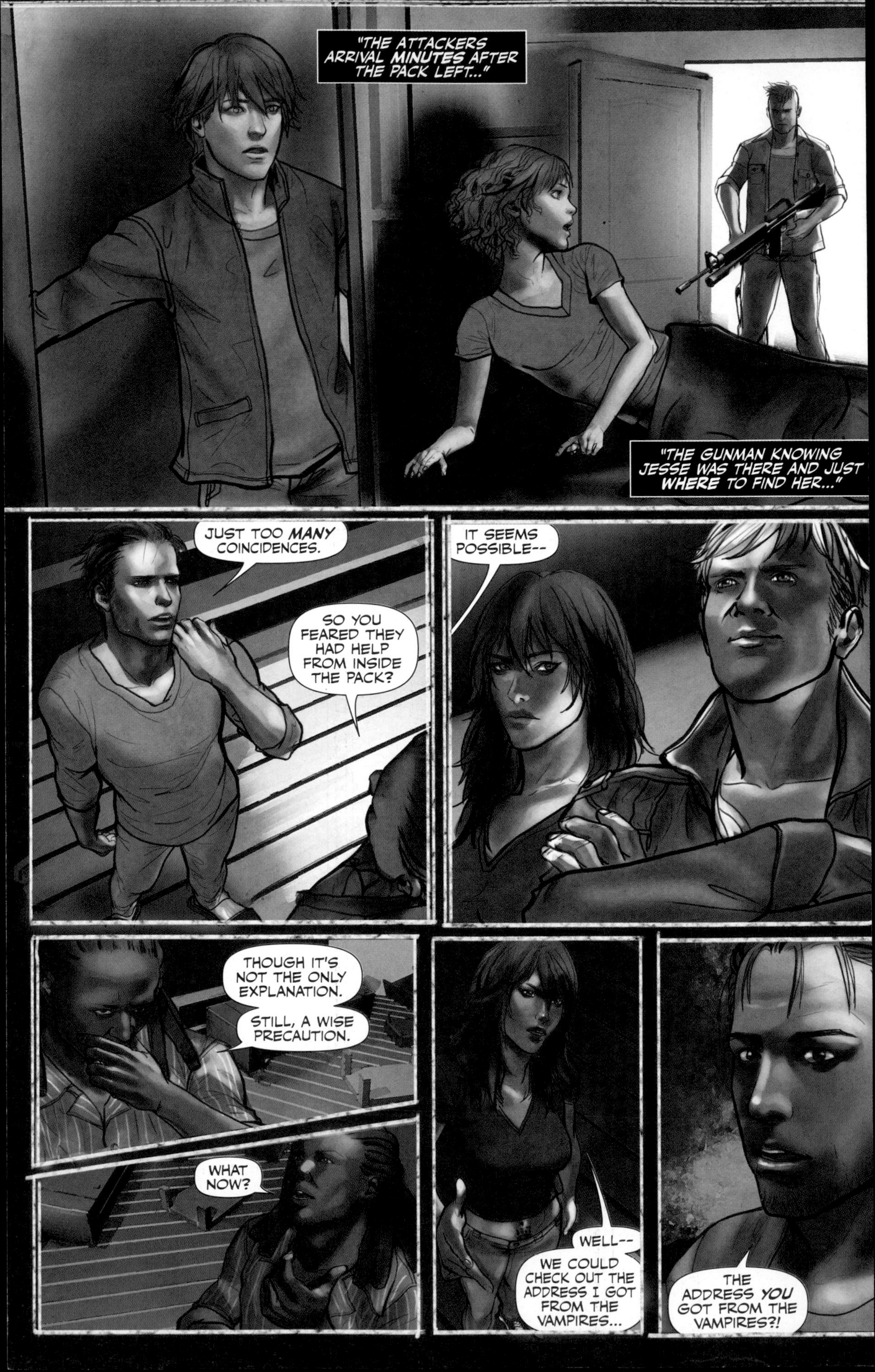
"THE ATTACKERS ARRIVAL MINUTES AFTER THE PACK LEFT..."
"THE GUNMAN KNOWING JESSE WAS THERE AND JUST WHERE TO FIND HER..."
JUST TOO MANY COINCIDENCES.
SO YOU FEARED THEY HAD HELP FROM INSIDE THE PACK?
IT SEEMS POSSIBLE--
THOUGH IT'S NOT THE ONLY EXPLANATION.
STILL, A WISE PRECAUTION.
WHAT NOW?
WELL--
WE COULD CHECK OUT THE ADDRESS I GOT FROM THE VAMPIRES...
THE ADDRESS YOU GOT FROM THE VAMPIRES?!

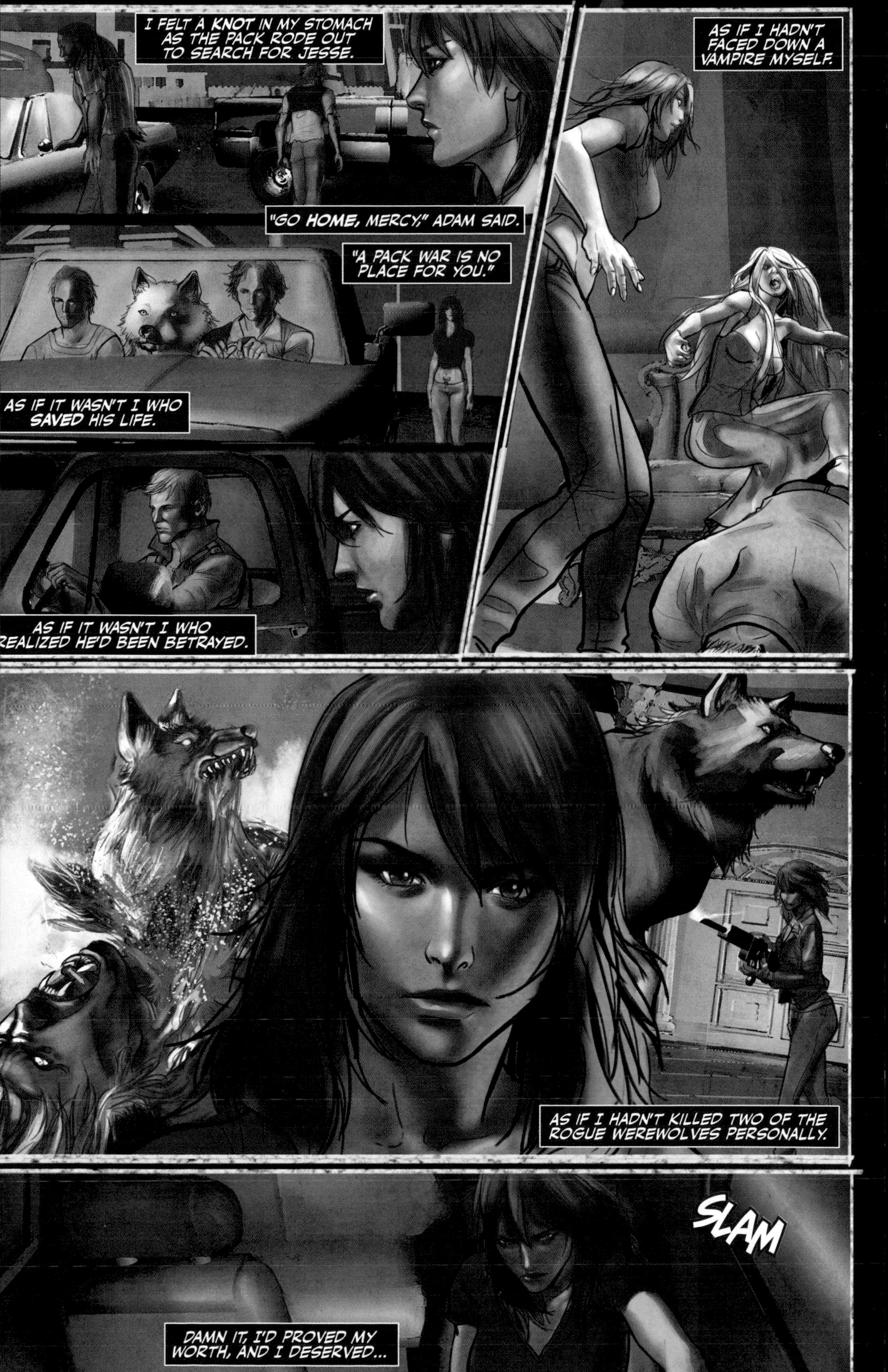
I FELT A KNOT IN MY STOMACH AS THE PACK RODE OUT TO SEARCH FOR JESSE.
"GO HOME, MERCY," ADAM SAID.
"A PACK WAR IS NO PLACE FOR YOU."
AS IF IT WASN'T I WHO SAVED HIS LIFE.
AS IF IT WASN'T I WHO REALIZED HE'D BEEN BETRAYED.
AS IF I HADN'T FACED DOWN A VAMPIRE MYSELF.
AS IF I HADN'T KILLED TWO OF THE ROGUE WEREWOLVES PERSONALLY.
SLAM
DAMN IT, I'D PROVED MY WORTH, AND I DESERVED...

DESERVED WHAT?

TO HELP PROTECT THE PEOPLE I LOVE--

OR TO BE IN ON THE KILL?

I'D BEEN SICKENED BY IT JUST DAYS BEFORE.

HAD I BECOME THAT BLOODTHIRSTY SO QUICKLY?

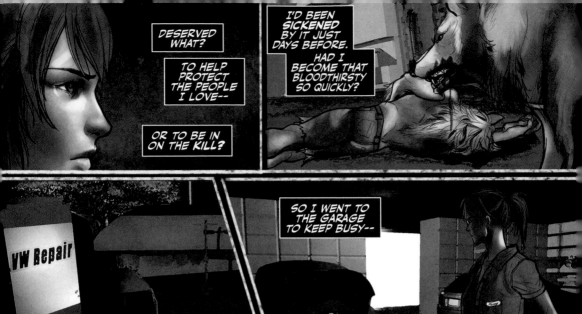

SO I WENT TO THE GARAGE TO KEEP BUSY--

SITTING BY, WAITING FOR NEWS SEEMED UNBEARABLE.

BUT MAC'S SCENT BROUGHT MEMORIES FLOODING BACK.

OF A POOR BOY CHANGED AGAINST HIS WILL--

CAGED AND TORTURED WITH EXPERIMENTAL DRUGS...

DRUGS? THAT'S IT.

IT SEEMED SO SIMPLE WHEN SAM EXPLAINED IT--

BUT WHO WOULD HAVE HAVE THE IMAGINATION...

THE MOTIVATION...

TO PUT IT ALL TOGETHER?

BRAN, IT'S MERCY. I HAVE A QUESTION...

COULD DR. WALLACE HAVE BEEN WORKING ON A DRUG TO *CONTROL* WEREWOLVES?

MERCY, CARTER IS ONE OF THE *GENTLEST* MEN I'VE EVER MET--

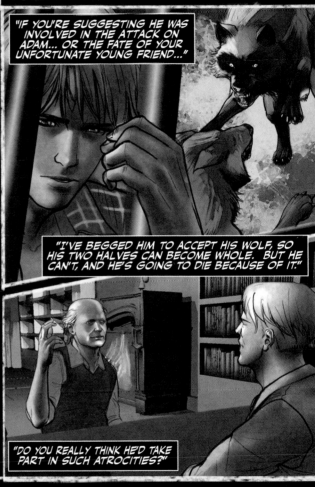

"IF YOU'RE SUGGESTING HE WAS INVOLVED IN THE ATTACK ON ADAM... OR THE FATE OF YOUR UNFORTUNATE YOUNG FRIEND..."

"I'VE BEGGED HIM TO ACCEPT HIS WOLF, SO HIS TWO HALVES CAN BECOME WHOLE. BUT HE CAN'T, AND HE'S GOING TO DIE BECAUSE OF IT."

"DO YOU REALLY THINK HE'D TAKE PART IN SUCH ATROCITIES?"

OF COURSE NOT. BUT...

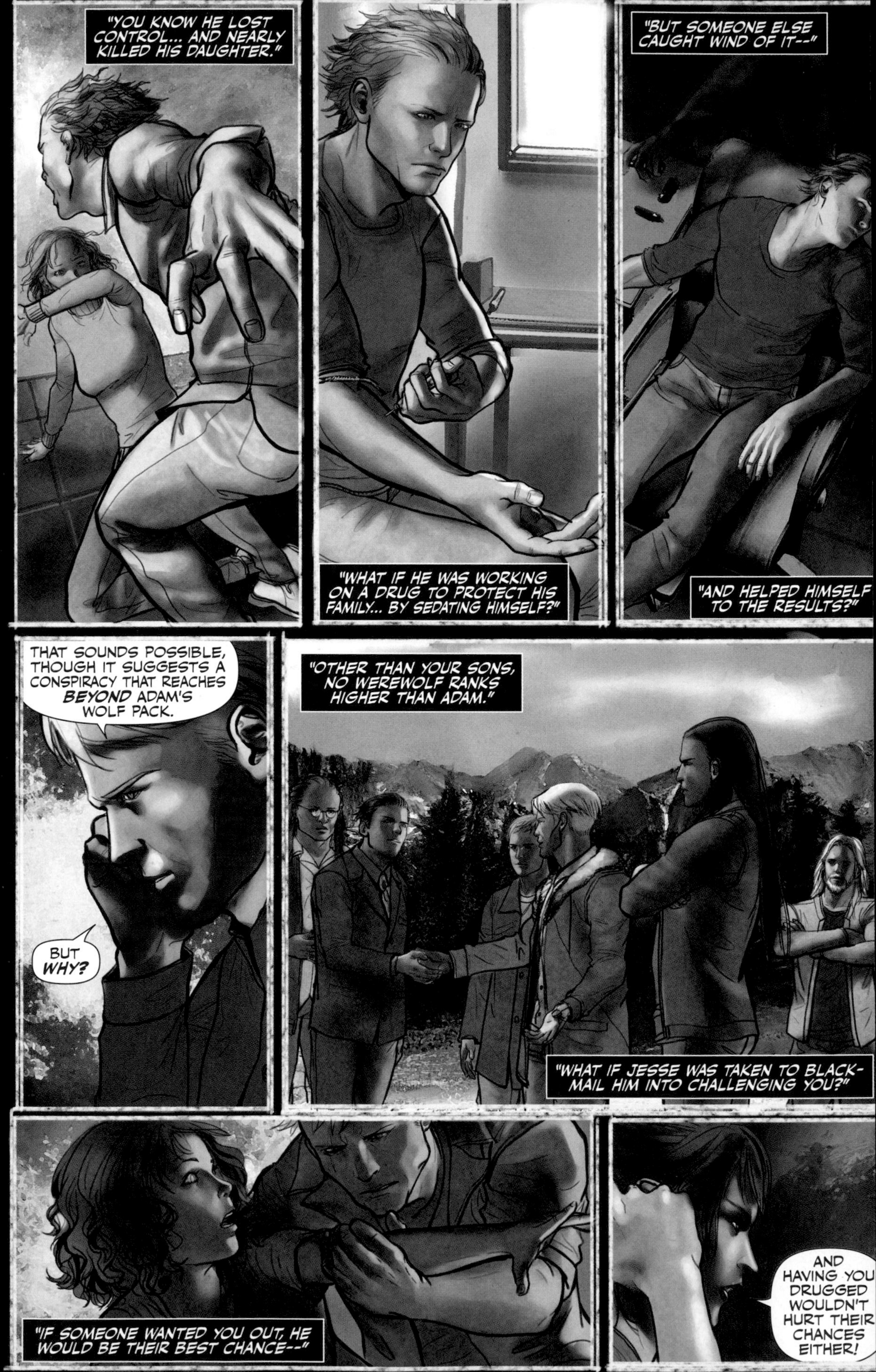
"YOU KNOW HE LOST CONTROL... AND NEARLY KILLED HIS DAUGHTER."
"WHAT IF HE WAS WORKING ON A DRUG TO PROTECT HIS FAMILY... BY SEDATING HIMSELF?"
"BUT SOMEONE ELSE CAUGHT WIND OF IT--"
"AND HELPED HIMSELF TO THE RESULTS?"
THAT SOUNDS POSSIBLE, THOUGH IT SUGGESTS A CONSPIRACY THAT REACHES BEYOND ADAM'S WOLF PACK.
BUT WHY?
"OTHER THAN YOUR SONS, NO WEREWOLF RANKS HIGHER THAN ADAM."
"WHAT IF JESSE WAS TAKEN TO BLACK-MAIL HIM INTO CHALLENGING YOU?"
"IF SOMEONE WANTED YOU OUT, HE WOULD BE THEIR BEST CHANCE--"
AND HAVING YOU DRUGGED WOULDN'T HURT THEIR CHANCES EITHER!

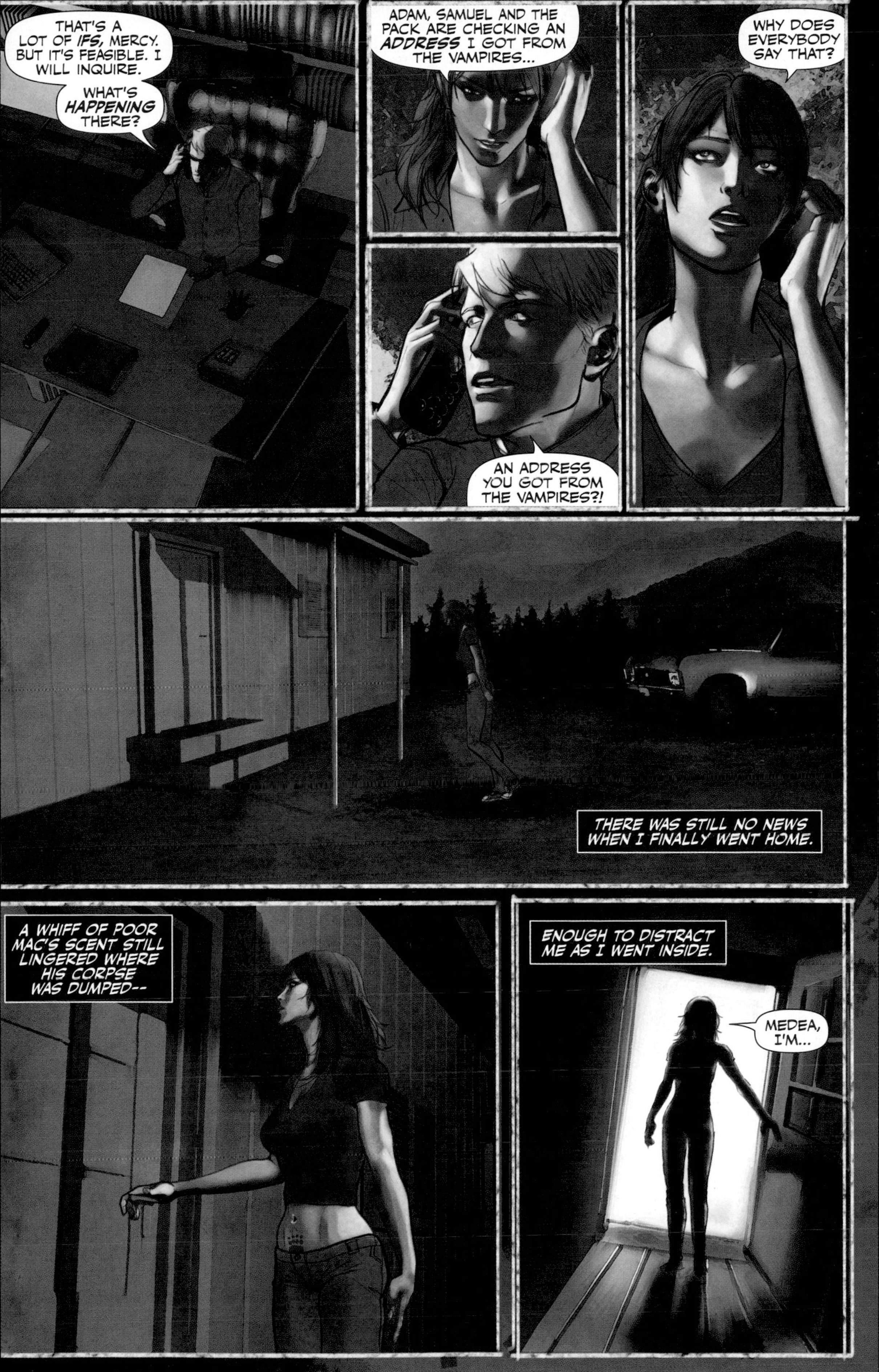
THAT'S A LOT OF *IFS,* MERCY. BUT IT'S FEASIBLE. I WILL INQUIRE.
WHAT'S *HAPPENING* THERE?
ADAM, SAMUEL AND THE PACK ARE CHECKING AN *ADDRESS* I GOT FROM THE VAMPIRES...
AN ADDRESS YOU GOT FROM THE VAMPIRES?!
WHY DOES EVERYBODY SAY THAT?
THERE WAS STILL NO NEWS WHEN I FINALLY WENT HOME.
A WHIFF OF POOR MAC'S SCENT STILL LINGERED WHERE HIS CORPSE WAS DUMPED--
ENOUGH TO DISTRACT ME AS I WENT INSIDE.
MEDEA, I'M...

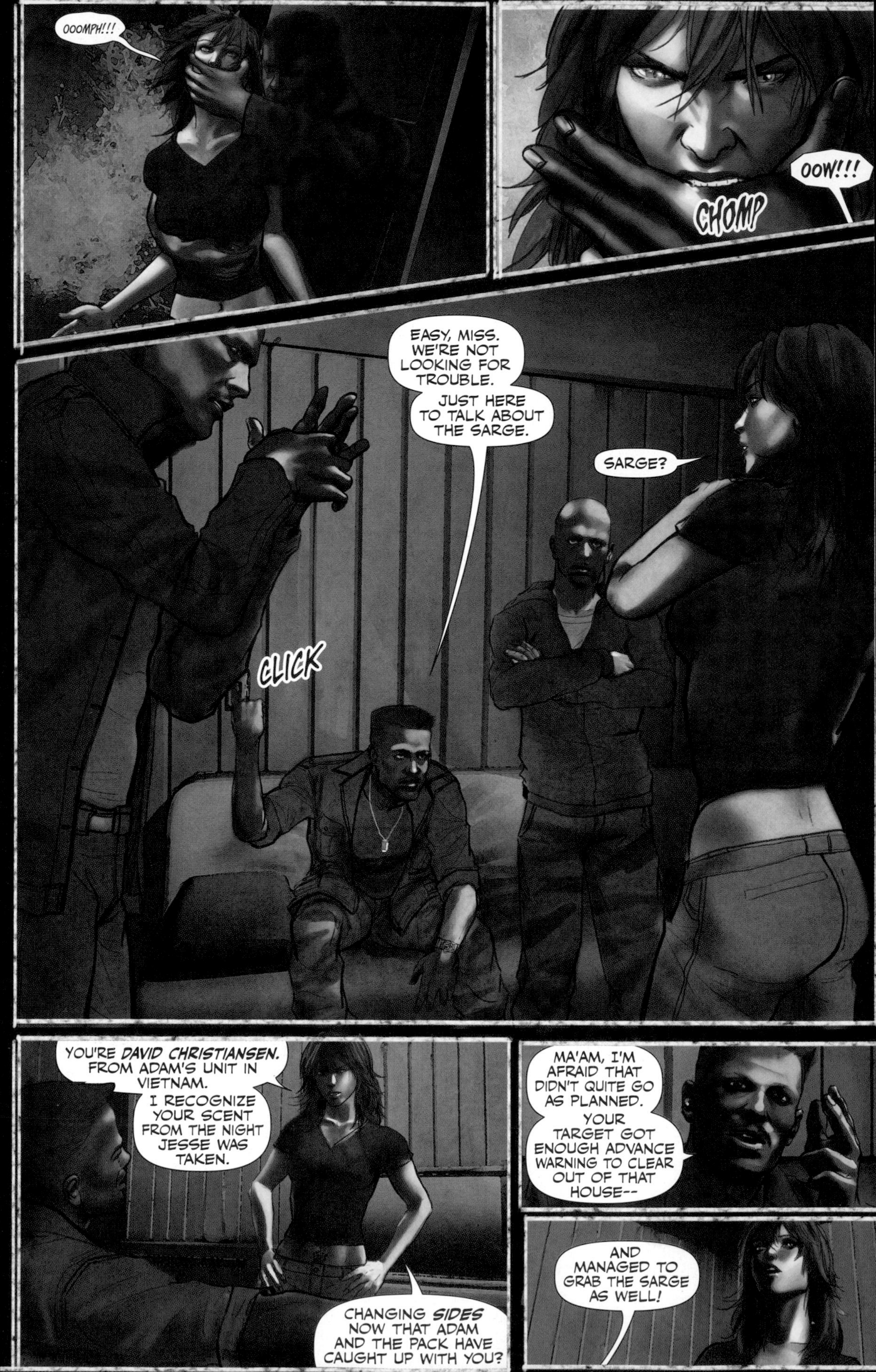
OOOMPH!!!
CHOMP
OOW!!!
EASY, MISS. WE'RE NOT LOOKING FOR TROUBLE.
JUST HERE TO TALK ABOUT THE SARGE.
SARGE?
CLICK
YOU'RE *DAVID CHRISTIANSEN.* FROM ADAM'S UNIT IN VIETNAM.
I RECOGNIZE YOUR SCENT FROM THE NIGHT JESSE WAS TAKEN.
CHANGING *SIDES* NOW THAT ADAM AND THE PACK HAVE CAUGHT UP WITH YOU?
MA'AM, I'M AFRAID THAT DIDN'T QUITE GO AS PLANNED.
YOUR TARGET GOT ENOUGH ADVANCE WARNING TO CLEAR OUT OF THAT HOUSE--
AND MANAGED TO GRAB THE SARGE AS WELL!

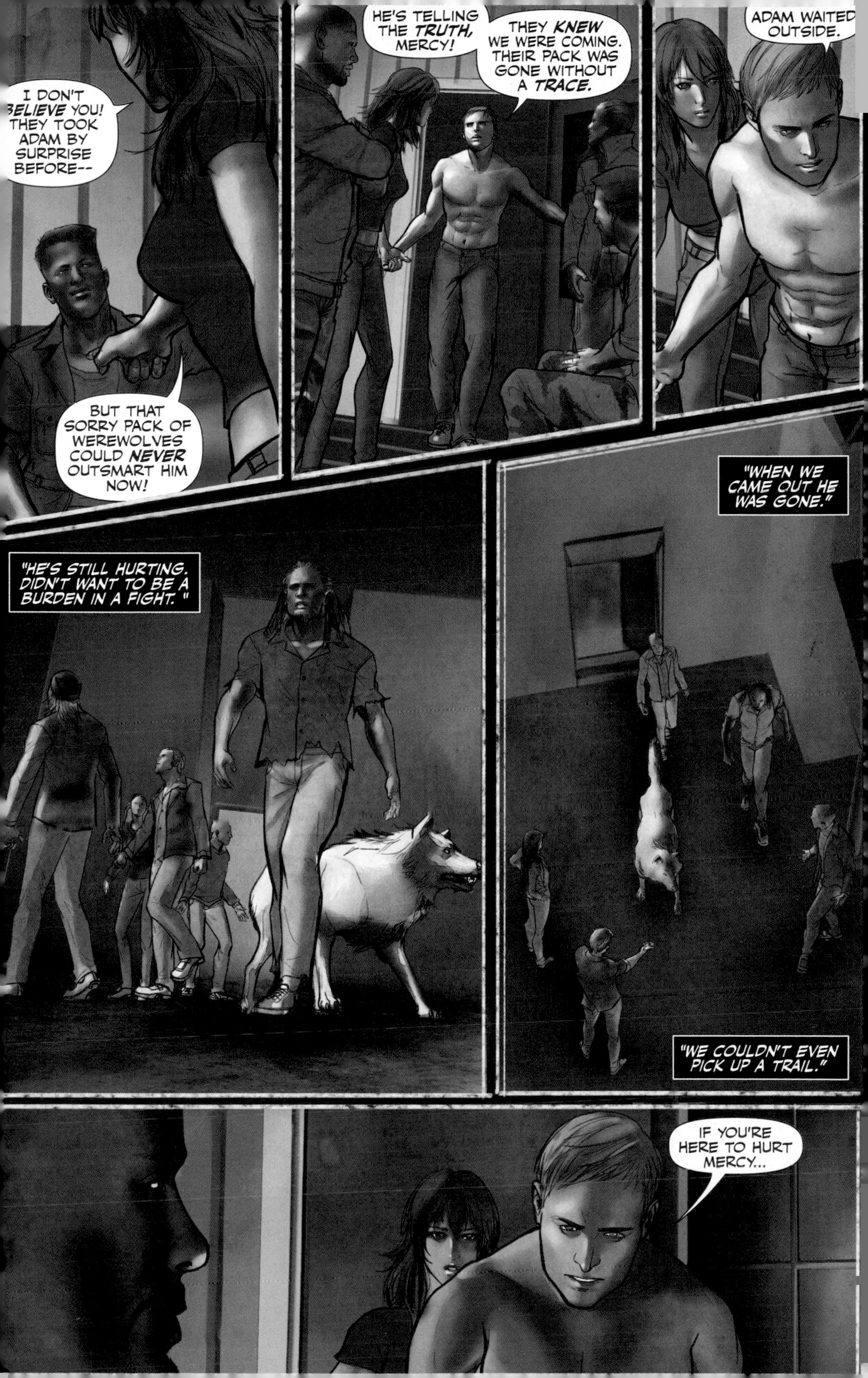

I DON'T BELIEVE YOU! THEY TOOK ADAM BY SURPRISE BEFORE--
BUT THAT SORRY PACK OF WEREWOLVES COULD NEVER OUTSMART HIM NOW!
HE'S TELLING THE TRUTH, MERCY!
THEY KNEW WE WERE COMING. THEIR PACK WAS GONE WITHOUT A TRACE.
ADAM WAITED OUTSIDE.
"HE'S STILL HURTING. DIDN'T WANT TO BE A BURDEN IN A FIGHT."
"WHEN WE CAME OUT HE WAS GONE."
"WE COULDN'T EVEN PICK UP A TRAIL."
IF YOU'RE HERE TO HURT MERCY...

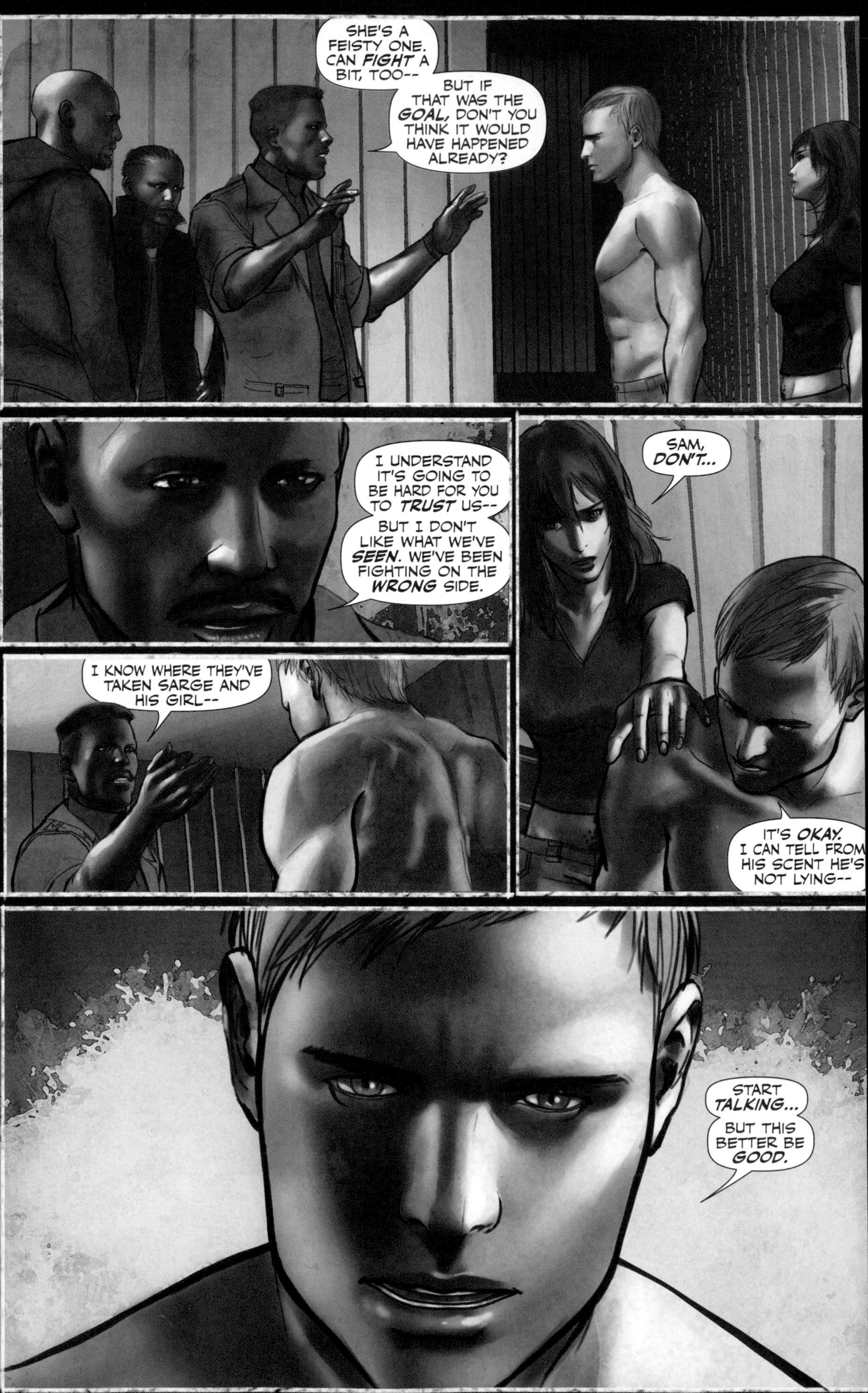
SHE'S A FEISTY ONE. CAN FIGHT A BIT, TOO--
BUT IF THAT WAS THE GOAL, DON'T YOU THINK IT WOULD HAVE HAPPENED ALREADY?
I UNDERSTAND IT'S GOING TO BE HARD FOR YOU TO TRUST US--
BUT I DON'T LIKE WHAT WE'VE SEEN. WE'VE BEEN FIGHTING ON THE WRONG SIDE.
I KNOW WHERE THEY'VE TAKEN SARGE AND HIS GIRL--
SAM, DON'T...
IT'S OKAY. I CAN TELL FROM HIS SCENT HE'S NOT LYING--
START TALKING...
BUT THIS BETTER BE GOOD.

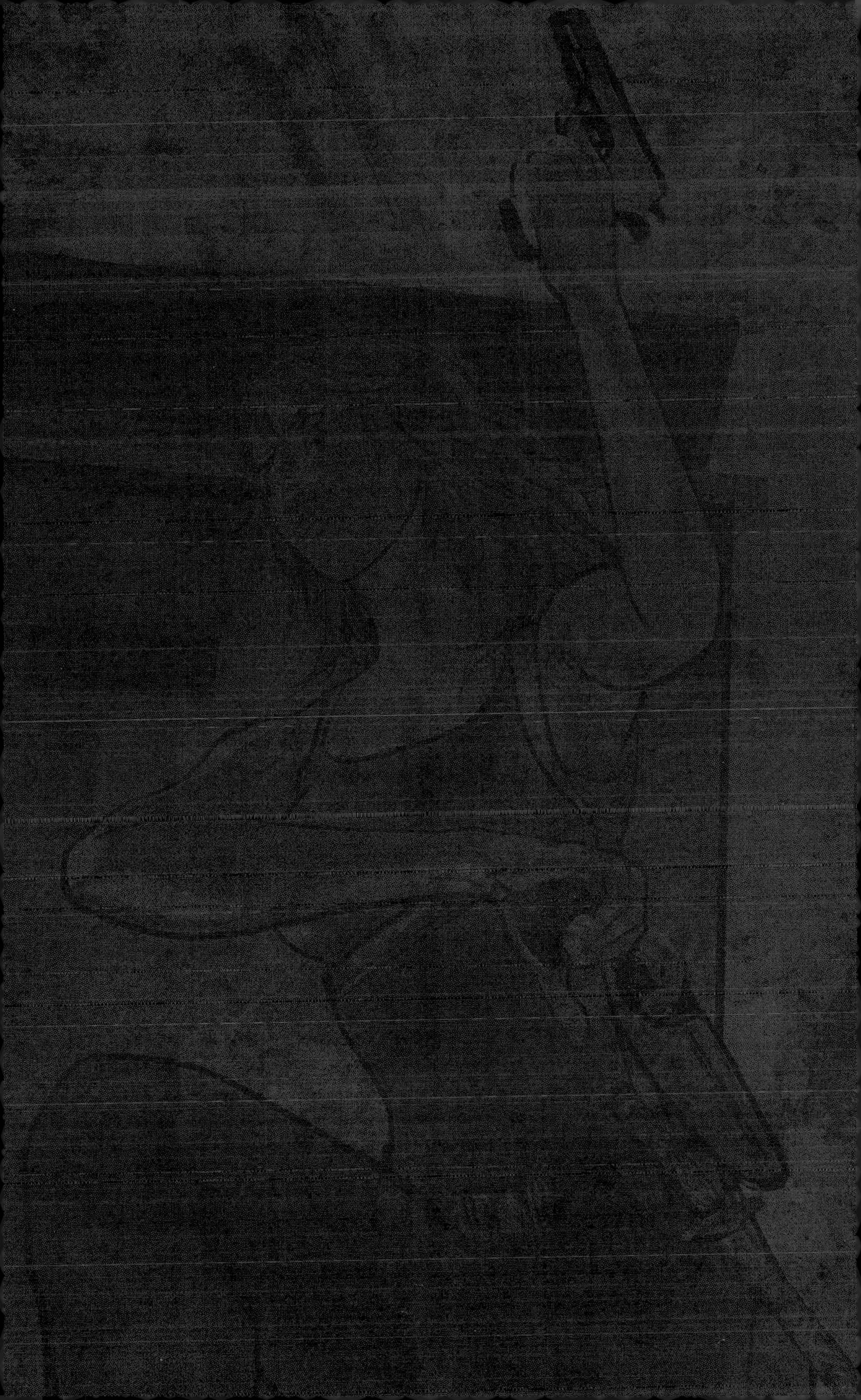

ISSUE EIGHT COVER BY:
**TYLER WALPOLE**

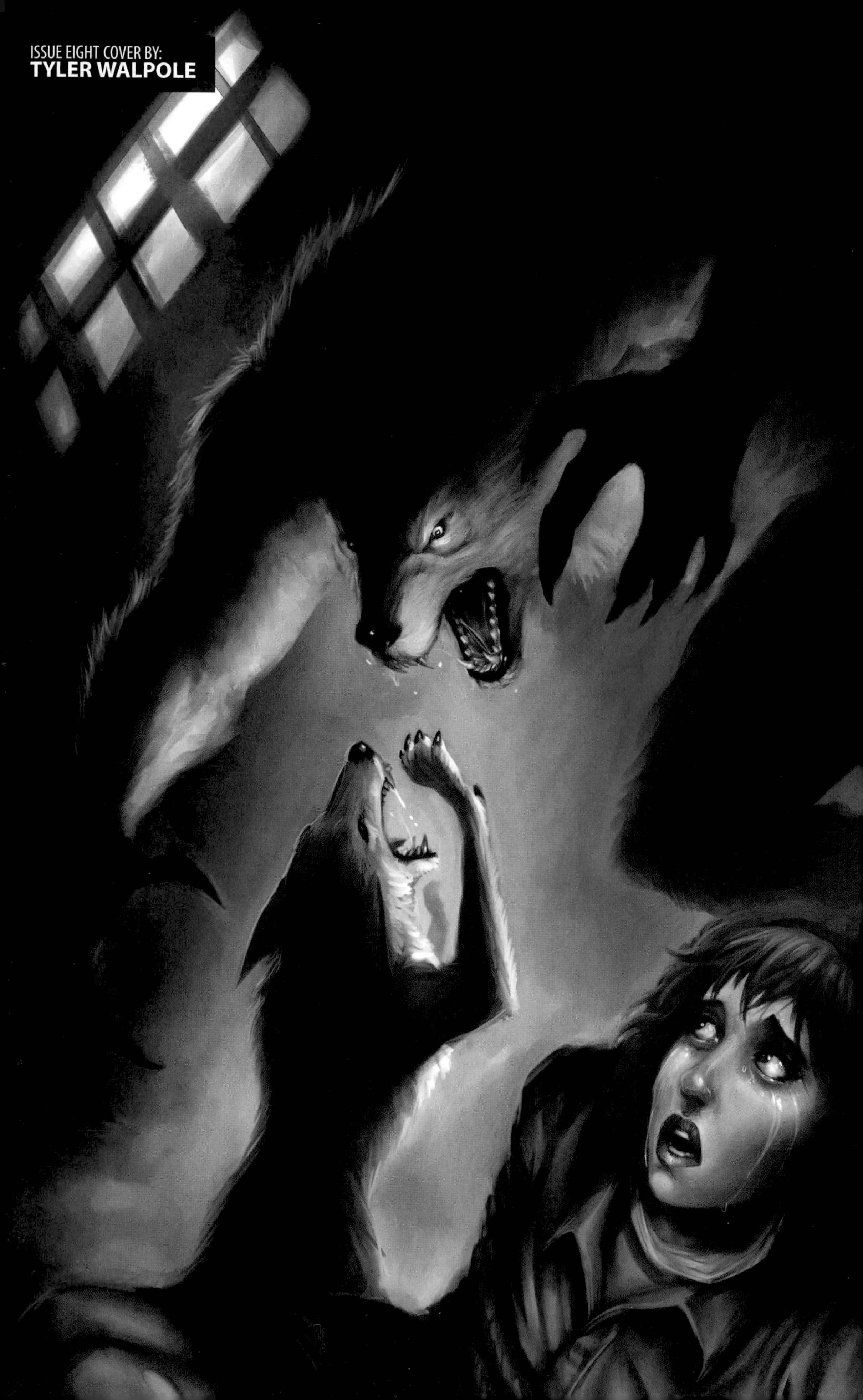

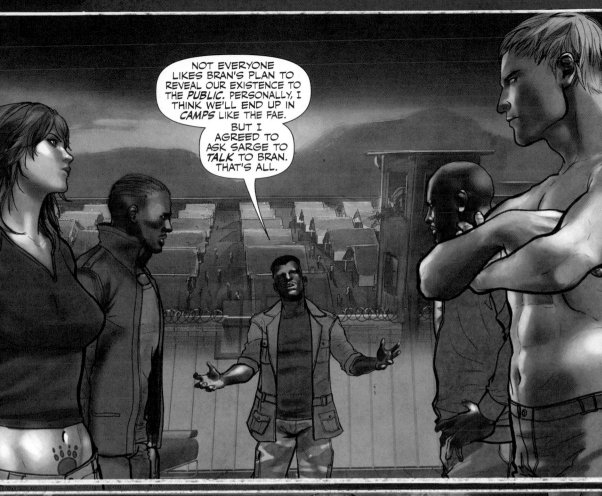

NOT EVERYONE LIKES BRAN'S PLAN TO REVEAL OUR EXISTENCE TO THE *PUBLIC.* PERSONALLY, I THINK WE'LL END UP IN *CAMPS* LIKE THE FAE.

BUT I AGREED TO ASK SARGE TO *TALK* TO BRAN. THAT'S ALL.

"WE DIDN'T SIGN ON FOR KIDNAPPING AND KILLING."

IF WE ALL WORK TOGETHER, WE CAN END THIS--

AND GET SARGE AND HIS GIRL OUT ALIVE.

WHO TOLD YOU ABOUT DA'S PLANS?

IT'S NOT A *SECRET* AROUND ASPEN CREEK, BUT YOU'RE NOT PART OF THE PACK.

A LONE WOLF LIKE YOU WOULD ONLY HAVE *CONTACT* WITH...

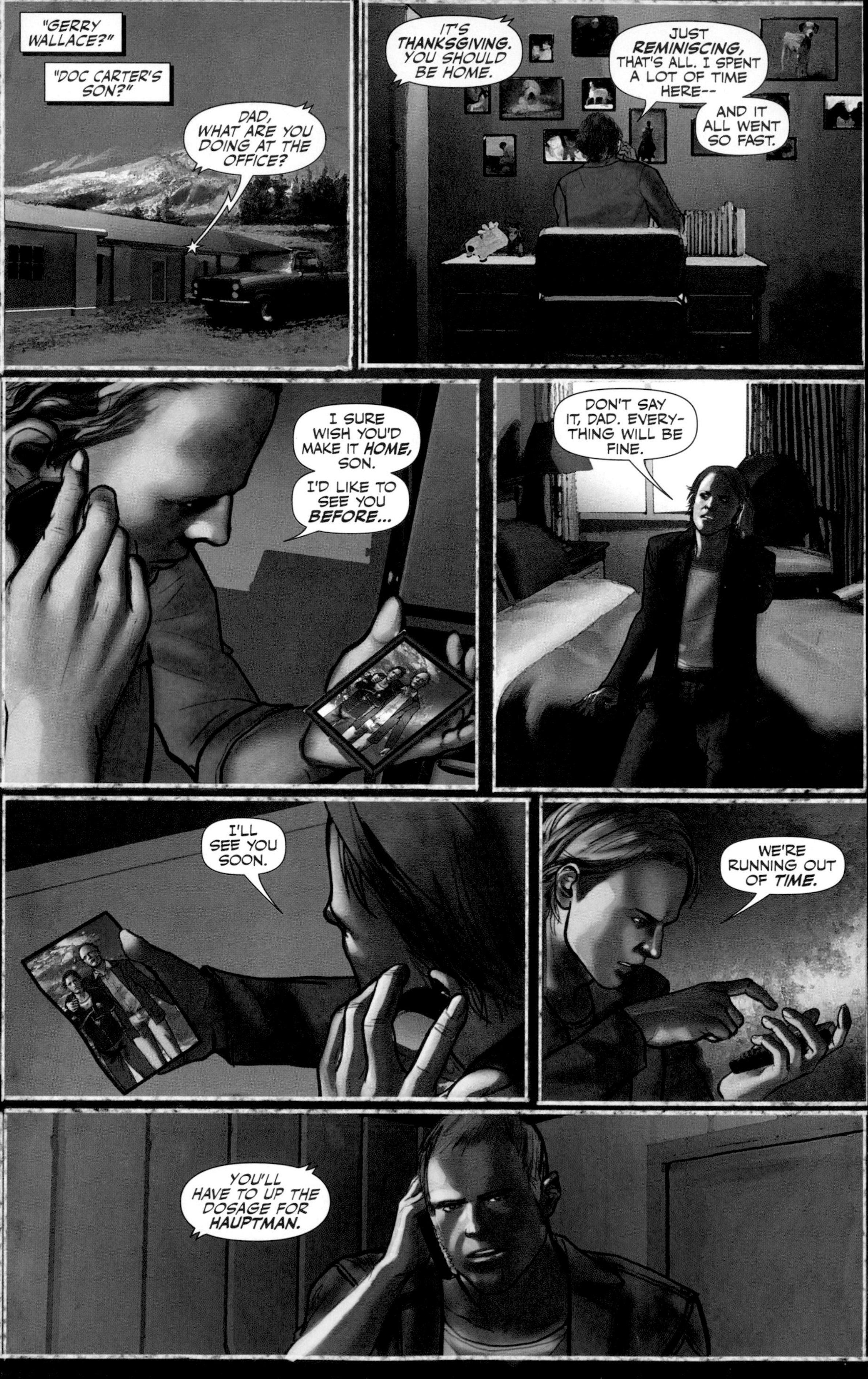
"GERRY WALLACE?"
"DOC CARTER'S SON?"
DAD, WHAT ARE YOU DOING AT THE OFFICE?
IT'S THANKSGIVING. YOU SHOULD BE HOME.
JUST REMINISCING, THAT'S ALL. I SPENT A LOT OF TIME HERE--
AND IT ALL WENT SO FAST.
I SURE WISH YOU'D MAKE IT HOME, SON.
I'D LIKE TO SEE YOU BEFORE...
DON'T SAY IT, DAD. EVERYTHING WILL BE FINE.
I'LL SEE YOU SOON.
WE'RE RUNNING OUT OF TIME.
YOU'LL HAVE TO UP THE DOSAGE FOR HAUPTMAN.

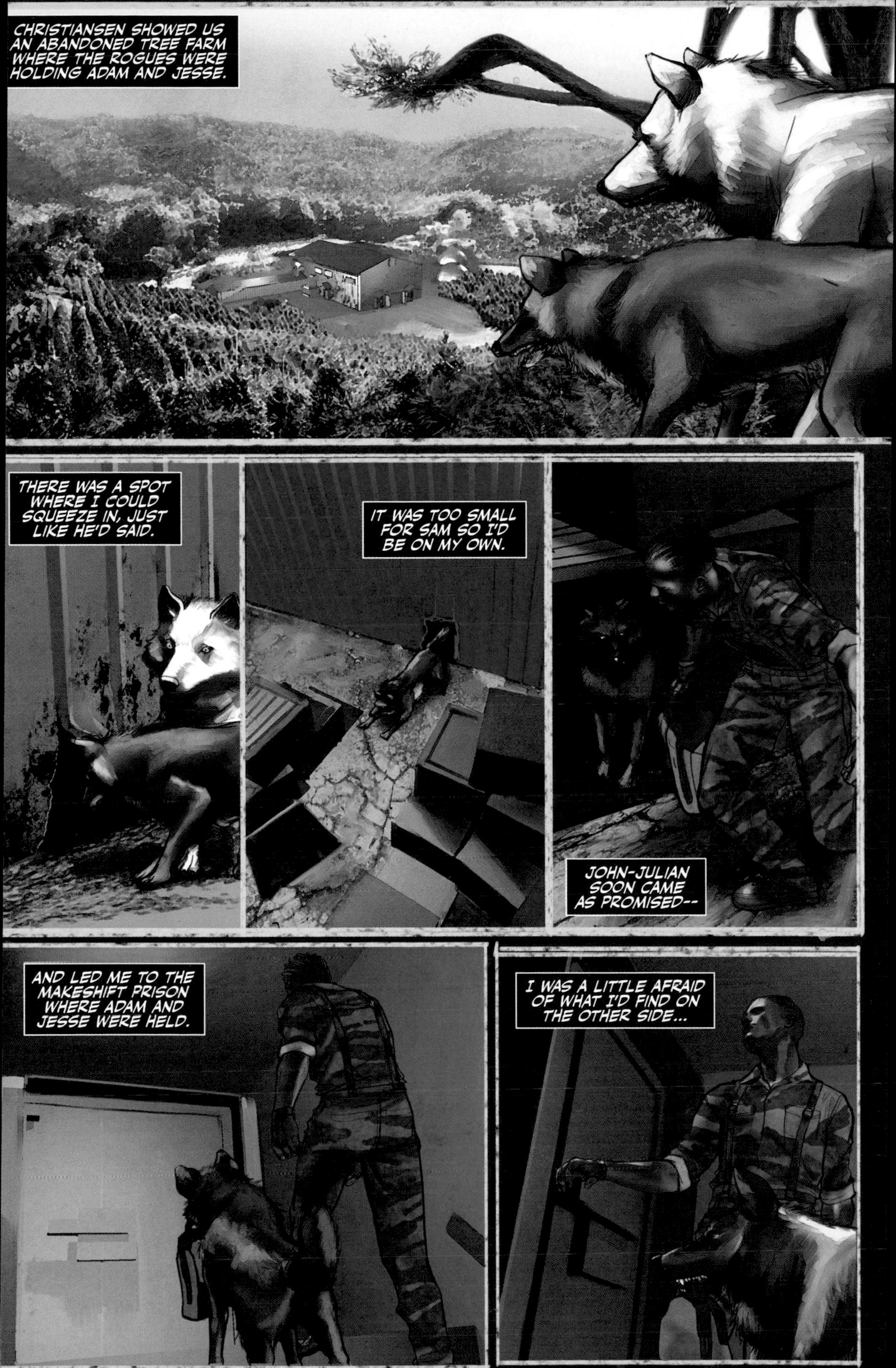
CHRISTIANSEN SHOWED US AN ABANDONED TREE FARM WHERE THE ROGUES WERE HOLDING ADAM AND JESSE.
THERE WAS A SPOT WHERE I COULD SQUEEZE IN, JUST LIKE HE'D SAID.
IT WAS TOO SMALL FOR SAM SO I'D BE ON MY OWN.
JOHN-JULIAN SOON CAME AS PROMISED--
AND LED ME TO THE MAKESHIFT PRISON WHERE ADAM AND JESSE WERE HELD.
I WAS A LITTLE AFRAID OF WHAT I'D FIND ON THE OTHER SIDE...

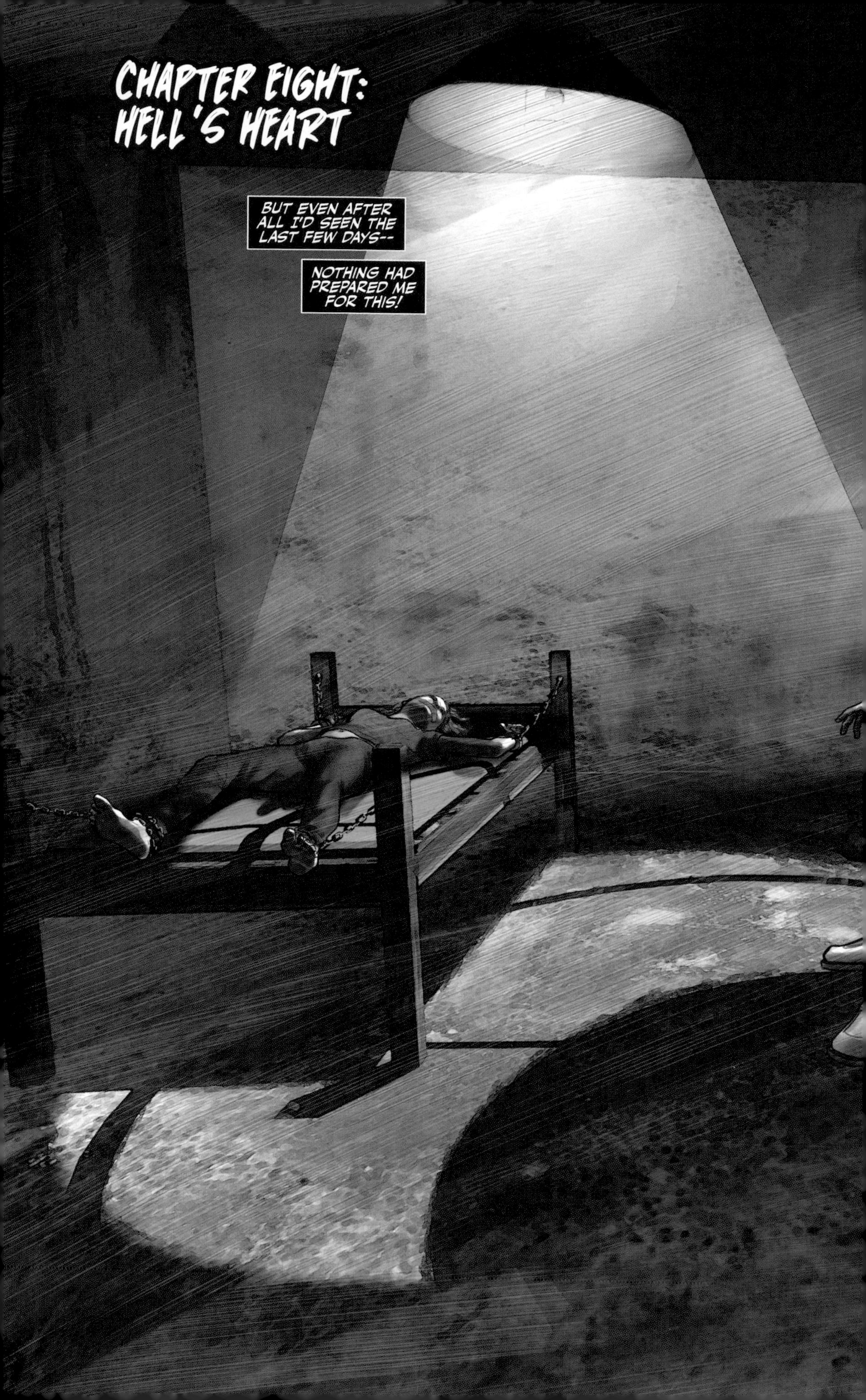
CHAPTER EIGHT: HELL'S HEART
BUT EVEN AFTER ALL I'D SEEN THE LAST FEW DAYS--
NOTHING HAD PREPARED ME FOR THIS!

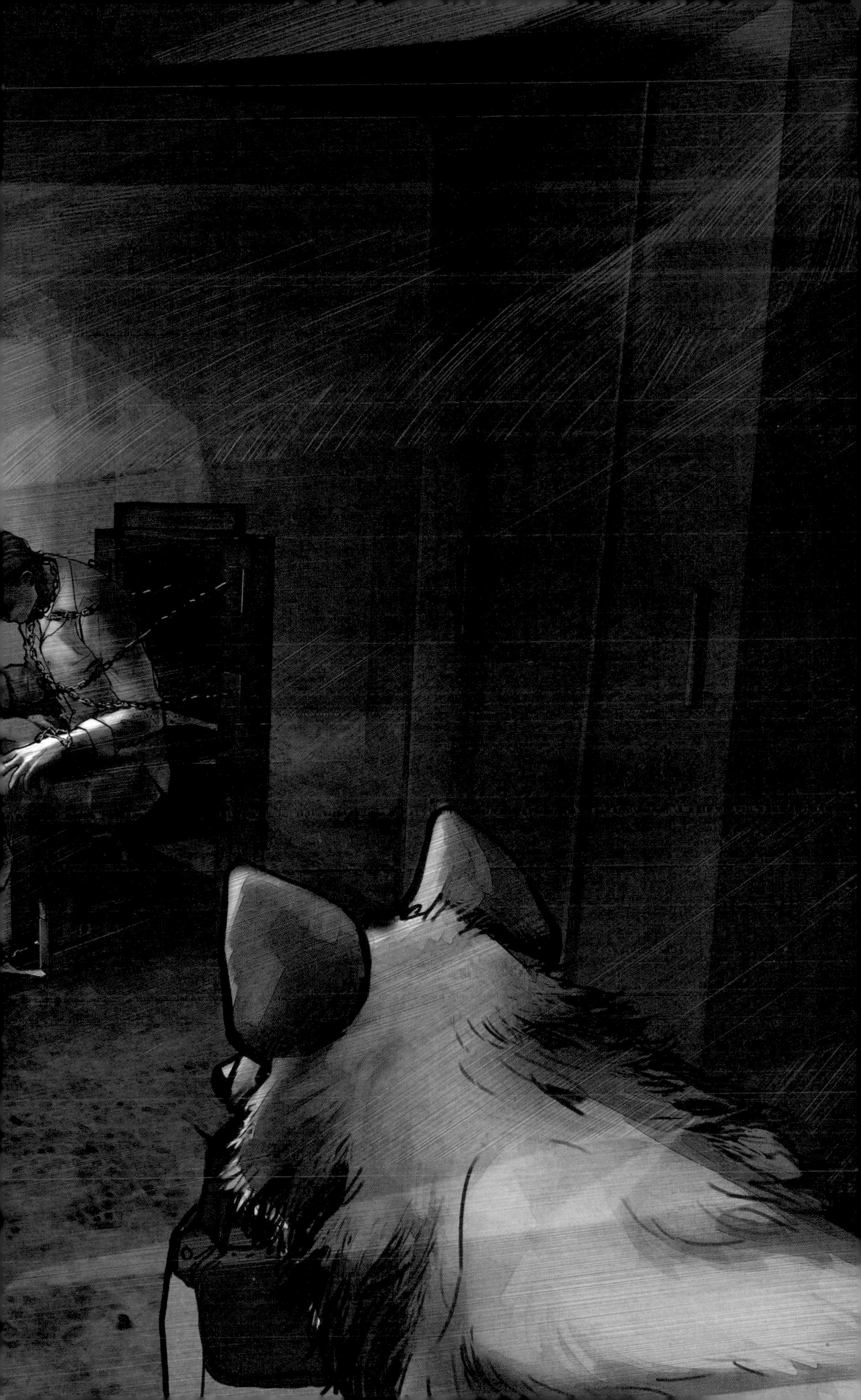

IT WOULD BE A WHILE UNTIL CHRISTIANSEN'S MEN CAME TO GET US OUT.
I COULDN'T RISK FREEING THEM. THE ROGUES COULD CHECK IN AT ANY TIME.
BUT AT LEAST I COULD WATCH OVER THEM--
SCREEEE
IF I DIDN'T GET CAUGHT!
HELLO, ANGEL.

BUT *THIS* TIME I'M HERE FOR YOUR FATHER.

I'D *LOVE* TO TAKE CARE OF YOU--

WOULDN'T DO FOR HIM TO WAKE UP AND START MAKING TROUBLE.

BUT I'LL BE BACK FOR YOU *LATER.*

I PROMISE.

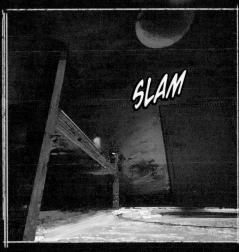

SLAM

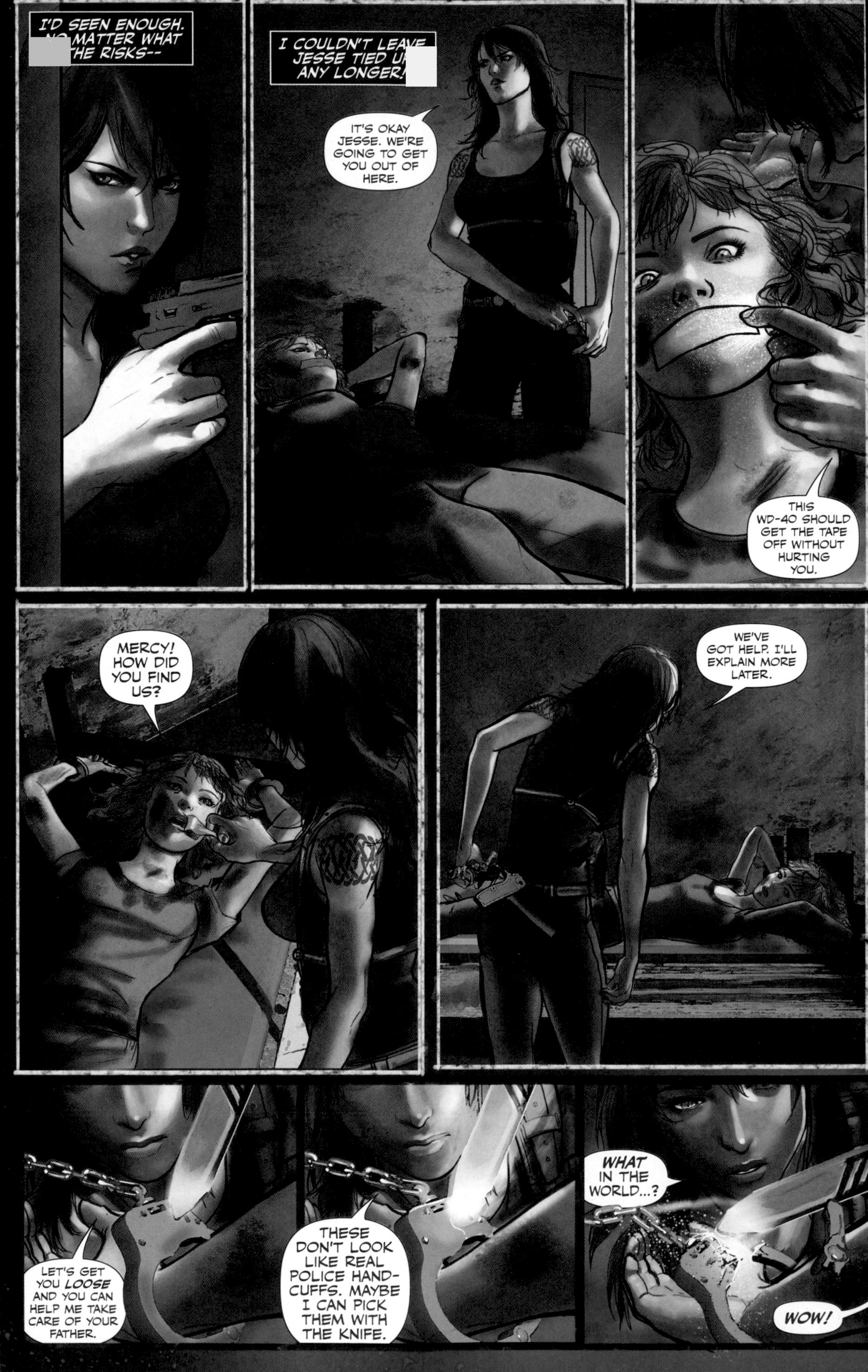
I'D SEEN ENOUGH.
MATTER WHAT
RISKS--
I COULDN'T LEAVE JESSE TIED UP ANY LONGER!
IT'S OKAY JESSE. WE'RE GOING TO GET YOU OUT OF HERE.
THIS WD-40 SHOULD GET THE TAPE OFF WITHOUT HURTING YOU.
MERCY! HOW DID YOU FIND US?
WE'VE GOT HELP. I'LL EXPLAIN MORE LATER.
LET'S GET YOU LOOSE AND YOU CAN HELP ME TAKE CARE OF YOUR FATHER.
THESE DON'T LOOK LIKE REAL POLICE HAND-CUFFS. MAYBE I CAN PICK THEM WITH THE KNIFE.
WHAT IN THE WORLD...?
WOW!

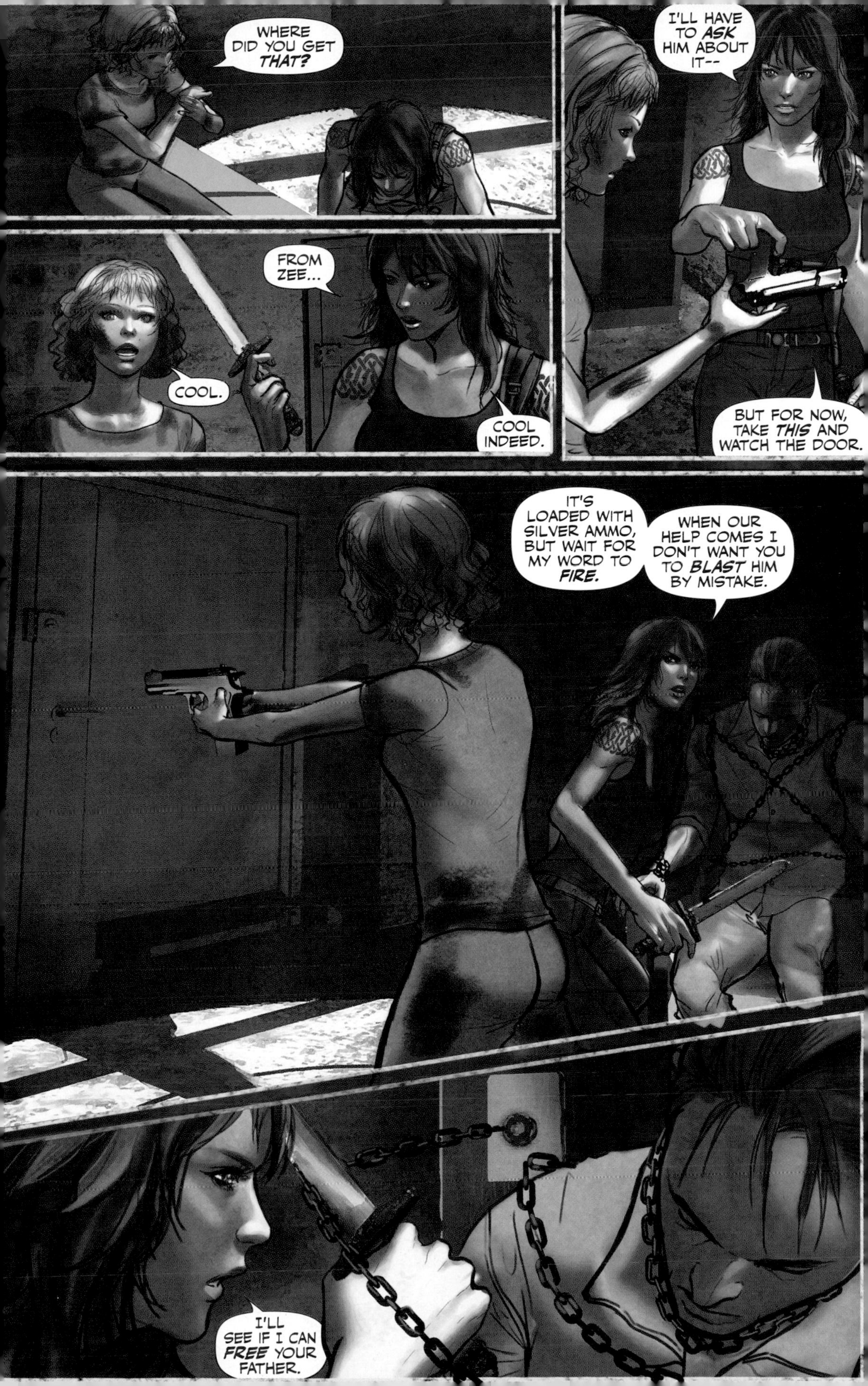
WHERE DID YOU GET THAT?
FROM ZEE...
COOL.
COOL INDEED.
I'LL HAVE TO ASK HIM ABOUT IT--
BUT FOR NOW, TAKE THIS AND WATCH THE DOOR.
IT'S LOADED WITH SILVER AMMO, BUT WAIT FOR MY WORD TO FIRE.
WHEN OUR HELP COMES I DON'T WANT YOU TO BLAST HIM BY MISTAKE.
I'LL SEE IF I CAN FREE YOUR FATHER.

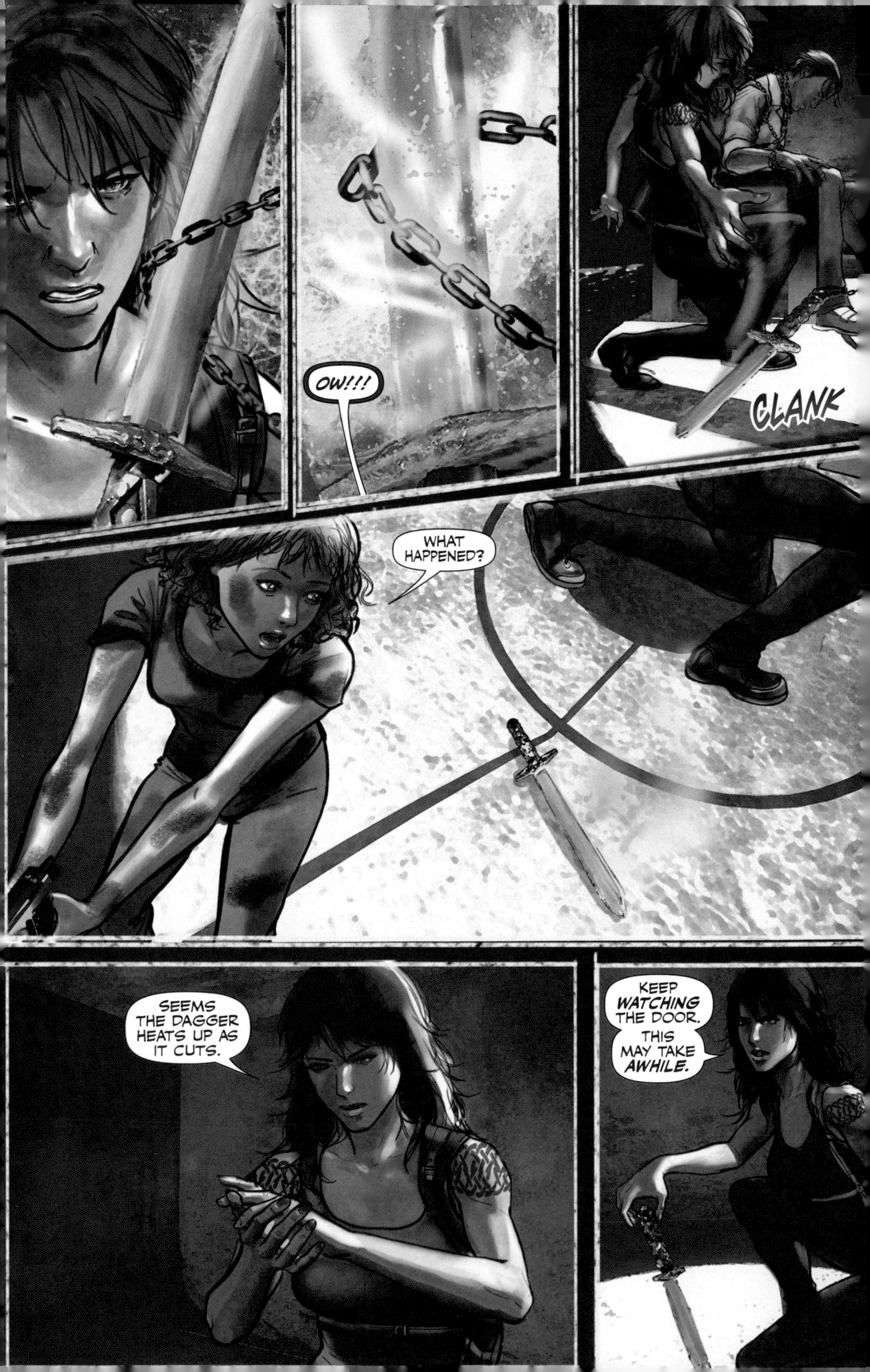
OW!!!
CLANK
WHAT HAPPENED?
SEEMS THE DAGGER HEATS UP AS IT CUTS.
KEEP WATCHING THE DOOR. THIS MAY TAKE AWHILE.

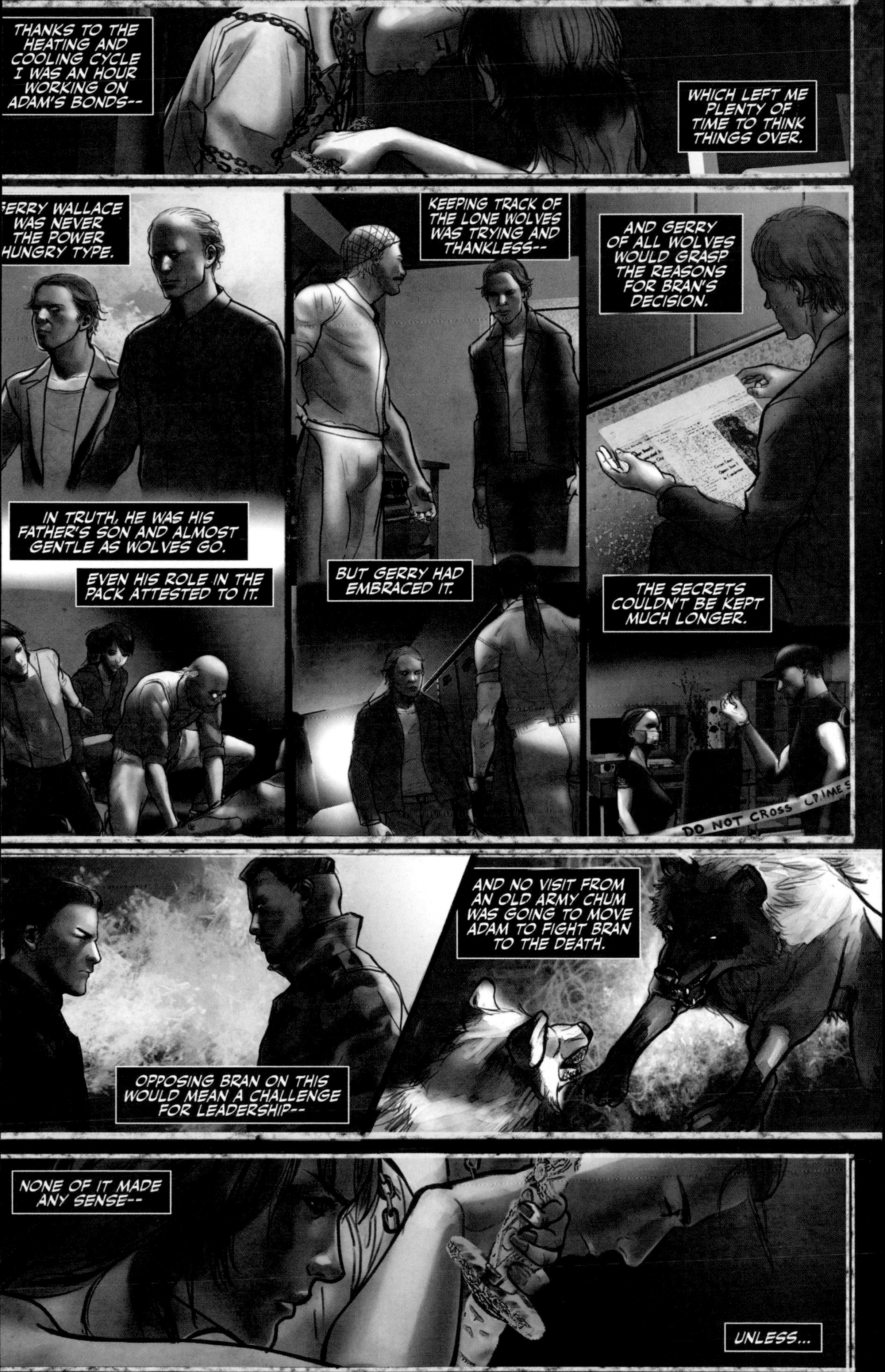

THANKS TO THE HEATING AND COOLING CYCLE I WAS AN HOUR WORKING ON ADAM'S BONDS--
WHICH LEFT ME PLENTY OF TIME TO THINK THINGS OVER.
GERRY WALLACE WAS NEVER THE POWER HUNGRY TYPE.
IN TRUTH, HE WAS HIS FATHER'S SON AND ALMOST GENTLE AS WOLVES GO.
EVEN HIS ROLE IN THE PACK ATTESTED TO IT.
KEEPING TRACK OF THE LONE WOLVES WAS TRYING AND THANKLESS--
BUT GERRY HAD EMBRACED IT.
AND GERRY OF ALL WOLVES WOULD GRASP THE REASONS FOR BRAN'S DECISION.
THE SECRETS COULDN'T BE KEPT MUCH LONGER.
DO NOT CROSS CRIMES
OPPOSING BRAN ON THIS WOULD MEAN A CHALLENGE FOR LEADERSHIP--
AND NO VISIT FROM AN OLD ARMY CHUM WAS GOING TO MOVE ADAM TO FIGHT BRAN TO THE DEATH.
NONE OF IT MADE ANY SENSE--
UNLESS...

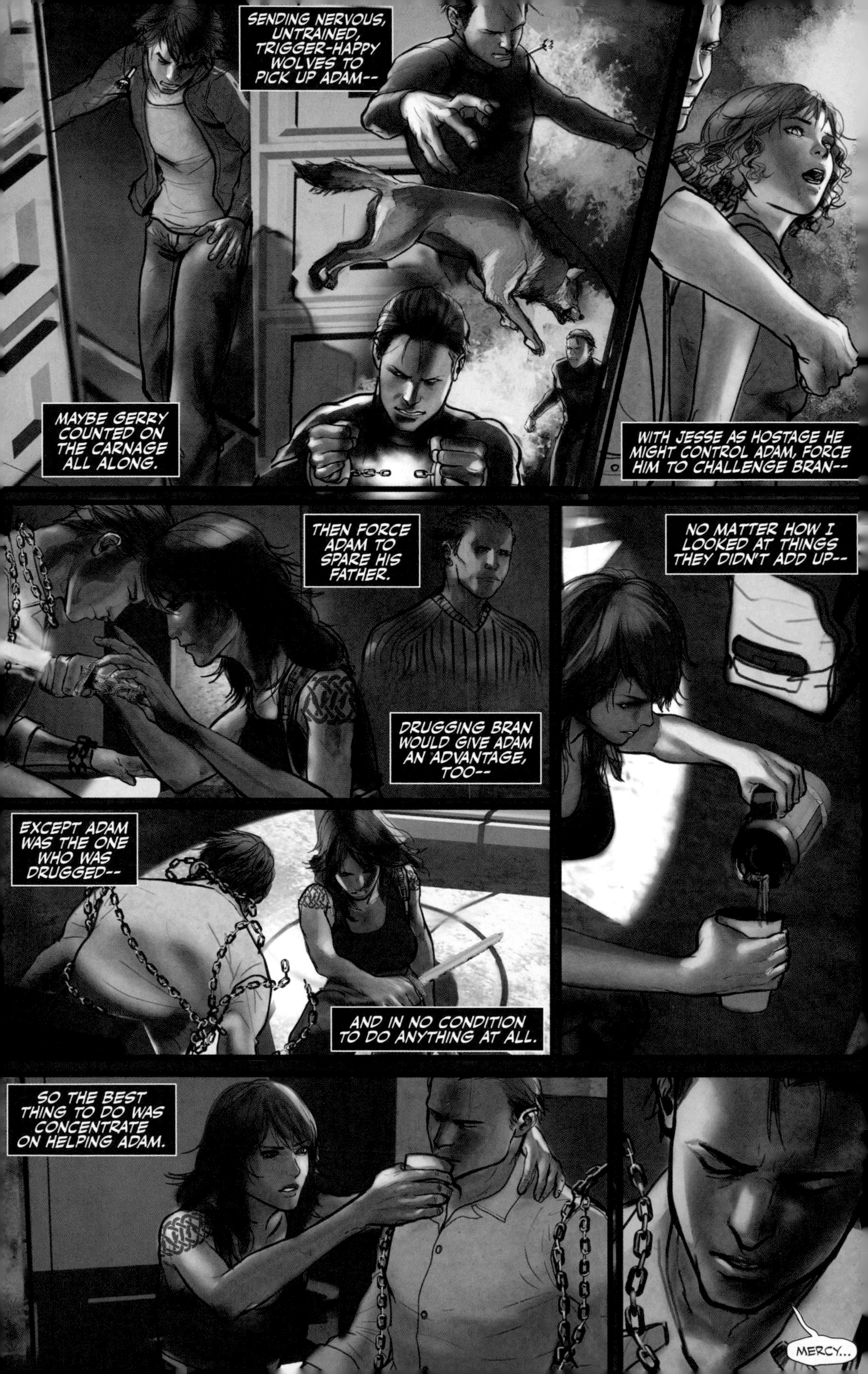
SENDING NERVOUS, UNTRAINED, TRIGGER-HAPPY WOLVES TO PICK UP ADAM--
MAYBE GERRY COUNTED ON THE CARNAGE ALL ALONG.
WITH JESSE AS HOSTAGE HE MIGHT CONTROL ADAM, FORCE HIM TO CHALLENGE BRAN--
THEN FORCE ADAM TO SPARE HIS FATHER.
DRUGGING BRAN WOULD GIVE ADAM AN ADVANTAGE, TOO--
NO MATTER HOW I LOOKED AT THINGS THEY DIDN'T ADD UP--
EXCEPT ADAM WAS THE ONE WHO WAS DRUGGED--
AND IN NO CONDITION TO DO ANYTHING AT ALL.
SO THE BEST THING TO DO WAS CONCENTRATE ON HELPING ADAM.
MERCY...

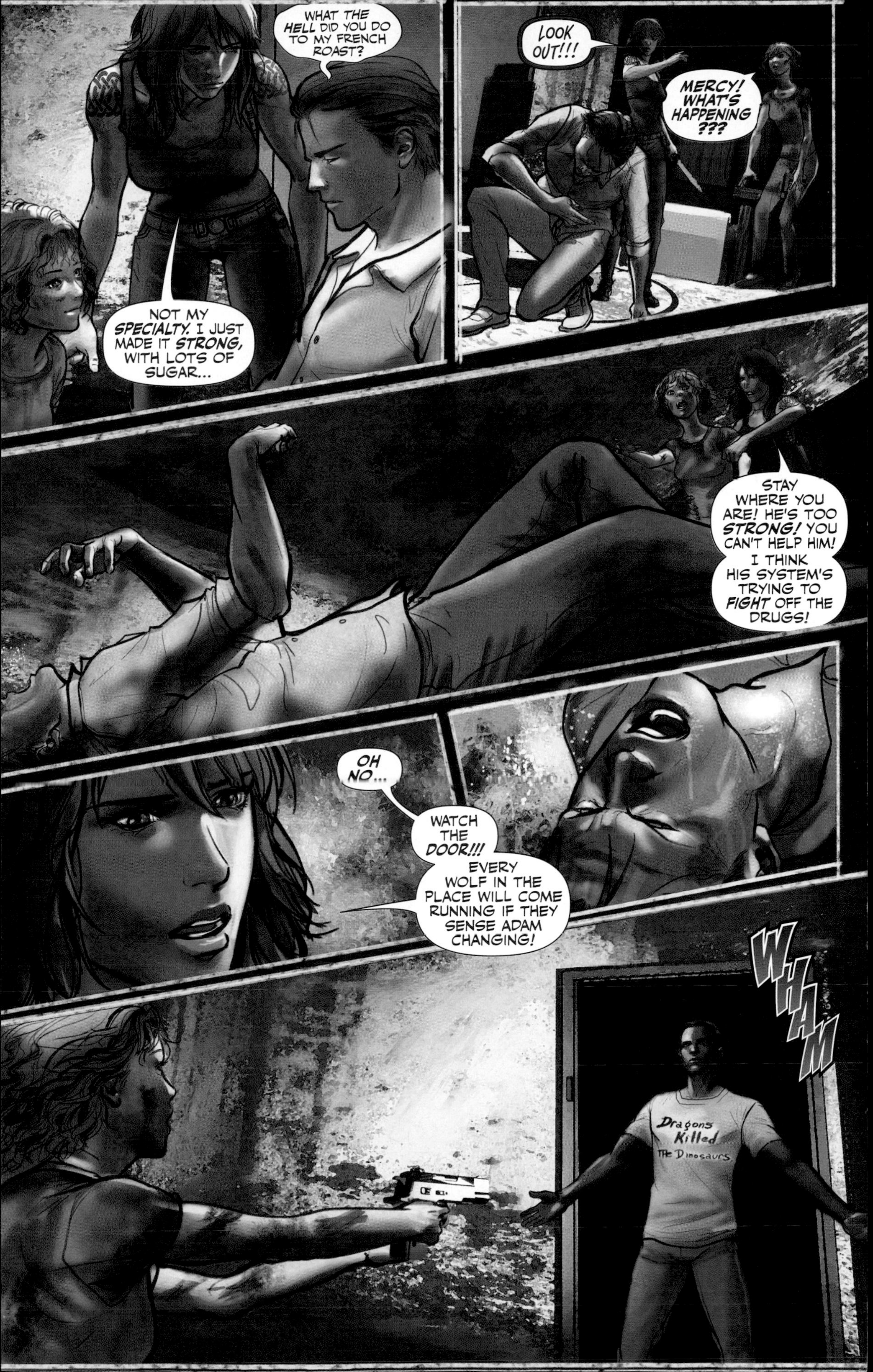
WHAT THE HELL DID YOU DO TO MY FRENCH ROAST?
NOT MY SPECIALTY. I JUST MADE IT STRONG, WITH LOTS OF SUGAR...
LOOK OUT!!!
MERCY! WHAT'S HAPPENING???
STAY WHERE YOU ARE! HE'S TOO STRONG! YOU CAN'T HELP HIM!
I THINK HIS SYSTEM'S TRYING TO FIGHT OFF THE DRUGS!
OH NO...
WATCH THE DOOR!!!
EVERY WOLF IN THE PLACE WILL COME RUNNING IF THEY SENSE ADAM CHANGING!
WHAM
Dragons Killed The Dinosaurs.

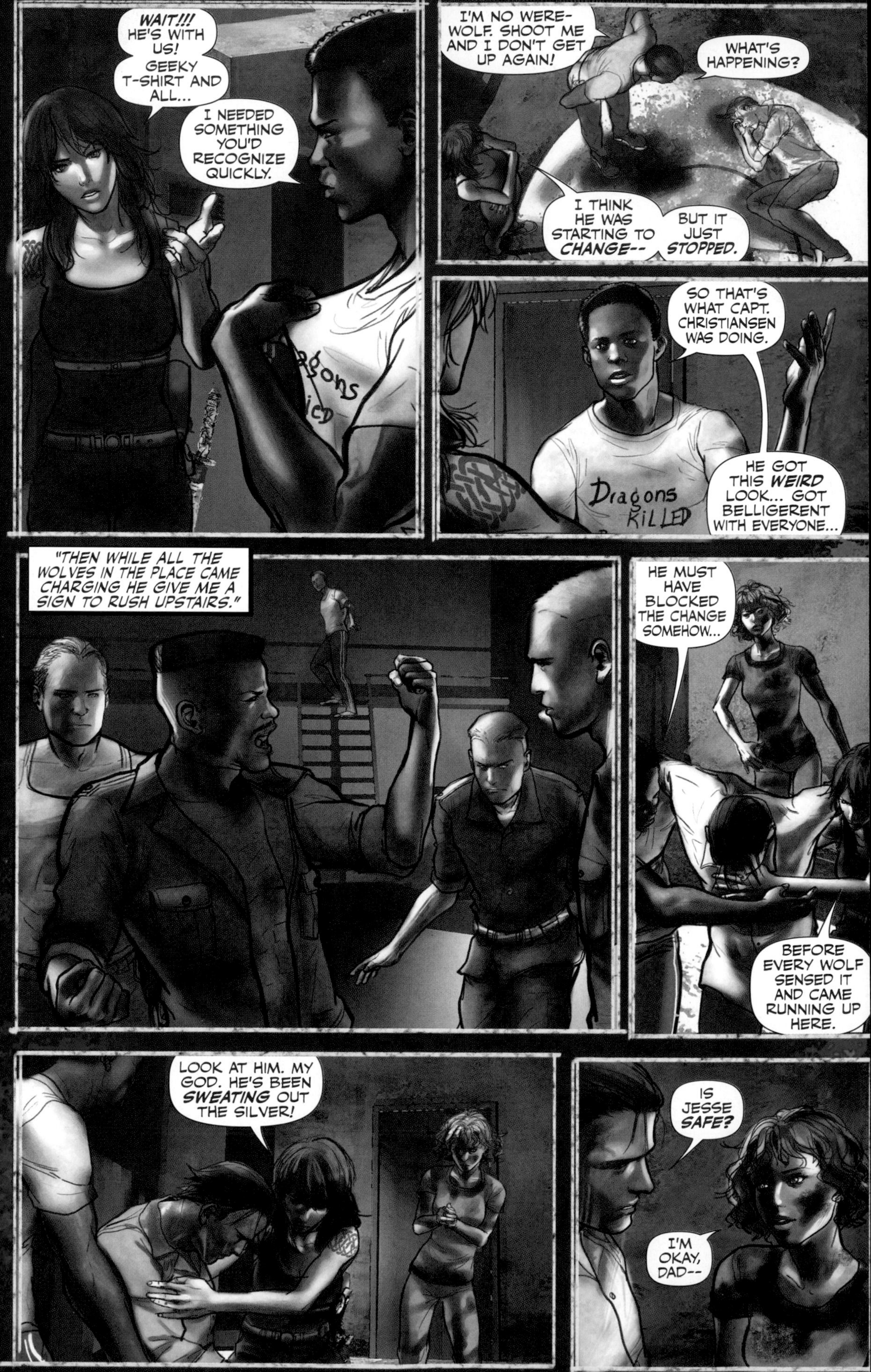
WAIT!!! HE'S WITH US! GEEKY T-SHIRT AND ALL...
I NEEDED SOMETHING YOU'D RECOGNIZE QUICKLY.
Dragons
I'M NO WERE-WOLF. SHOOT ME AND I DON'T GET UP AGAIN!
WHAT'S HAPPENING?
I THINK HE WAS STARTING TO CHANGE--
BUT IT JUST STOPPED.
SO THAT'S WHAT CAPT. CHRISTIANSEN WAS DOING.
Dragons KILLED
HE GOT THIS WEIRD LOOK... GOT BELLIGERENT WITH EVERYONE...
"THEN WHILE ALL THE WOLVES IN THE PLACE CAME CHARGING HE GIVE ME A SIGN TO RUSH UPSTAIRS."
HE MUST HAVE BLOCKED THE CHANGE SOMEHOW...
BEFORE EVERY WOLF SENSED IT AND CAME RUNNING UP HERE.
LOOK AT HIM. MY GOD. HE'S BEEN SWEATING OUT THE SILVER!
IS JESSE SAFE?
I'M OKAY, DAD--

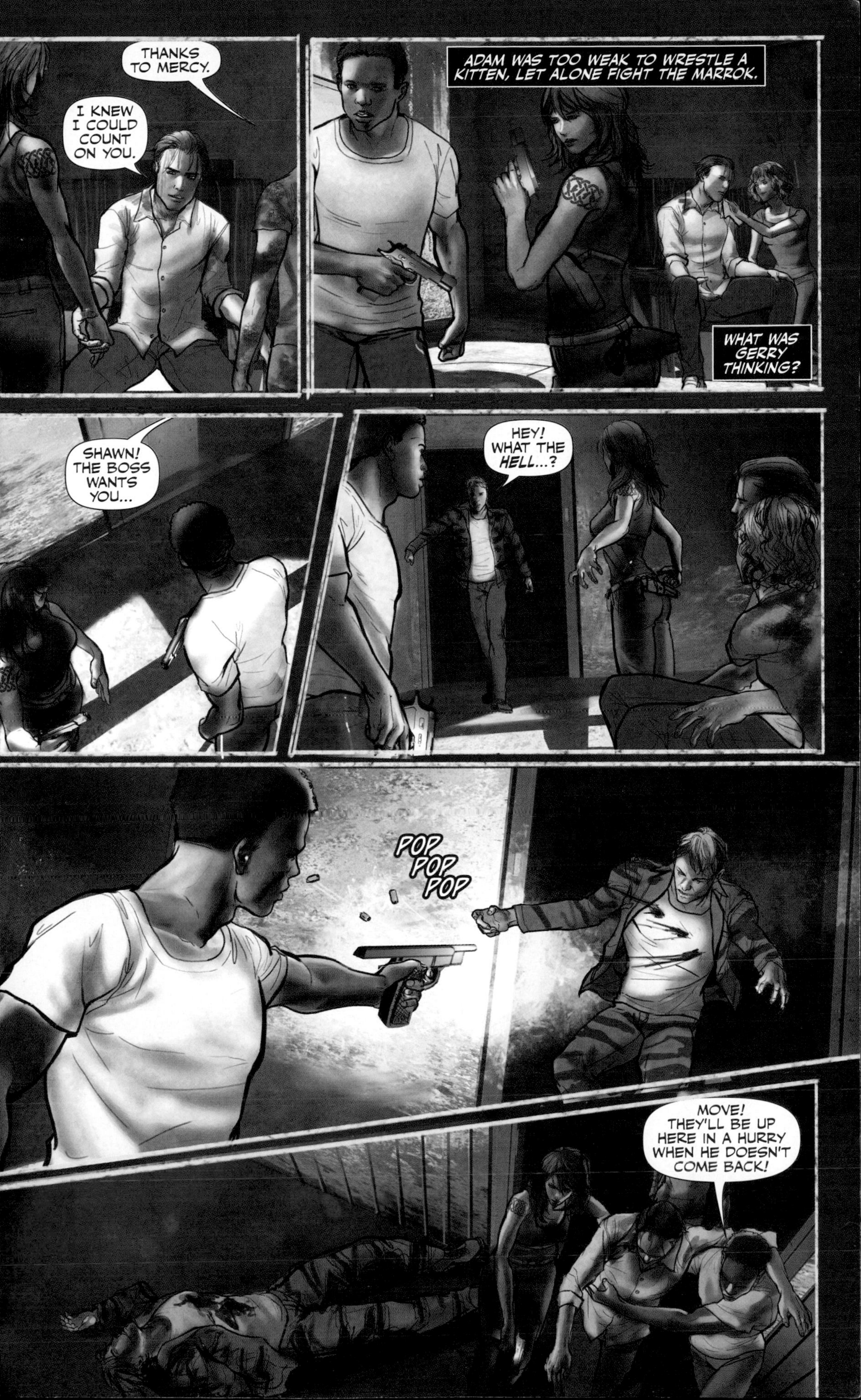
I KNEW I COULD COUNT ON YOU.
THANKS TO MERCY.
ADAM WAS TOO WEAK TO WRESTLE A KITTEN, LET ALONE FIGHT THE MARROK.
WHAT WAS GERRY THINKING?
SHAWN! THE BOSS WANTS YOU...
HEY! WHAT THE HELL...?
POP POP POP
MOVE! THEY'LL BE UP HERE IN A HURRY WHEN HE DOESN'T COME BACK!

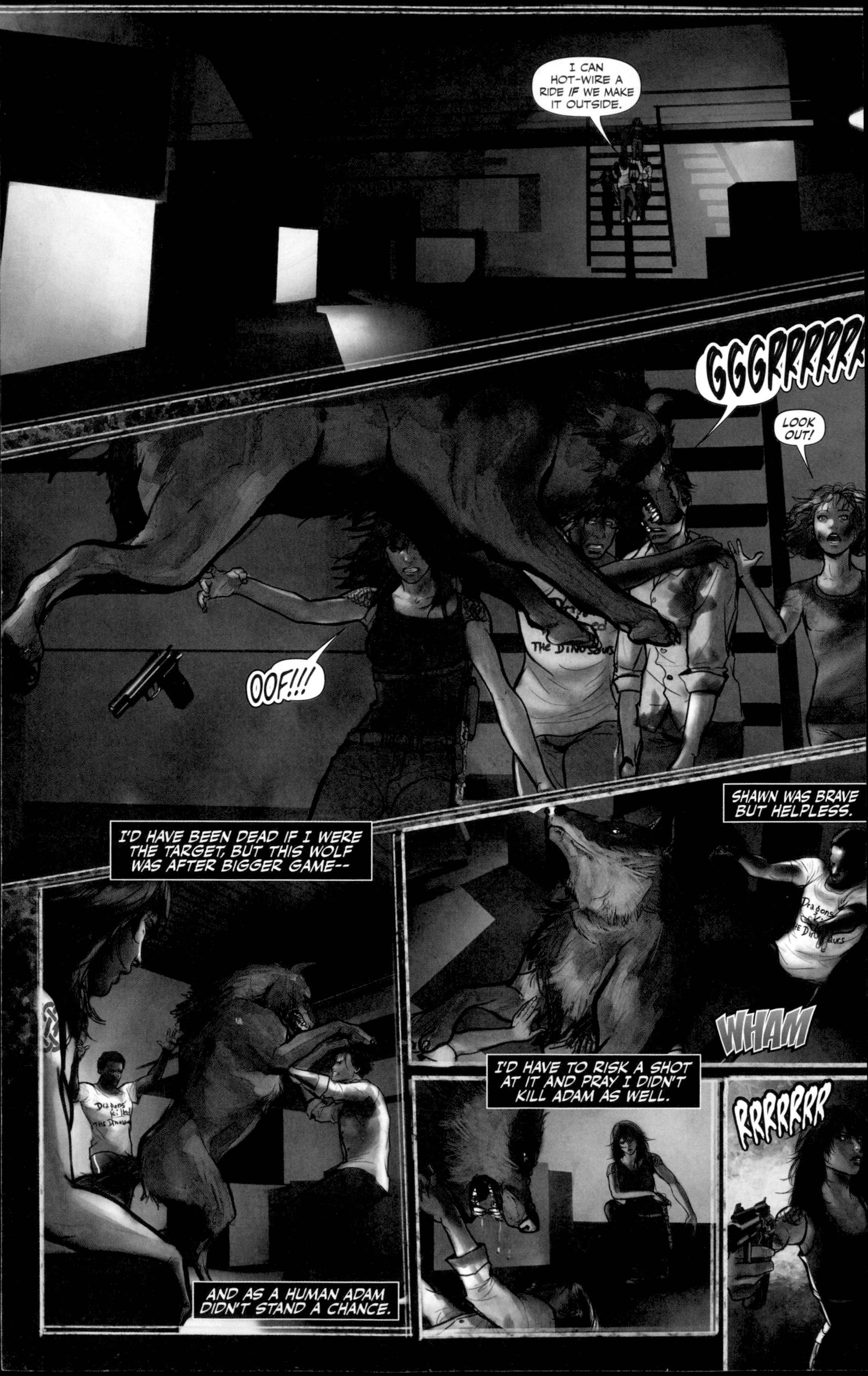
I CAN HOT-WIRE A RIDE *IF* WE MAKE IT OUTSIDE.
GGGRRRRR
LOOK OUT!
OOF!!!
I'D HAVE BEEN DEAD IF I WERE THE TARGET, BUT THIS WOLF WAS AFTER BIGGER GAME--
SHAWN WAS BRAVE BUT HELPLESS.
WHAM
AND AS A HUMAN ADAM DIDN'T STAND A CHANCE.
I'D HAVE TO RISK A SHOT AT IT AND PRAY I DIDN'T KILL ADAM AS WELL.
RRRRRR

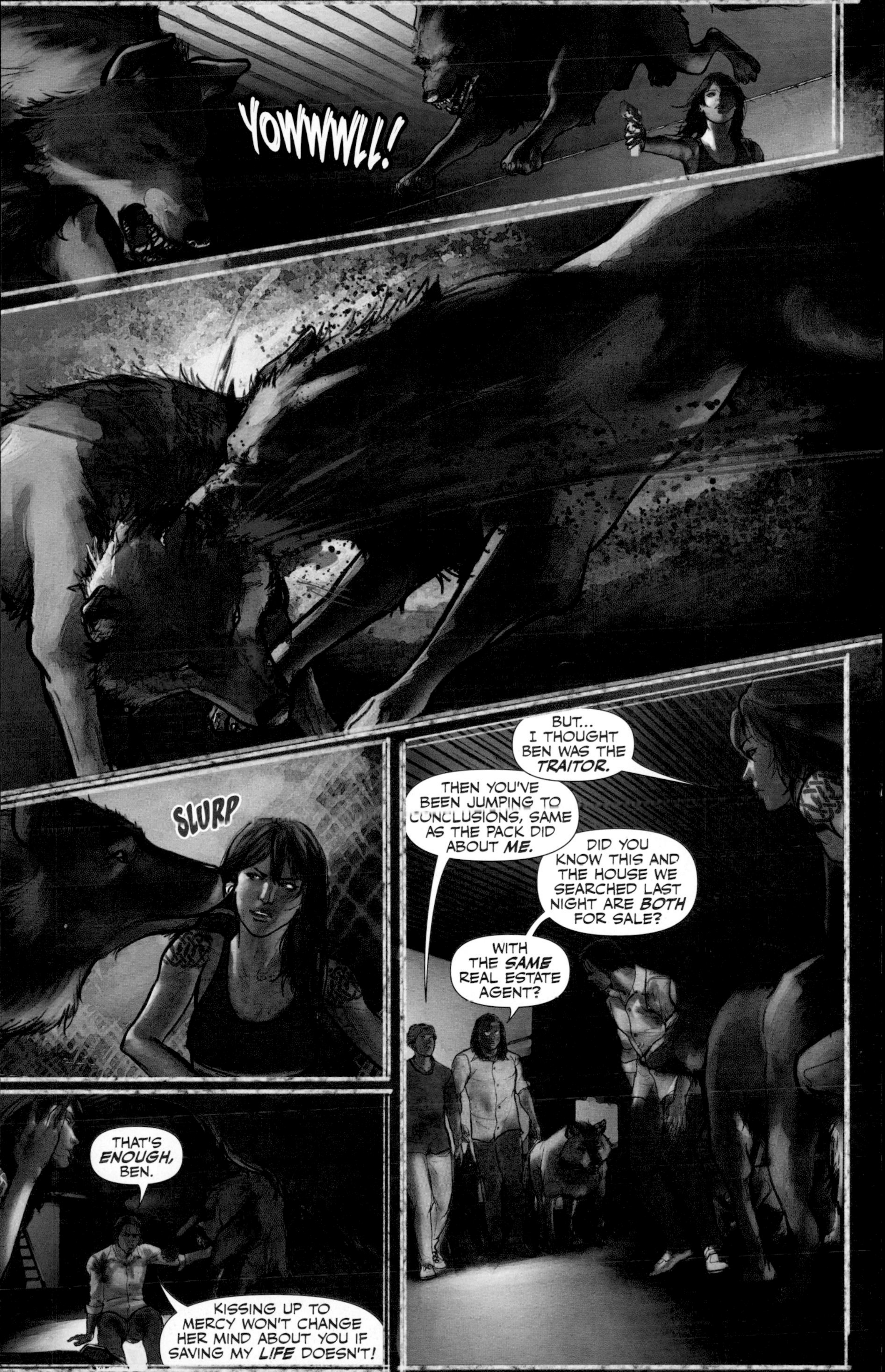
YOWWWLL!
SLURP
BUT... I THOUGHT BEN WAS THE TRAITOR.
THEN YOU'VE BEEN JUMPING TO CONCLUSIONS, SAME AS THE PACK DID ABOUT ME.
DID YOU KNOW THIS AND THE HOUSE WE SEARCHED LAST NIGHT ARE BOTH FOR SALE?
WITH THE SAME REAL ESTATE AGENT?
THAT'S ENOUGH, BEN.
KISSING UP TO MERCY WON'T CHANGE HER MIND ABOUT YOU IF SAVING MY LIFE DOESN'T!

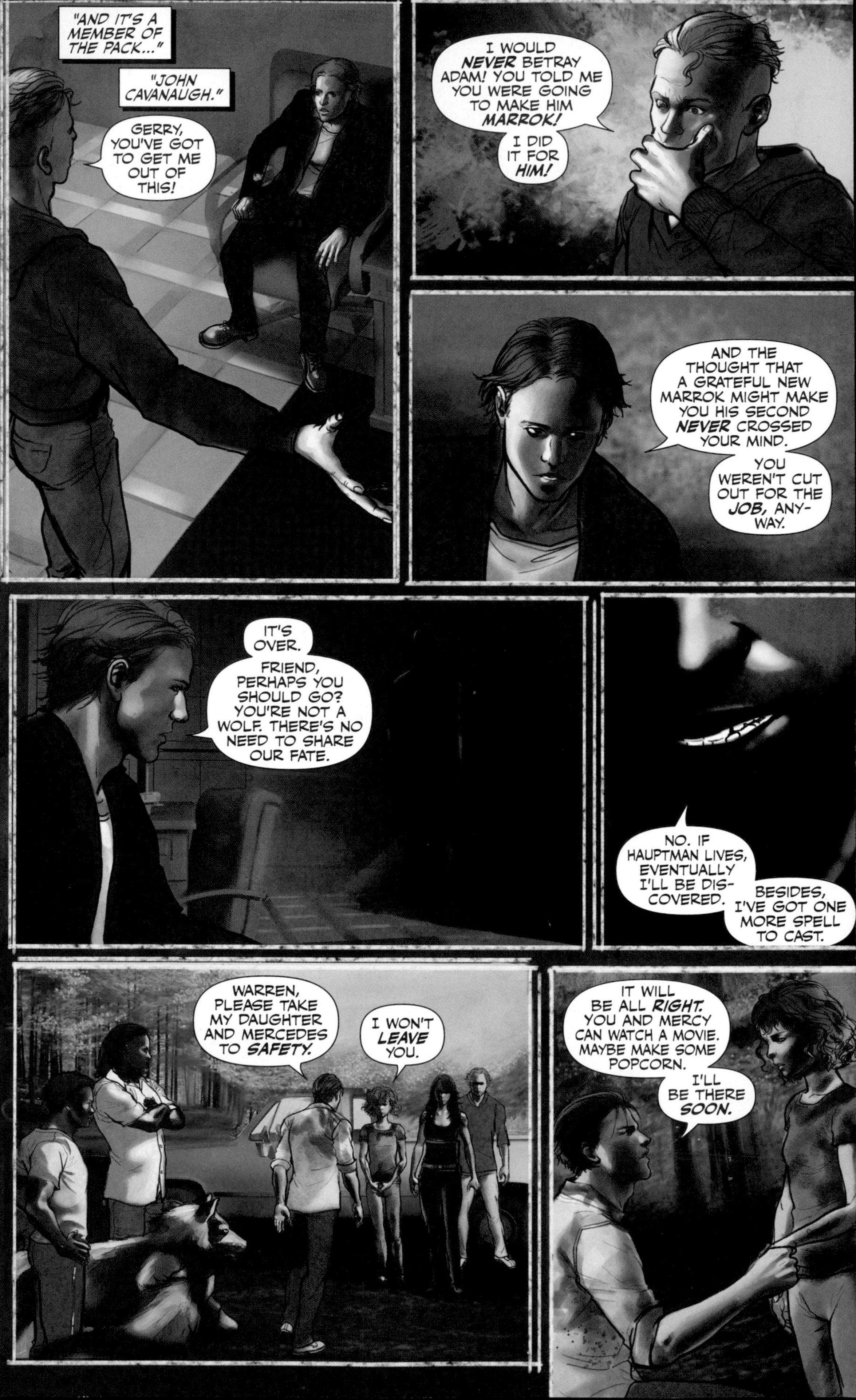
"AND IT'S A MEMBER OF THE PACK..."
"JOHN CAVANAUGH."
GERRY, YOU'VE GOT TO GET ME OUT OF THIS!
I WOULD NEVER BETRAY ADAM! YOU TOLD ME YOU WERE GOING TO MAKE HIM MARROK!
I DID IT FOR HIM!
AND THE THOUGHT THAT A GRATEFUL NEW MARROK MIGHT MAKE YOU HIS SECOND NEVER CROSSED YOUR MIND.
YOU WEREN'T CUT OUT FOR THE JOB, ANY-WAY.
IT'S OVER.
FRIEND, PERHAPS YOU SHOULD GO? YOU'RE NOT A WOLF. THERE'S NO NEED TO SHARE OUR FATE.
NO. IF HAUPTMAN LIVES, EVENTUALLY I'LL BE DIS-COVERED.
BESIDES, I'VE GOT ONE MORE SPELL TO CAST.
WARREN, PLEASE TAKE MY DAUGHTER AND MERCEDES TO SAFETY.
I WON'T LEAVE YOU.
IT WILL BE ALL RIGHT. YOU AND MERCY CAN WATCH A MOVIE. MAYBE MAKE SOME POPCORN.
I'LL BE THERE SOON.

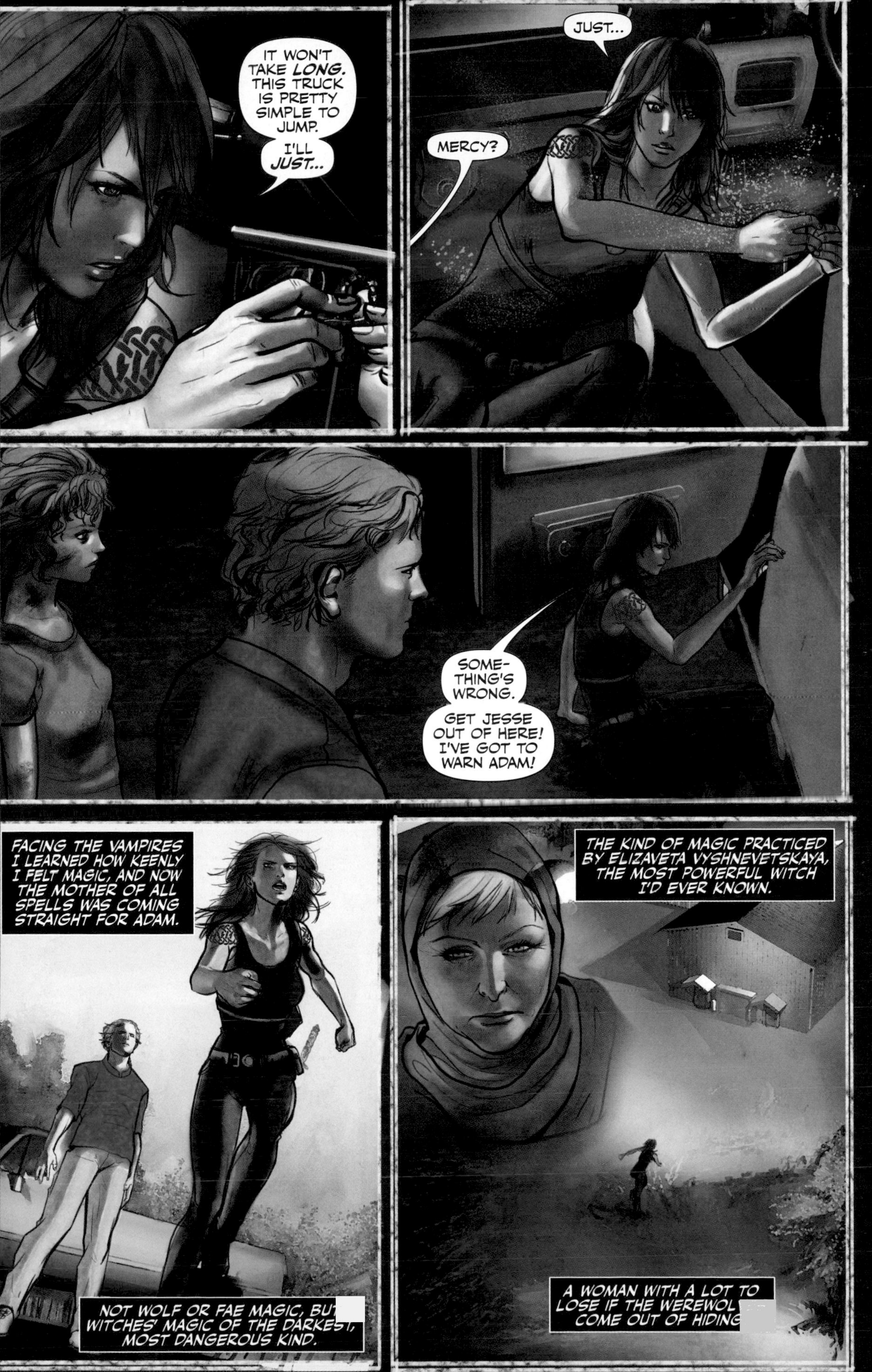
IT WON'T TAKE LONG. THIS TRUCK IS PRETTY SIMPLE TO JUMP.
I'LL JUST...
JUST...
MERCY?
SOME-THING'S WRONG.
GET JESSE OUT OF HERE! I'VE GOT TO WARN ADAM!
FACING THE VAMPIRES I LEARNED HOW KEENLY I FELT MAGIC, AND NOW THE MOTHER OF ALL SPELLS WAS COMING STRAIGHT FOR ADAM.
NOT WOLF OR FAE MAGIC, BUT WITCHES' MAGIC OF THE DARKEST, MOST DANGEROUS KIND.
THE KIND OF MAGIC PRACTICED BY ELIZAVETA VYSHNEVETSKAYA, THE MOST POWERFUL WITCH I'D EVER KNOWN.
A WOMAN WITH A LOT TO LOSE IF THE WEREWOLV
COME OUT OF HIDING

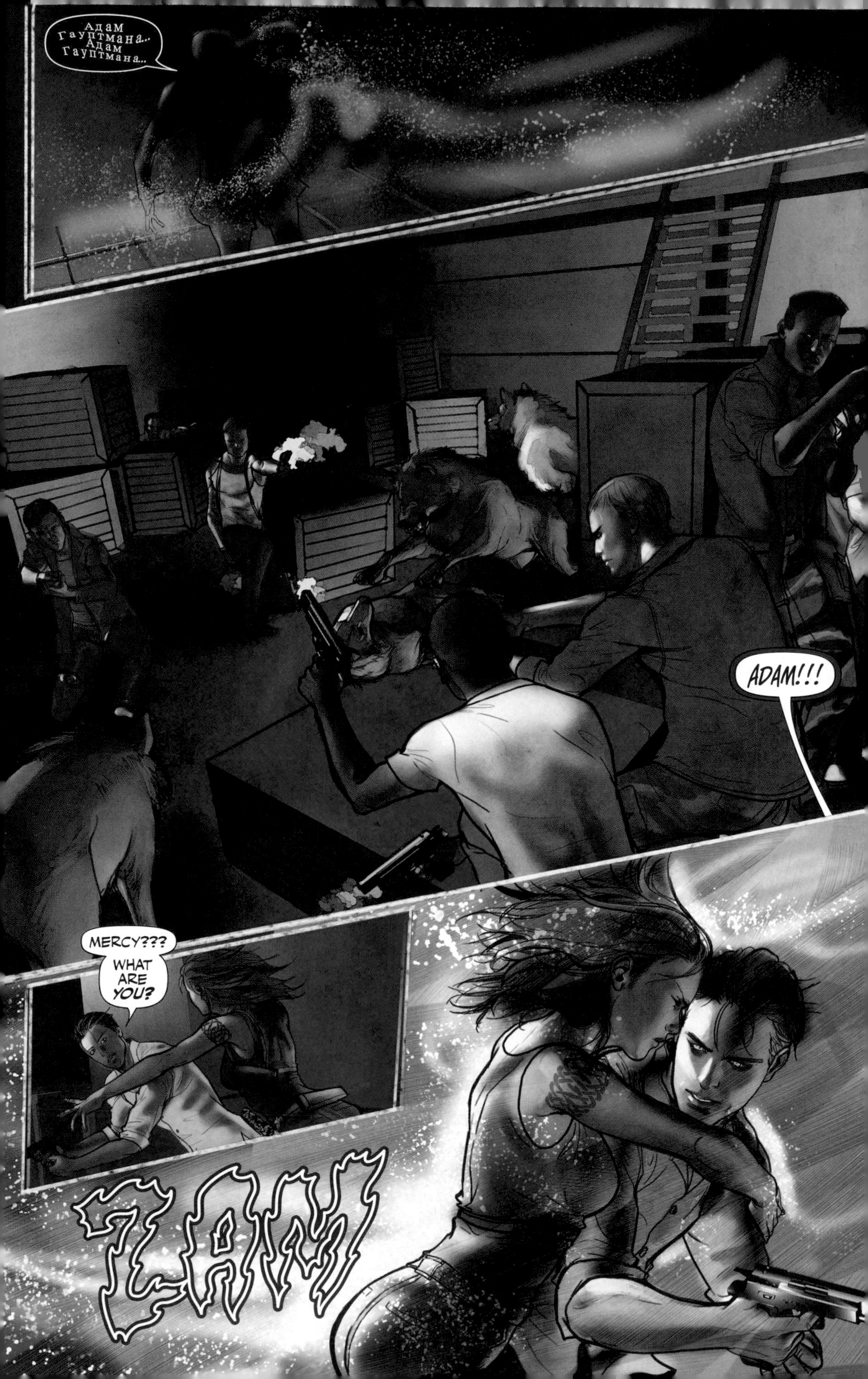
Адам Гауптмана... Адам Гауптмана...
ADAM!!!
MERCY??? WHAT ARE YOU?
ZAM

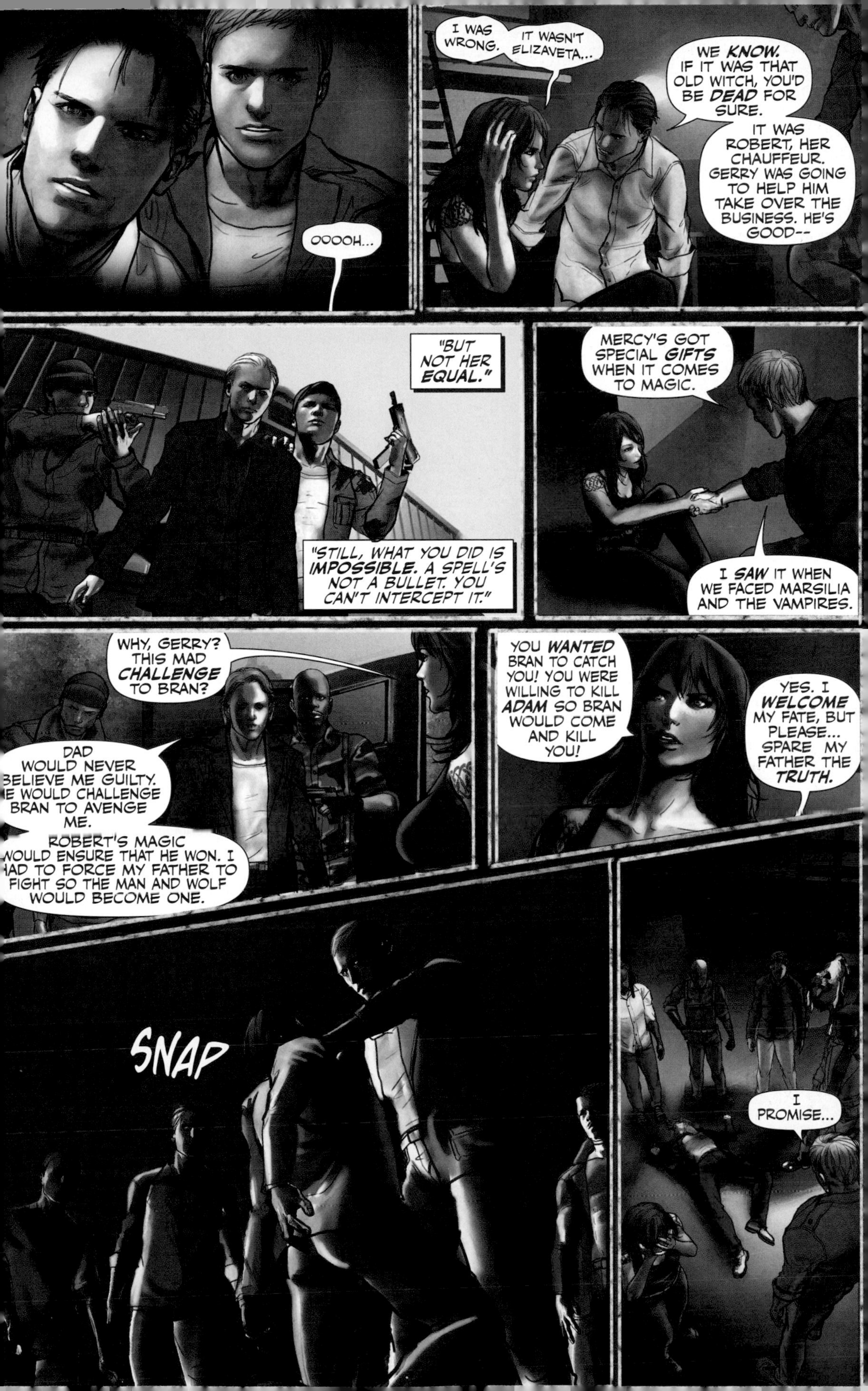
OOOOH...
I WAS WRONG.
IT WASN'T ELIZAVETA...
WE KNOW. IF IT WAS THAT OLD WITCH, YOU'D BE DEAD FOR SURE.
IT WAS ROBERT, HER CHAUFFEUR. GERRY WAS GOING TO HELP HIM TAKE OVER THE BUSINESS. HE'S GOOD--
"BUT NOT HER EQUAL."
"STILL, WHAT YOU DID IS IMPOSSIBLE. A SPELL'S NOT A BULLET. YOU CAN'T INTERCEPT IT."
MERCY'S GOT SPECIAL GIFTS WHEN IT COMES TO MAGIC.
I SAW IT WHEN WE FACED MARSILIA AND THE VAMPIRES.
WHY, GERRY? THIS MAD CHALLENGE TO BRAN?
DAD WOULD NEVER BELIEVE ME GUILTY. HE WOULD CHALLENGE BRAN TO AVENGE ME.
ROBERT'S MAGIC WOULD ENSURE THAT HE WON. I HAD TO FORCE MY FATHER TO FIGHT SO THE MAN AND WOLF WOULD BECOME ONE.
YOU WANTED BRAN TO CATCH YOU! YOU WERE WILLING TO KILL ADAM SO BRAN WOULD COME AND KILL YOU!
YES. I WELCOME MY FATE, BUT PLEASE... SPARE MY FATHER THE TRUTH.
SNAP
I PROMISE...

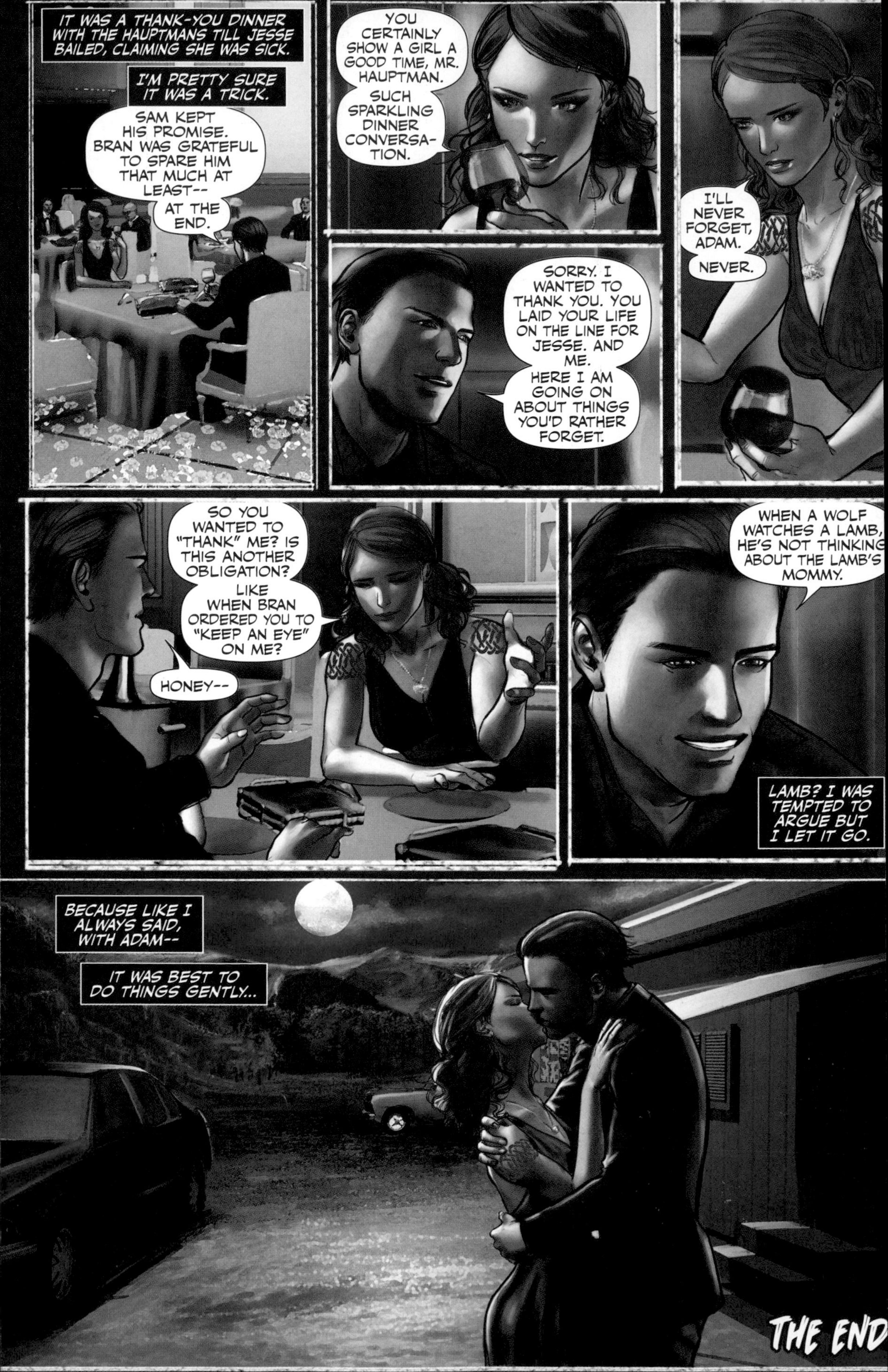
IT WAS A THANK-YOU DINNER WITH THE HAUPTMANS TILL JESSE BAILED, CLAIMING SHE WAS SICK.
I'M PRETTY SURE IT WAS A TRICK.
SAM KEPT HIS PROMISE. BRAN WAS GRATEFUL TO SPARE HIM THAT MUCH AT LEAST--
AT THE END.
YOU CERTAINLY SHOW A GIRL A GOOD TIME, MR. HAUPTMAN.
SUCH SPARKLING DINNER CONVERSA-TION.
SORRY. I WANTED TO THANK YOU. YOU LAID YOUR LIFE ON THE LINE FOR JESSE. AND ME.
HERE I AM GOING ON ABOUT THINGS YOU'D RATHER FORGET.
I'LL NEVER FORGET, ADAM.
NEVER.
SO YOU WANTED TO "THANK" ME? IS THIS ANOTHER OBLIGATION?
LIKE WHEN BRAN ORDERED YOU TO "KEEP AN EYE" ON ME?
HONEY--
WHEN A WOLF WATCHES A LAMB, HE'S NOT THINKING ABOUT THE LAMB'S MOMMY.
LAMB? I WAS TEMPTED TO ARGUE BUT I LET IT GO.
BECAUSE LIKE I ALWAYS SAID, WITH ADAM--
IT WAS BEST TO DO THINGS GENTLY...
THE END

# BONUS chapter

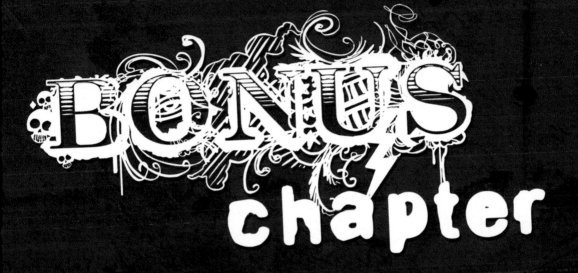

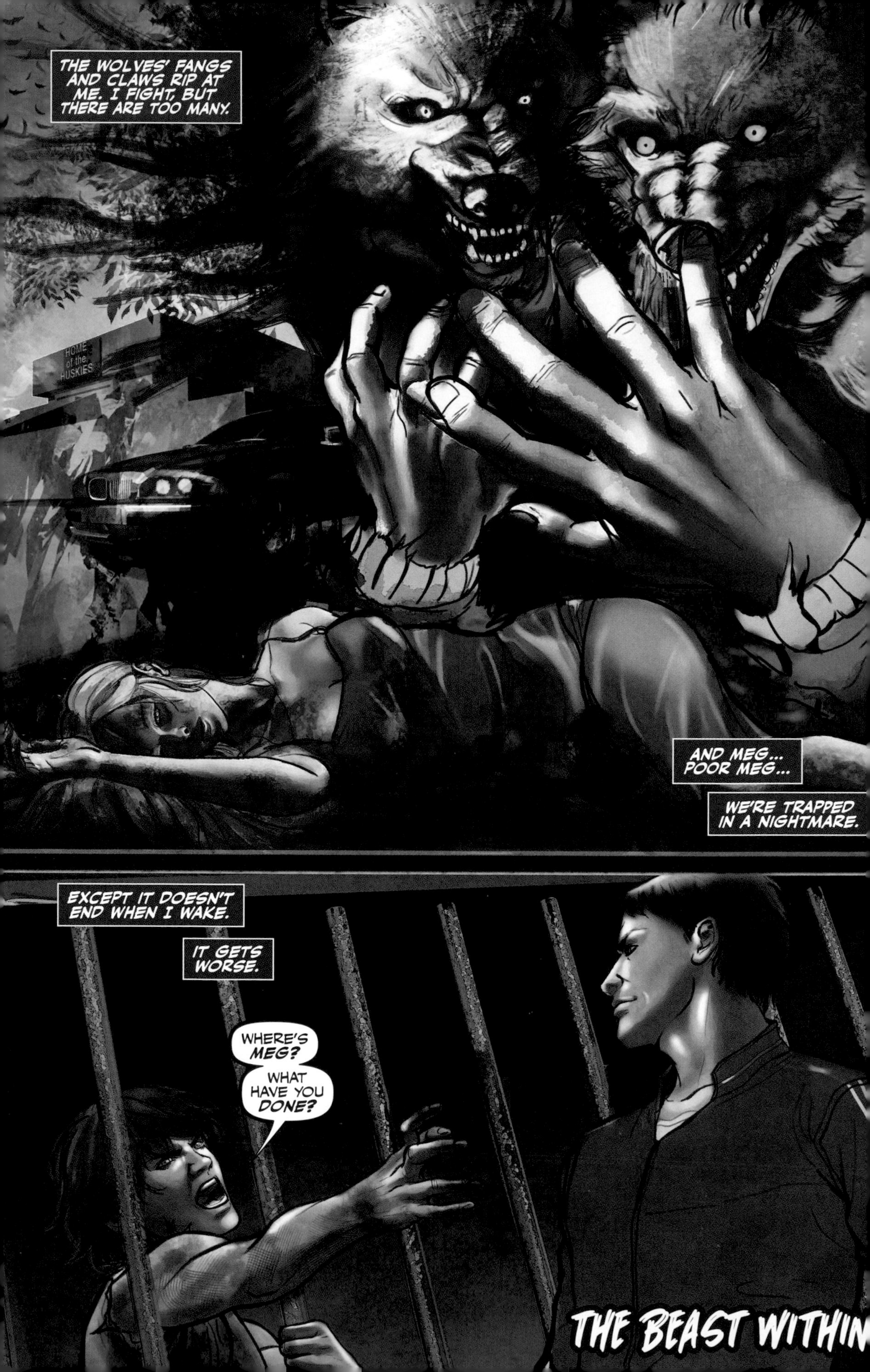
THE WOLVES' FANGS AND CLAWS RIP AT ME. I FIGHT, BUT THERE ARE TOO MANY.
HOME of the HUSKIES
AND MEG... POOR MEG...
WE'RE TRAPPED IN A NIGHTMARE.
EXCEPT IT DOESN'T END WHEN I WAKE.
IT GETS WORSE.
WHERE'S MEG?
WHAT HAVE YOU DONE?
THE BEAST WITHIN

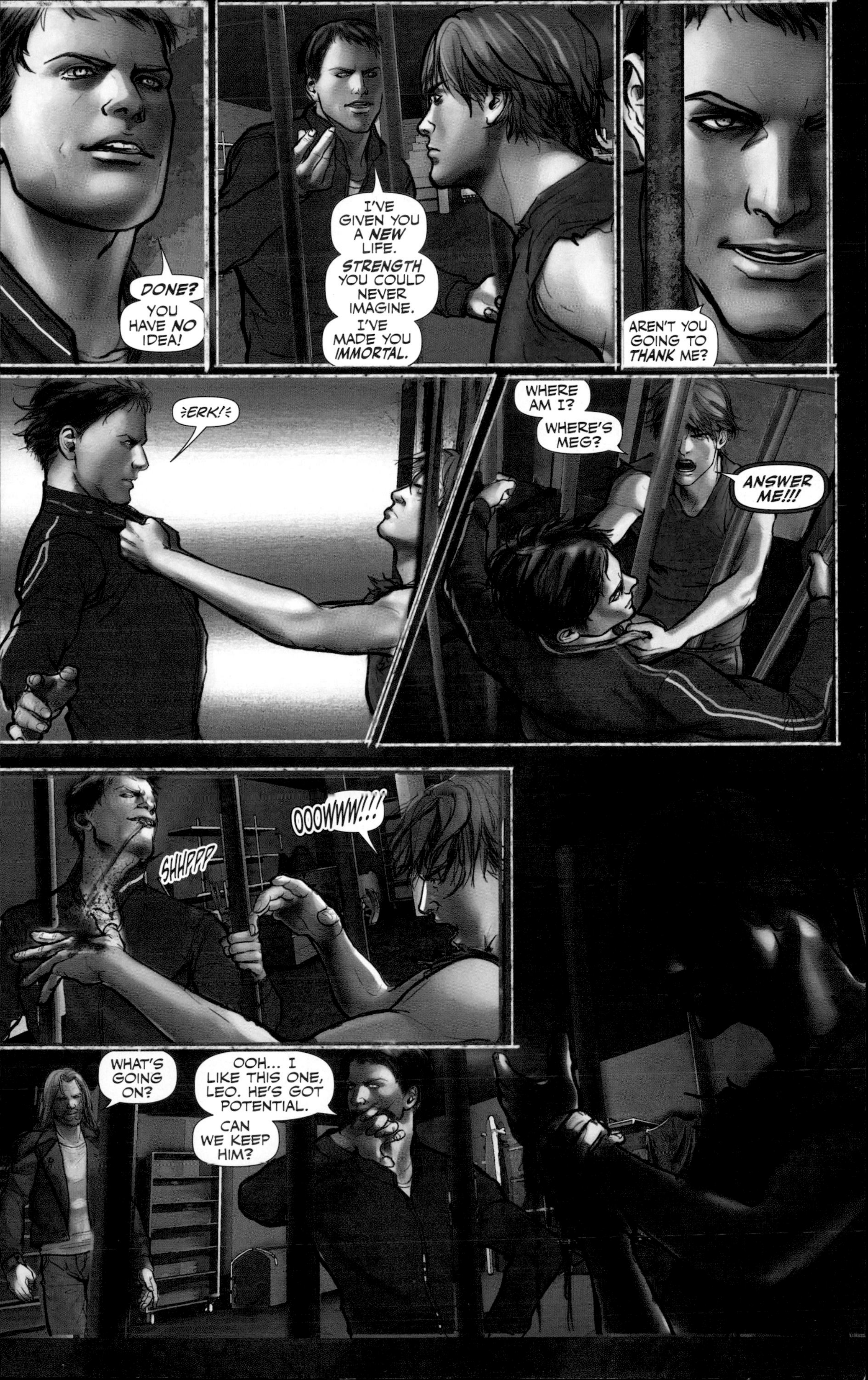
DONE? YOU HAVE NO IDEA!
I'VE GIVEN YOU A NEW LIFE.
STRENGTH YOU COULD NEVER IMAGINE.
I'VE MADE YOU IMMORTAL.
AREN'T YOU GOING TO THANK ME?
ERK!
WHERE AM I?
WHERE'S MEG?
ANSWER ME!!!
OOOWWW!!!
SHHPPP
WHAT'S GOING ON?
OOH... I LIKE THIS ONE, LEO. HE'S GOT POTENTIAL.
CAN WE KEEP HIM?

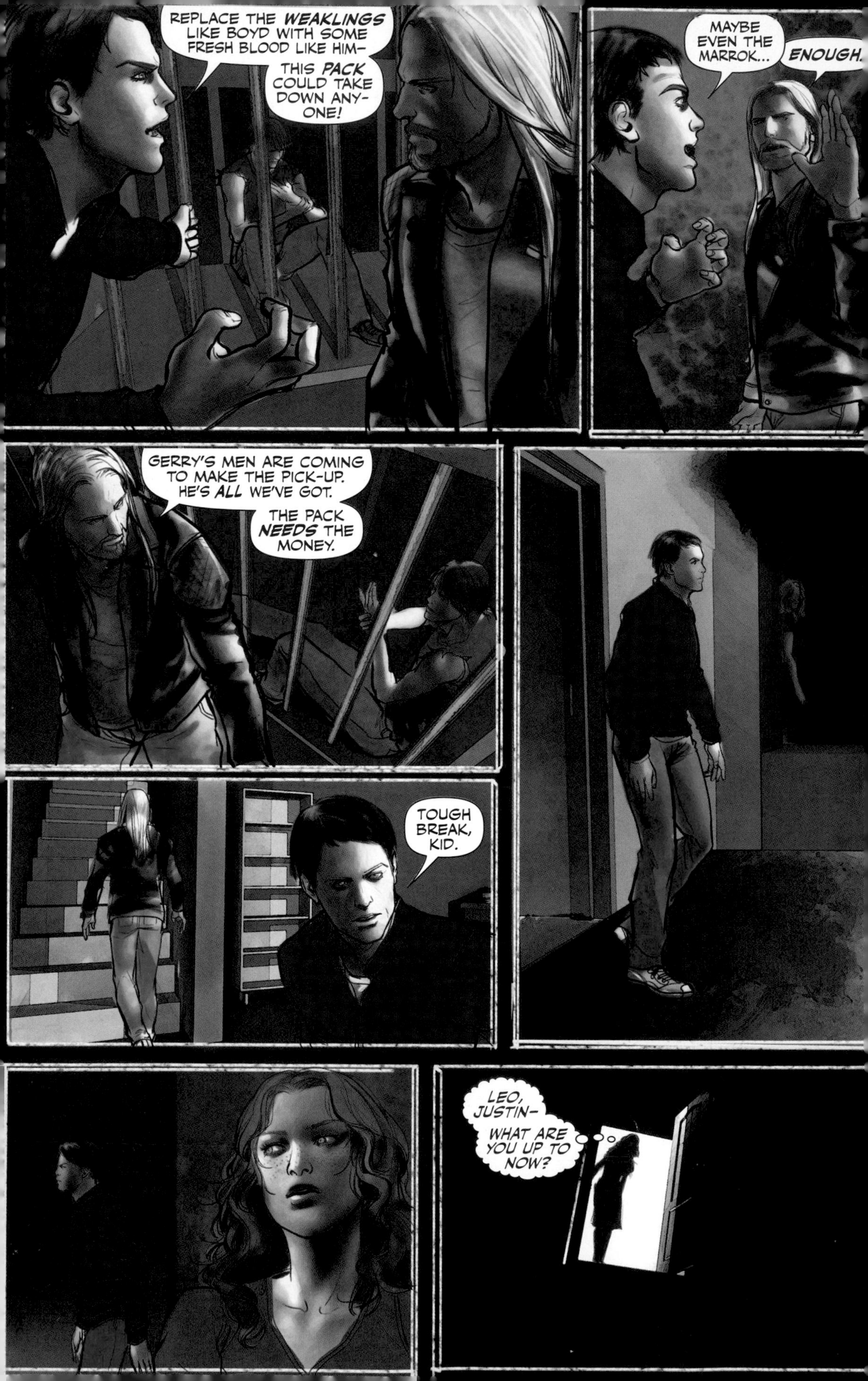
REPLACE THE WEAKLINGS LIKE BOYD WITH SOME FRESH BLOOD LIKE HIM–
THIS PACK COULD TAKE DOWN ANY-ONE!
MAYBE EVEN THE MARROK...
ENOUGH.
GERRY'S MEN ARE COMING TO MAKE THE PICK-UP. HE'S ALL WE'VE GOT.
THE PACK NEEDS THE MONEY.
TOUGH BREAK, KID.
LEO, JUSTIN–
WHAT ARE YOU UP TO NOW?

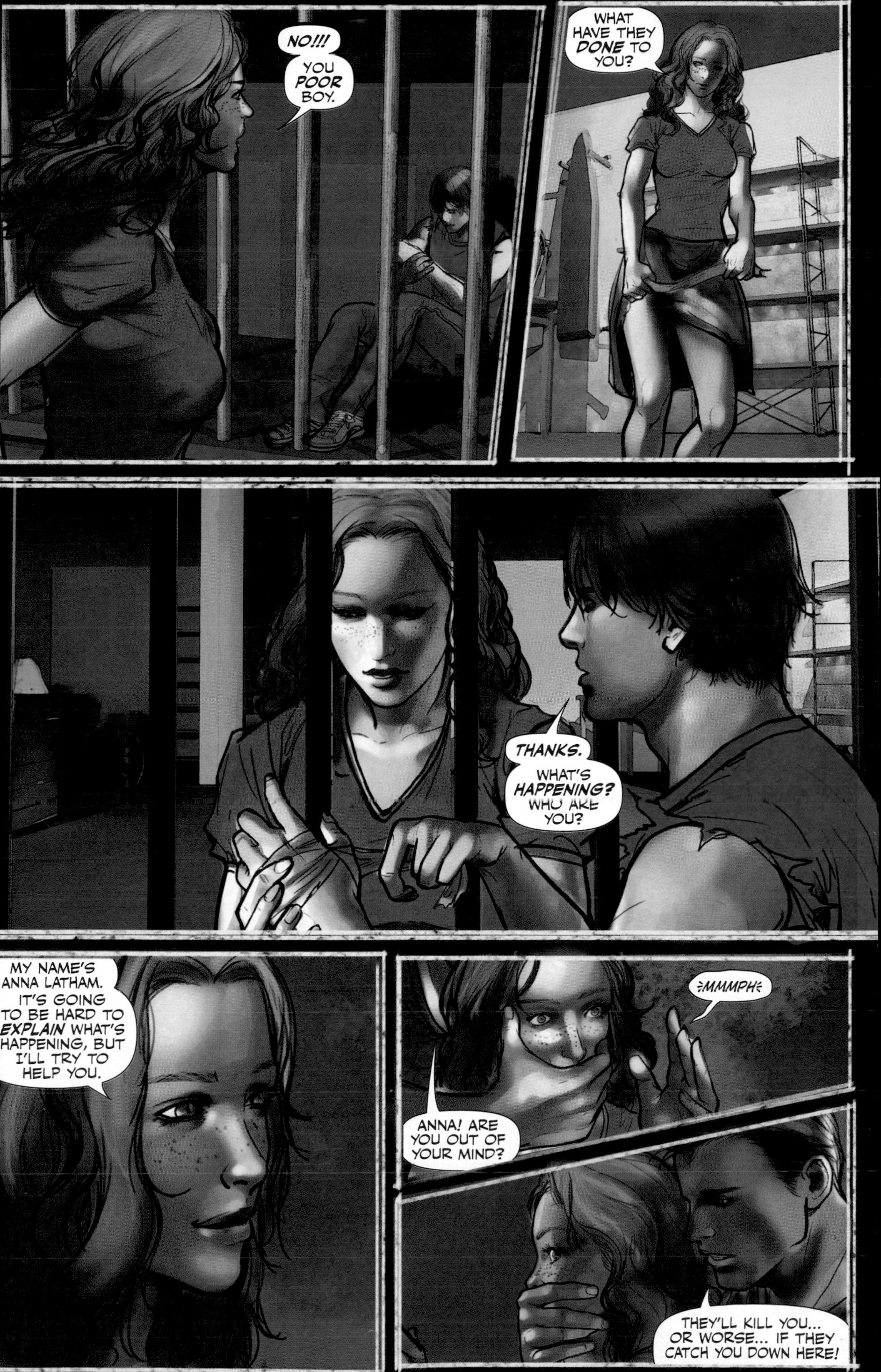

NO!!! YOU POOR BOY.
WHAT HAVE THEY DONE TO YOU?
THANKS. WHAT'S HAPPENING? WHO ARE YOU?
MY NAME'S ANNA LATHAM. IT'S GOING TO BE HARD TO EXPLAIN WHAT'S HAPPENING, BUT I'LL TRY TO HELP YOU.
MMMPH
ANNA! ARE YOU OUT OF YOUR MIND?
THEY'LL KILL YOU... OR WORSE... IF THEY CATCH YOU DOWN HERE!

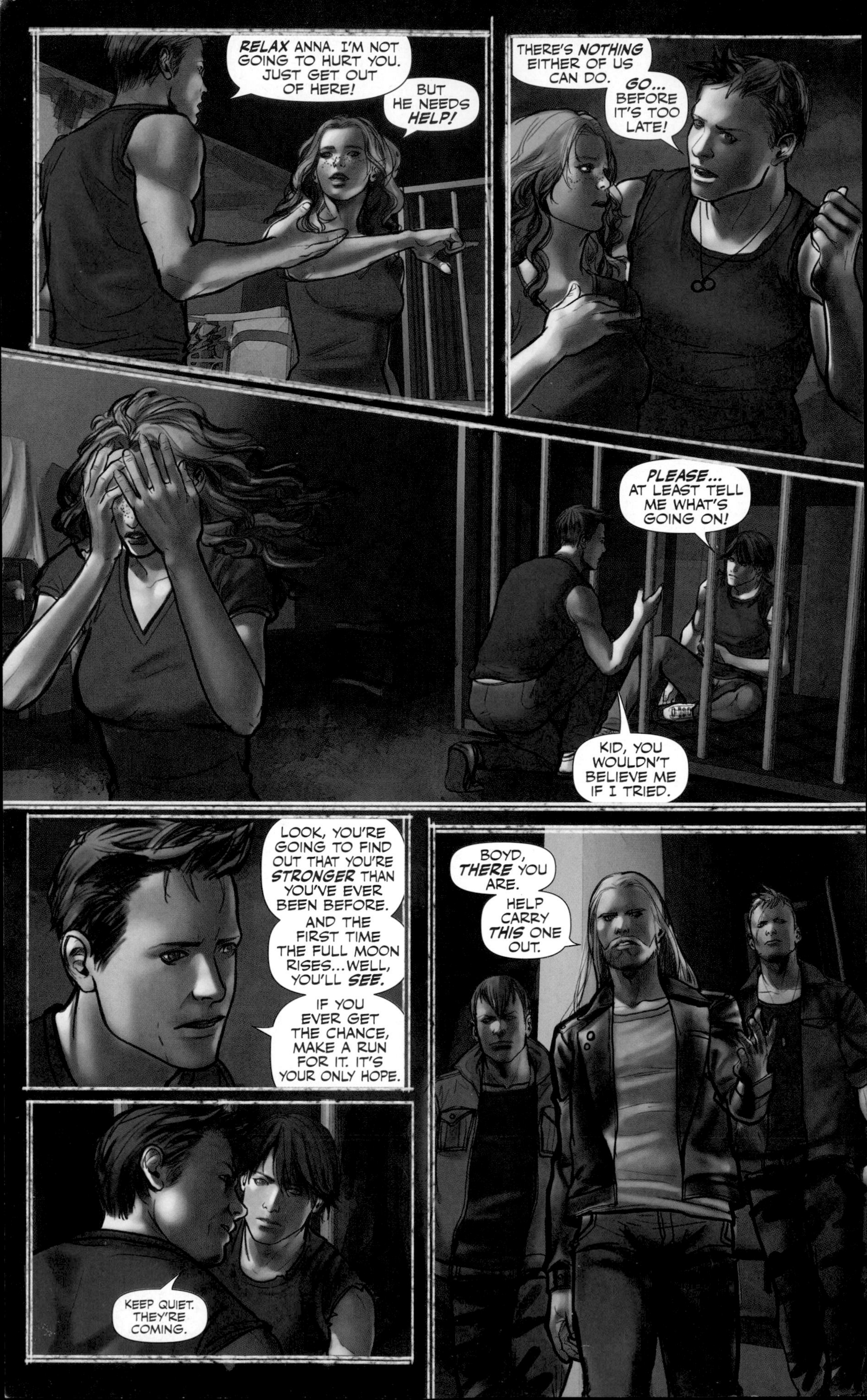
RELAX ANNA. I'M NOT GOING TO HURT YOU. JUST GET OUT OF HERE!
BUT HE NEEDS HELP!
THERE'S NOTHING EITHER OF US CAN DO.
GO... BEFORE IT'S TOO LATE!
PLEASE... AT LEAST TELL ME WHAT'S GOING ON!
KID, YOU WOULDN'T BELIEVE ME IF I TRIED.
LOOK, YOU'RE GOING TO FIND OUT THAT YOU'RE STRONGER THAN YOU'VE EVER BEEN BEFORE.
AND THE FIRST TIME THE FULL MOON RISES...WELL, YOU'LL SEE.
IF YOU EVER GET THE CHANCE, MAKE A RUN FOR IT. IT'S YOUR ONLY HOPE.
KEEP QUIET. THEY'RE COMING.
BOYD, THERE YOU ARE.
HELP CARRY THIS ONE OUT.

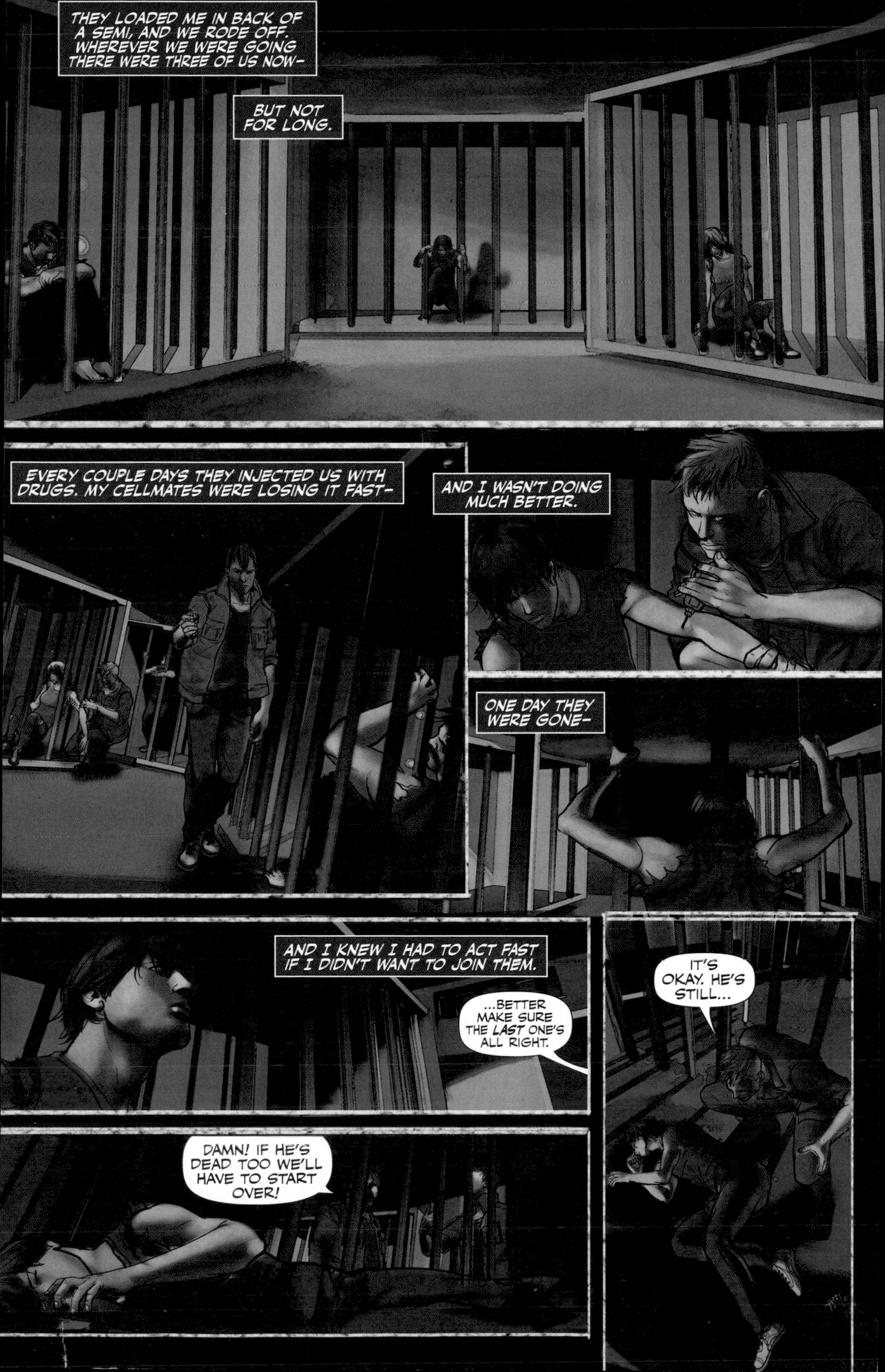
THEY LOADED ME IN BACK OF A SEMI, AND WE RODE OFF. WHEREVER WE WERE GOING THERE WERE THREE OF US NOW-
BUT NOT FOR LONG.
EVERY COUPLE DAYS THEY INJECTED US WITH DRUGS. MY CELLMATES WERE LOSING IT FAST-
AND I WASN'T DOING MUCH BETTER.
ONE DAY THEY WERE GONE-
AND I KNEW I HAD TO ACT FAST IF I DIDN'T WANT TO JOIN THEM.
...BETTER MAKE SURE THE LAST ONE'S ALL RIGHT.
IT'S OKAY. HE'S STILL...
DAMN! IF HE'S DEAD TOO WE'LL HAVE TO START OVER!

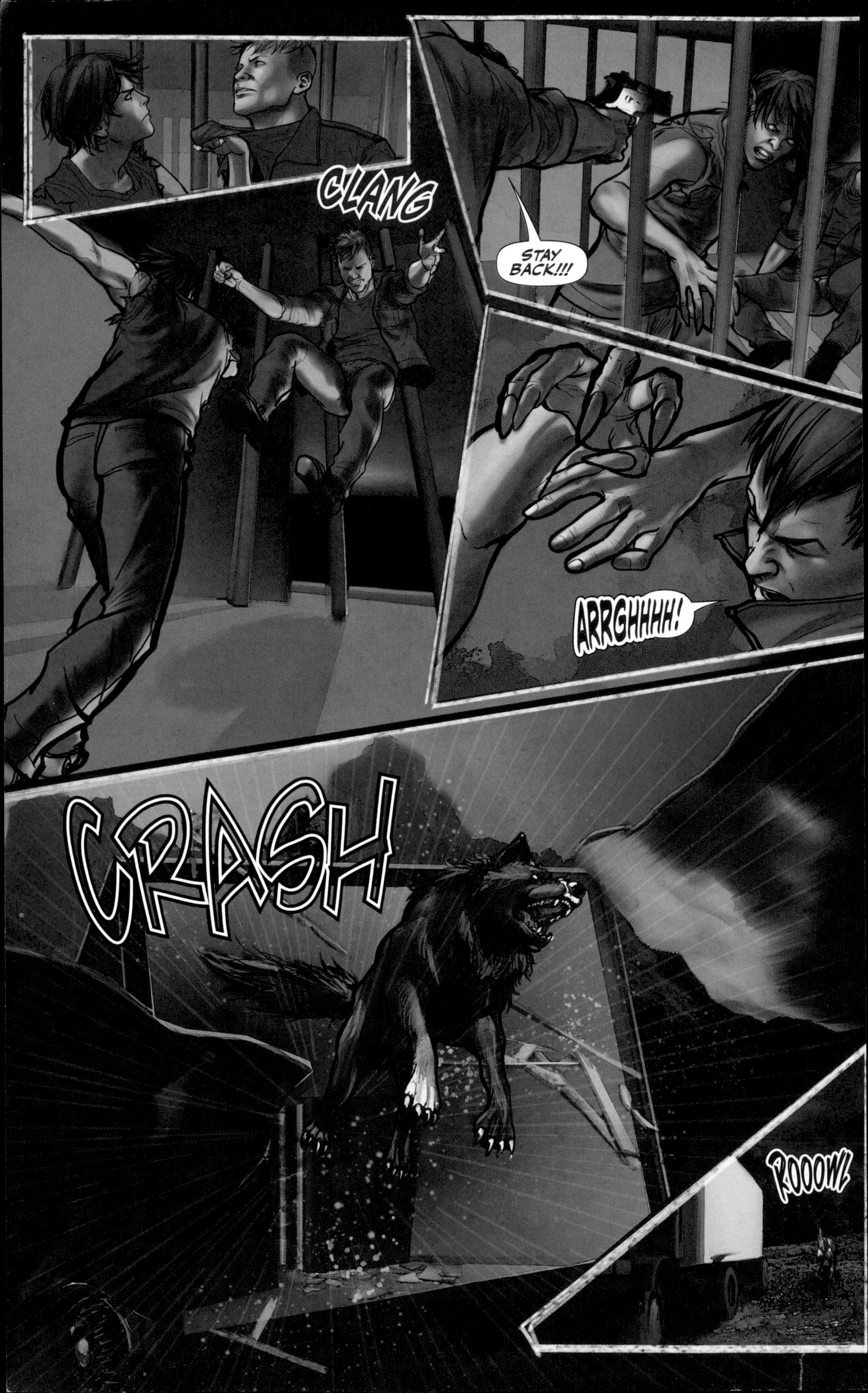
CLANG
STAY BACK!!!
ARRGHHHH!
CRASH
ROOOWL

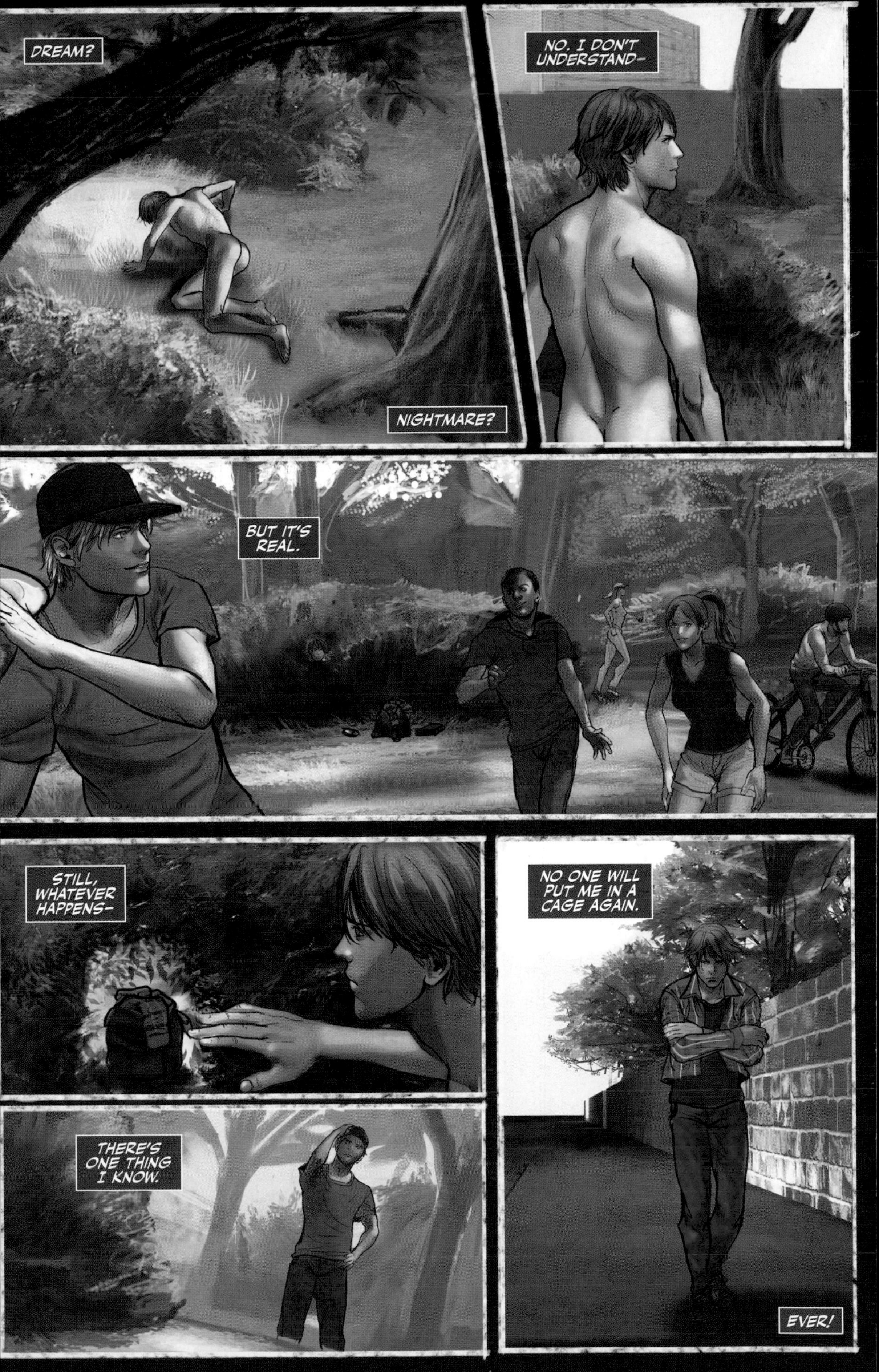
DREAM?
NIGHTMARE?
NO. I DON'T UNDERSTAND–
BUT IT'S REAL.
STILL, WHATEVER HAPPENS–
THERE'S ONE THING I KNOW.
NO ONE WILL PUT ME IN A CAGE AGAIN.
EVER!

# LAST CALLED
## An Afterword by David Lawrence

While putting the finishing touches on this volume, I finally met Patty Briggs.

This might surprise those of you who don't know how this crazy business called comics works. After all, Patty and I have been working together for three years now, beginning with the original Mercy Thompson graphic novel Homecoming, continuing through the volume you now hold in your hands, and ongoing with the adaptation of her first Alpha & Omega novel Cry Wolf.

But this isn't your standard workplace. There is no office to report to, no desk or cubicle or counter or anything to share.

I myself am in Pittsburgh, Pennsylvania, or I would be if I wasn't this moment visiting New York. Patty is centered in Washington State, though she likewise is visiting New York this weekend. Artist Amelia Woo, whom I have never had the pleasure of meeting, lives in the tropical paradise of Brazil. Letterer extraordinaire Zach Matheny, whom I once met in San Diego, is probably off raiding the lost ark or storming the temple of doom somewhere, adventurous type that he is.

So it's often a special treat in this line of work to finally meet somebody with whom you've worked, corresponded, perhaps chatted with on the phone, after many years of seeing your name beside theirs in the credits.

In this case, the catalyst was the New York City Comic Con, held annually at the Jacob Javits Center, in the Hell's Kitchen section of New York. (It's also not far from the Daily Show studios, but Jon Stewart was on vacation this week. Damn!)

New York City Comic Con is one of my favorite events of the year. First of all, it's in New York City, where I want to wake up and find I'm king of the hill, top of the heap. In short, I love the town and all the energy there. Whether I'm making a new friend or meeting a valued collaborator, sipping Irish Whiskey or watching helplessly while a drunk girl shatters a beer mug in my lap…it's New York.

And the show, though certainly large, lacks the large-scale, exhausting immensity of Comic Con in San Diego. It's actually possible to wander the aisles (most of the time) and browse the books, meet fans and fellow professionals, and even meet the professionals the professionals idolize. My most treasured New York moments were shaking hands with legends Joe Simon and Jerry Robinson, and having the chance to tell them how much their work meant to me.

I also, last year, met a girl dressed as the Black Widow who looked exactly like Scarlett Johansson. I usually ignore the costumes, but after stopping to compliment her on the likeness, I spent about ten minutes wondering if I had just told Scarlett Johansson that she looked like Scarlett Johansson.

Hey, a guy can dream, can't he?

But, back to my story…if I actually have one. On finally reaching my hotel the first day of the show, after a delayed flight (is there any other kind?) and a white-knuckle cab ride that made Space Mountain look like a merry-go-round, I checked my phone and found an e-mail from Amelia Woo.

Attached to the e-mail were several pages of artwork from the final material prepared for this album, the conclusion of the short story detailing poor Mac's journey from Naperville,

IL to the door of Mercy's garage.

I forwarded the artwork to Patty, along with a note that I wouldn't really be able to review it till Monday, since I was in New York without my laptop, and the pages on my phone were really, really small.

I quickly heard back from Patty, asking if I was in New York for the Con, because she was coming out too. It was a last minute decision for her, as she'd had a lot going on at El Rancho Briggs, but Barnes & Noble had really wanted her to come.

So as Patty and I were at long last going to be on the same coast, plans were made, and I met up with her yesterday afternoon at the Penguin booth, site of her book signing at the show.

She had a nice turn out for the signing, naturally, and her fans were thrilled to meet her. Most of those in line had brought her novels of course, but a handful had the first volume of the Moon Called graphic novel. Even I got to sign a couple, after Patty pointed me out. I won't let it go to my head, but it was nice for once to sign something that wasn't going out in the mail to the landlord.

We had about an hour to kill before a meeting with some of the nice folks at Dynamite. We found a quiet spot, no small feat in the crowded Javits Center, literally camping out on the floor. While there, we discussed some possibilities for Mercy's four-color future. Nothing set in stone, but we bounced around some ideas, always fun for a couple of writers. We spend so much of our time working alone.

After a very pleasant meeting with Dynamite head honchos Nick Barrucci and Juan Collado we headed out for some dinner. Wandering aimlessly among the endless rows of Irish Pubs (seriously, there must be one on every block) we settled on one called the Wee Molly, mostly because we liked the name.

(It also met one of my very important requirements: there was no ATM right inside the door. Trust me, if when you walk into a restaurant that is the first thing that greets you, run! It's one of the many lessons learned over my time in the hospitality field. The food will be lousy, the silverware dirty, and the crowd surly.)

So over a hearty meal and a couple cold pints of Smithwick's (both drank by me; Patty had iced tea) we at long last had the chance to get better acquainted. Though we've talked on the phone from time to time there is no substitute for sitting down and breaking bread.

It will come as no surprise to Patty's many fans that she is as warm and genuine in person as she appears to be in print. If she wasn't a wildly talented writer she would probably be content to spend her time fixing up her home and raising horses.

But lucky for all the rest of us, Patty is wildly talented. Hence the volume you hold in your hands, along with her many other works.

After discussing some possibilities for Mercy's four-color future, the conversation wandered amiably from writing and art to politics and religion, with detours to discuss horses and the wondrous world of bartending.

After finishing up, I walked Patty to her hotel and then headed back to my own, about 40 blocks away. It might sound long, but it was another chance to soak up the sights and sounds of Manhattan, including interestingly enough an Occupy Wall Street march. All in all, it was what I'd call a good day.

So as I conclude this last little piece of this book, I prefer to think that we are not at the end of an adventure but at its beginning; that this little coda is not so much an afterward to Mercy's latest adventure as a preamble to adventures to come.

We all look forward to bringing you Mercy's adventures…and the occasional meeting at conventions, for a long time to come!

David Lawrence
November 2011

# from script, to page...

**PAGE FOUR**

**Panel one:**
Flashback ends.     Tight close-up on Adam.  His expression & eyes are haunted as he recalls that day from long ago.

1 ADAM:
Only two of us, <u>Dave Christiansen</u> and I, survived.

2 ADAM:
Somehow we made it back to base.  The Army docs shipped us stateside in a <u>hurry</u>—

**Panel two:**
Establishing shot.  Mercy, Sam, WARREN & Adam are gathered in Warren's living room.  Adam sits on the couch.  He's still tired and haggard, slumping forward a bit as though it's difficult for him to remain upright.  The rest of the group is gathered around Adam, listening to his story.  Mercy sits across from him, leaning forward, head in her hands, listening attentive.  Sam & Warren stand back, against opposite walls, maintaining a wary distance from one another.

3 ADAM:
Before our ranting and rapid healing brought on <u>questions</u> they couldn't answer.

4 MERCY:
<u>Hmm</u>...

**Panel three:**
Two-shot of Adam & Mercy, a knowing look on her face that suggests she already knows the answer to her question.

5 MERCY:
And you're telling us this now <u>because</u>...?

6 ADAM:
Uh-huh.  Because Christiansen took part in the <u>attack</u> at my house.

**Panel four:**
Sam chimes in.  He looks a bit puzzled as he tries to make sense of the recent events.

7 ADAM:
Didn't come in but I caught his scent.

8 SAM:
Were you the target all along?

**Panel five:**
Adam shakes his head weakly.

9 ADAM:
Why the <u>kidnap</u> attempt at the garage if they wanted to use Mac to get to me?

10 ADAM:
I can't make <u>sense</u> of any of it.

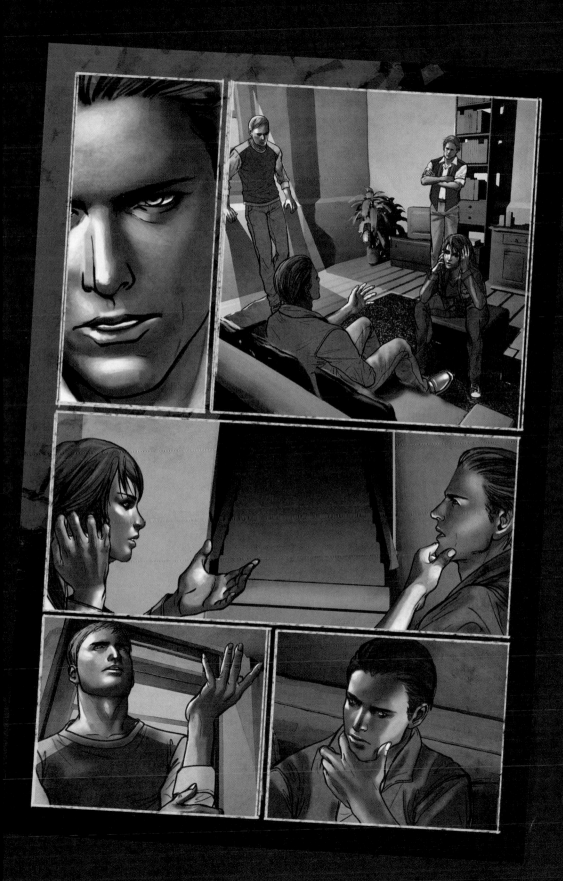

## PAGE FIVE

**Panel one:**
Montage panel, b&w flashback scenes.  Scenes include:
1)      the pack in Adam's living room (Adam addresses them; include Darryl & Ben, Warren, toss in a couple of others.
2)      Mac getting shot with tranquilizer darts and collapsing as he opens the door.
3)      Adam charging in and getting shot as well.
4)      Adam locked up in silver leg & hand cuffs.

1 CAPTION (Adam):
I brought in the pack to discuss the <u>attack</u> at Mercy's garage.   After they left there was a knock at the door--

2 CAPTION (Adam):
Mac answered it before I could <u>stop</u> him.  Someone shot him with a tran-quilizer gun—

3 CAPTION (Adam):
And when I <u>ran</u> in they got me.

4 CAPTION (Adam):
I woke up bound in <u>silver</u>.

**Panel two:**
B&W flashback.  Adam breaks out of the cuffs as begins to transform into a wolf.  The human gunman from #1 is dragging a struggling Jesse away.

5 CAPTION (Adam):
I broke free when I heard <u>Jesse</u> scream—

6 CAPTION (Adam):
But it was too <u>late</u> to prevent them from taking her.

**Panel three:**
End of flashback.  Close-up Mercy.

7 CAPTION:
And I arrived just a little <u>later</u>—

8 CAPTION:
After they dumped Mac's <u>body</u> at my door.

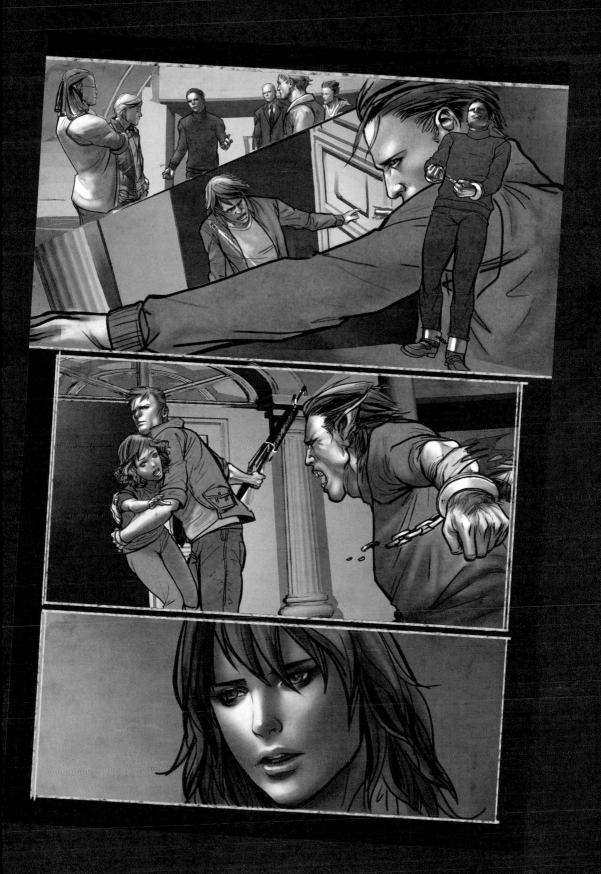

**Panel one:**
Two-shot of Sam & Mercy.

1 ADAM:
Don't understand why the <u>drug</u> worked on us—

2 ADAM:
Or why it <u>killed</u> Mac while I survived…

**Panel two:**
Cut to Sam, alongside a ghostly image of him in a lab running tests.

3 SAM:
I had a chance to analyze the drug.

4 SAM:
It's an <u>interesting</u> cocktail—

**Panel three:**
Sam continues to speak.

5 SAM:
And <u>all</u> stuff that's readily available.

6 SAM:
Silver nitrate, Ketamine and Dimethyl Sulfoxide, better known as <u>DMSO</u>.

**Panel four:**
All eyes in the group are on Sam as he continues his explanation.

7 SAM:
The ketamine is an animal <u>tranquilizer</u>, and we all know how silver affects werewolves—

8 SAM:
But the <u>key</u> is the DMSO.

**Panel five:**
B&W.  A finger is dipped in a beaker.  Behind it are two small bottles, one labeled "PEPPERMINT" and on labeled "DMSO"

9 CAPTION (Sam):
There's an old <u>experiment</u>.  Mix DMSO with some peppermint and dip in your finger.

10 CAPTION (Sam):
You'll be able to <u>taste</u> it—

**Panel six:**
View of the group from over Sam's shoulder.

11 SAM:
Because DMSO can <u>cross</u> cell membranes, and take other substances with it.

12 SAM:
So <u>mix</u> silver nitrate with DMSO…

**Panel seven:**
An "a-ha!" look on Adam's face as he finishes Sam's sentence.

13 ADAM:
And it carries the <u>silver</u> throughout a werewolves' body!

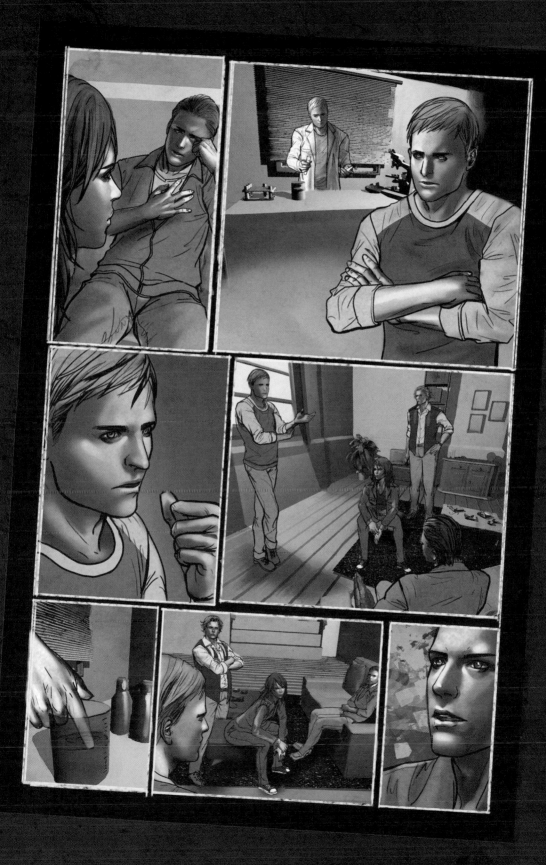

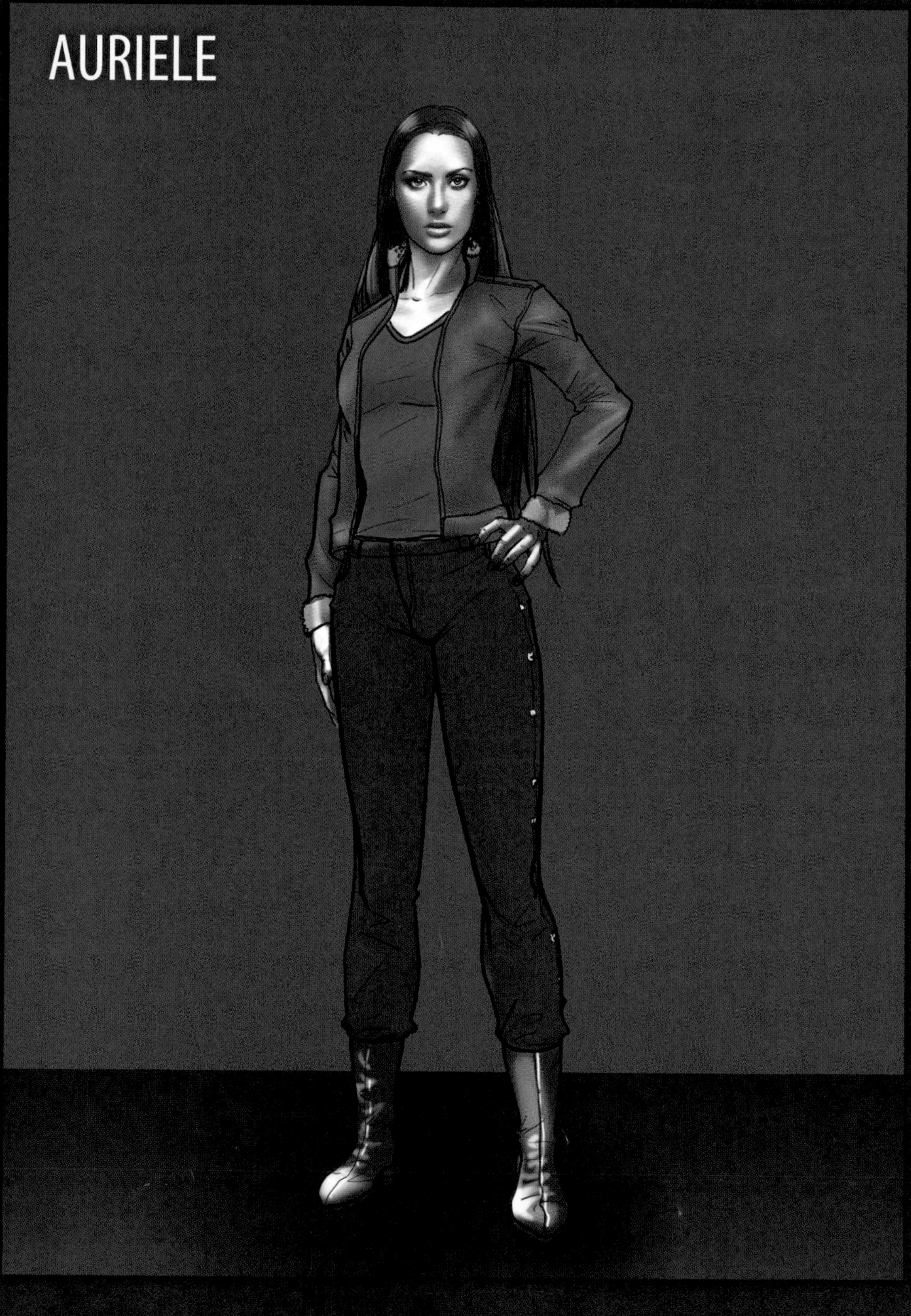
AURIELE

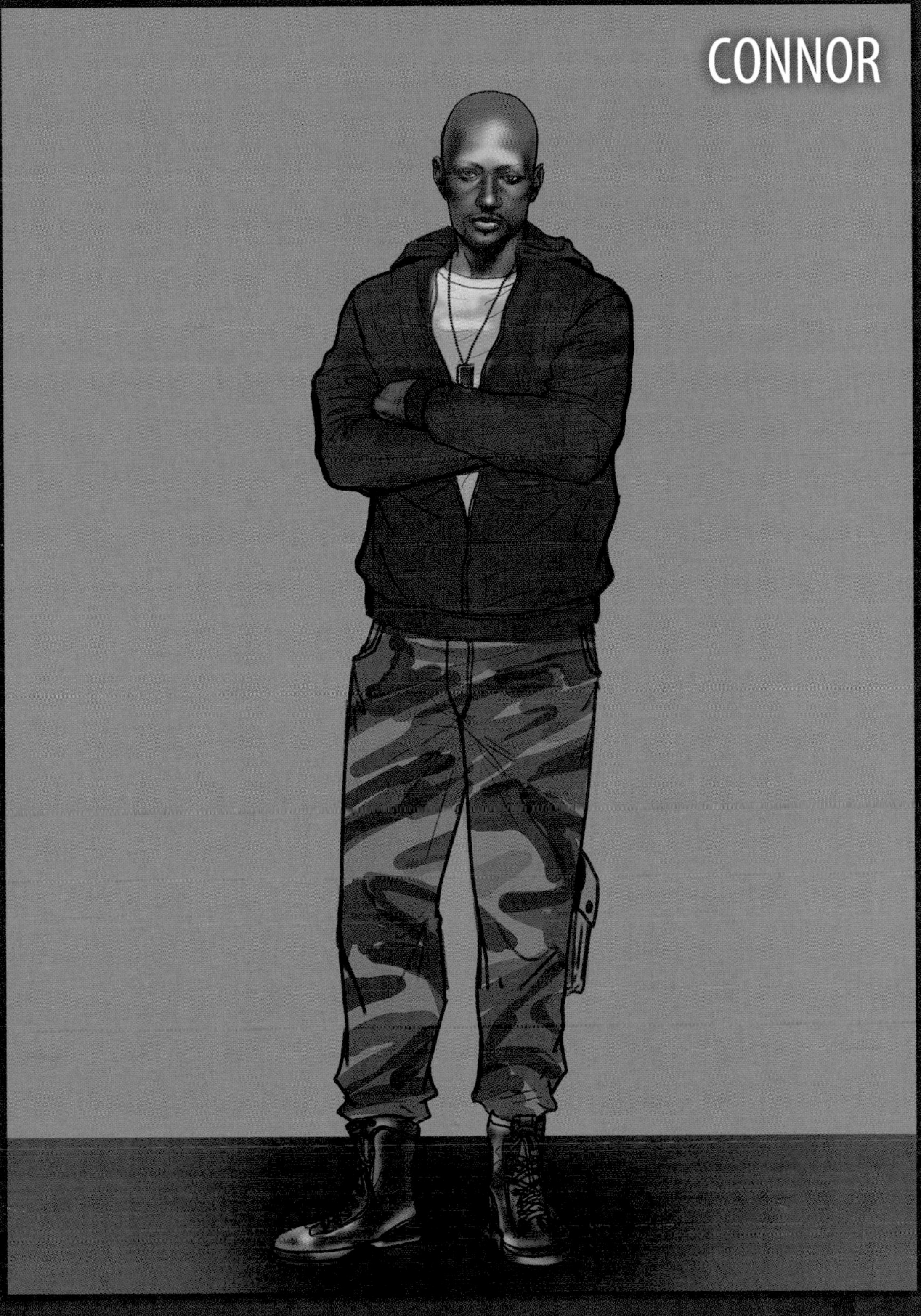
CONNOR

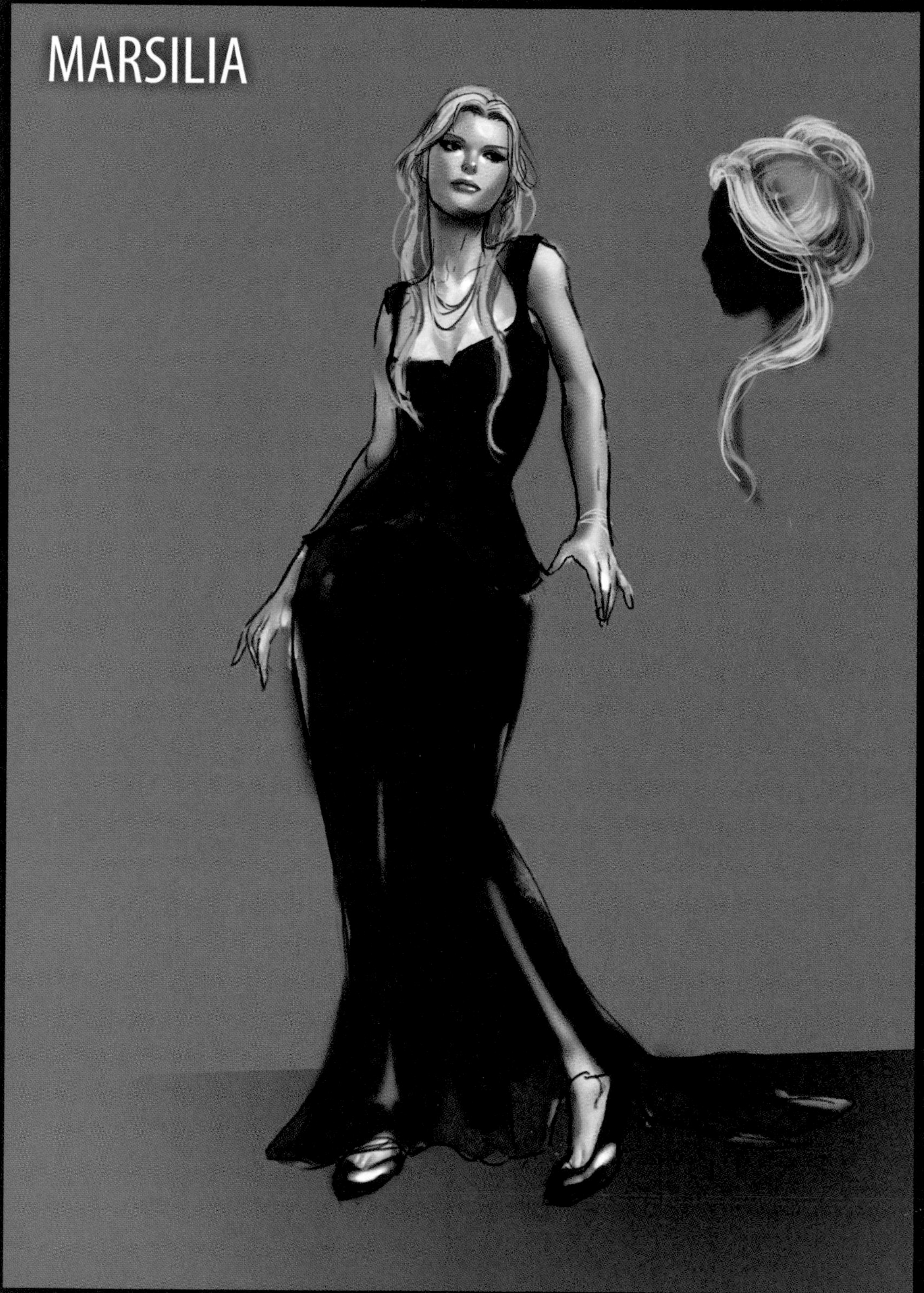
MARSILIA

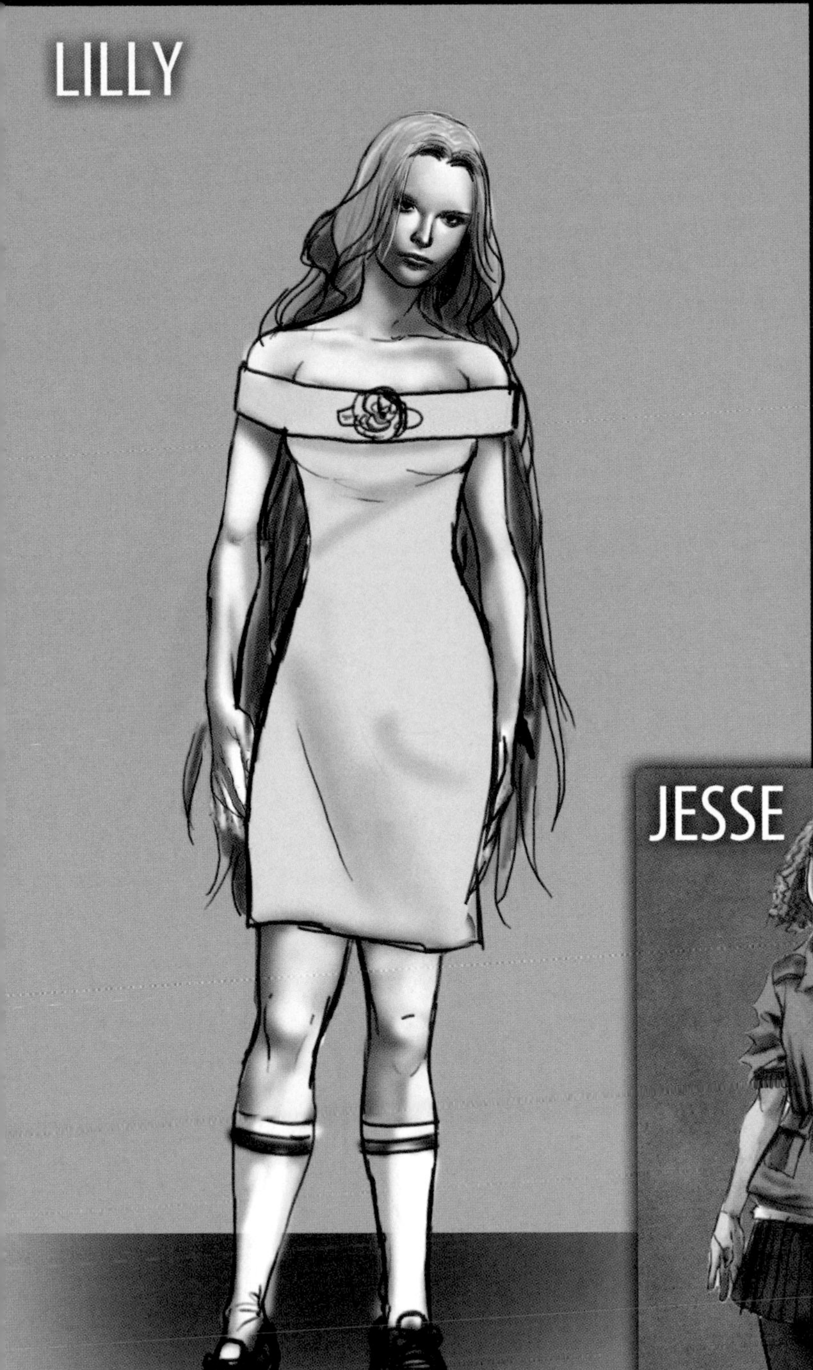
LILLY

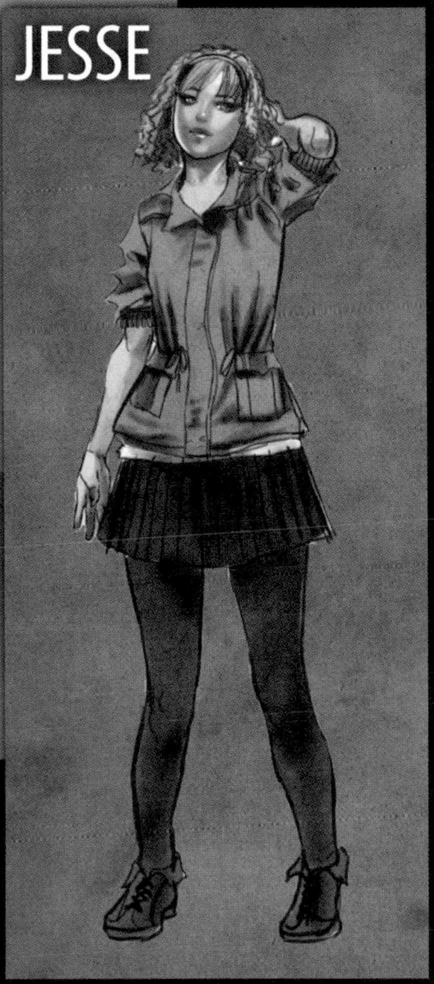
JESSE

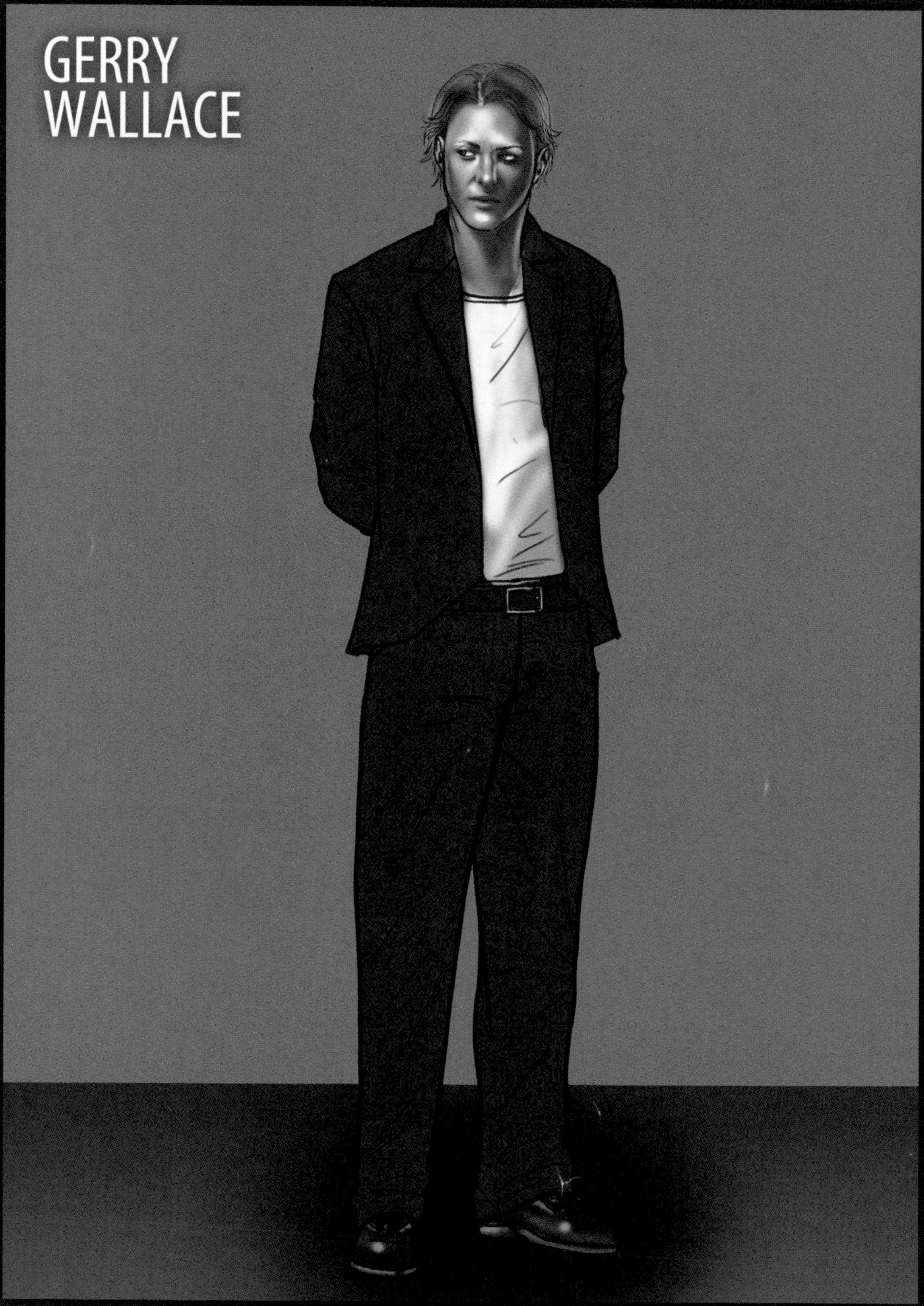
GERRY
WALLACE

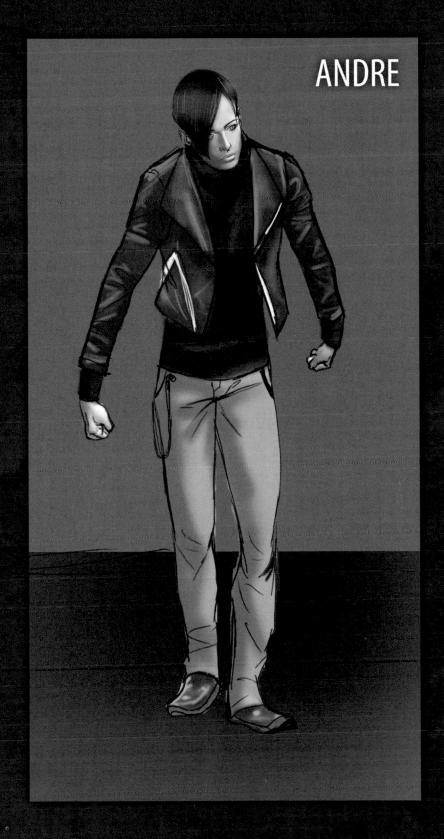

ANDRE

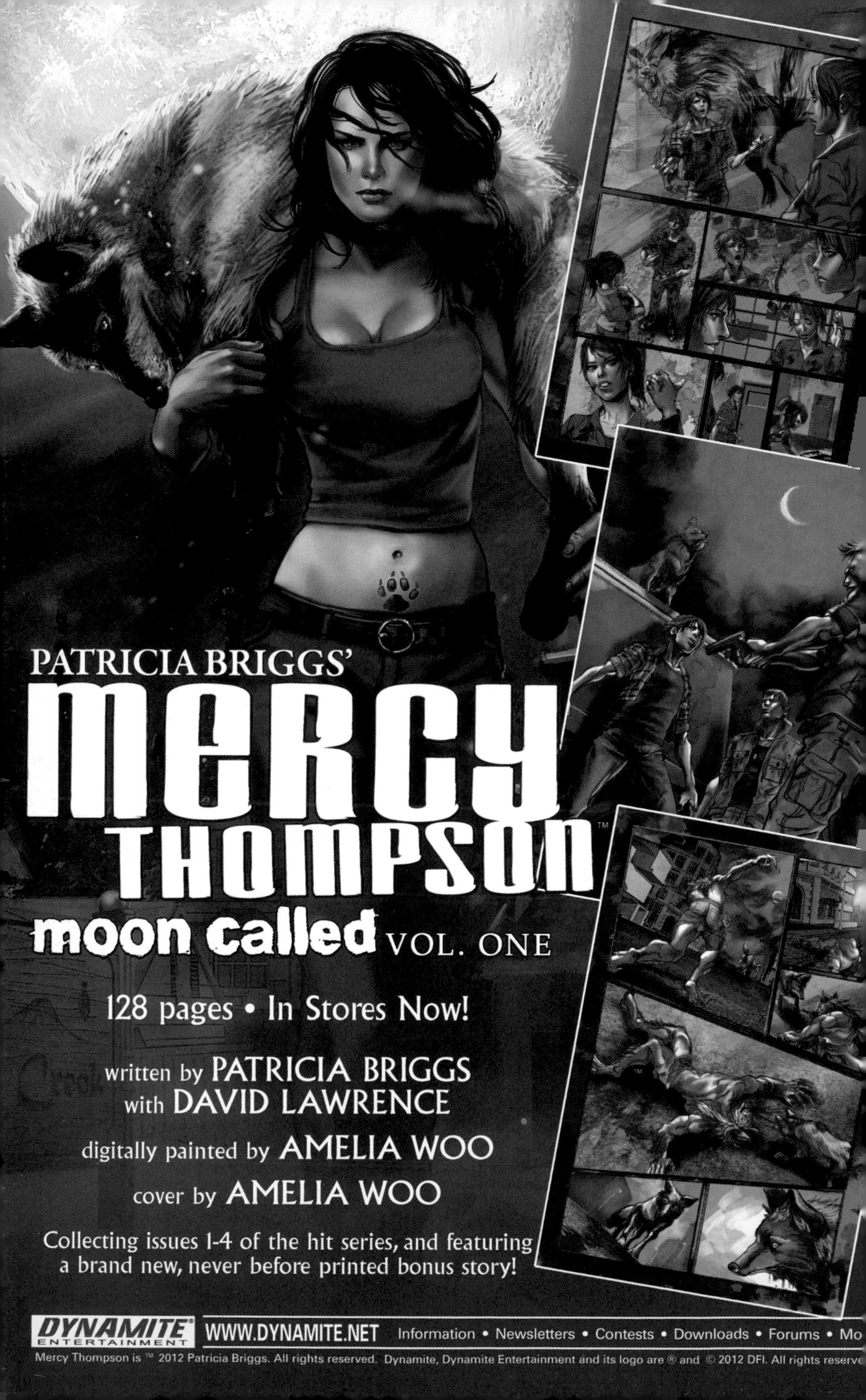
PATRICIA BRIGGS'
MERCY THOMPSON™
moon called VOL. ONE
128 pages • In Stores Now!
written by PATRICIA BRIGGS
with DAVID LAWRENCE
digitally painted by AMELIA WOO
cover by AMELIA WOO
Collecting issues 1-4 of the hit series, and featuring a brand new, never before printed bonus story!
DYNAMITE ENTERTAINMENT
WWW.DYNAMITE.NET
Information • Newsletters • Contests • Downloads • Forums • Mo
Mercy Thompson is ™ 2012 Patricia Briggs. All rights reserved. Dynamite, Dynamite Entertainment and its logo are ® and © 2012 DFI. All rights reserve

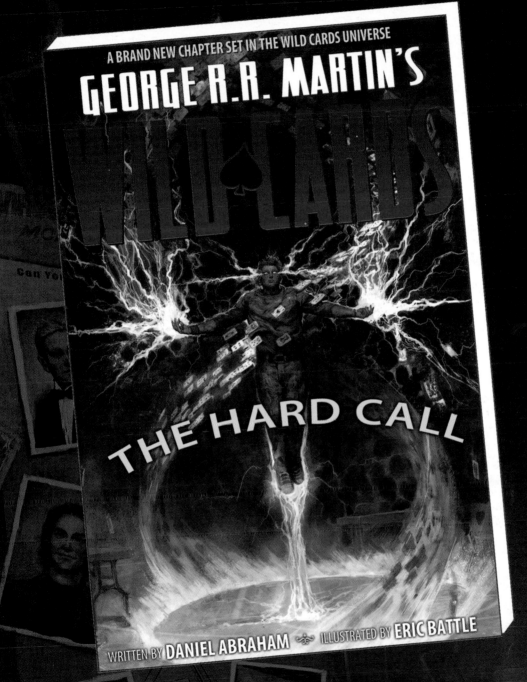